Edgar Allan Poe

Edgar Allan Poe

Beyond Gothicism

Edited by James M. Hutchisson

UNIVERSITY OF DELAWARE PRESS
Newark

Published by University of Delaware Press
Co-published with The Rowman & Littlefield Publishing Group, Inc.
4501 Forbes Boulevard, Suite 200, Lanham, Maryland 20706
http://www.rowmanlittlefield.com

Estover Road, Plymouth PL6 7PY, United Kingdom

British Library Cataloguing in Publication Information Available

Library of Congress Cataloging-in-Publication Data

Edgar Allan Poe : beyond gothicism / edited by James M. Hutchisson.
p. cm.
"Co-published with The Rowman & Littlefield Publishing Group."
Includes bibliographical references and index.
ISBN 978-1-61149-068-8 (cloth : alk. paper) -- ISBN 978-1-61149-069-5 (electronic)
1. Poe, Edgar Allan, 1809-1849--Criticism and interpretation. I. Hutchisson, James M.
PS2638.E335 2011
818'.309--dc22
2011003372

The paper used in this publication meets the minimum requirements of American National Standard for Information Sciences Permanence of Paper for Printed Library Materials, ANSI/NISO Z39.48-1992.

Printed in the United States of America

Contents

Acknowledgments

Chapter 6 originally appeared in a slightly different form in *Southern Literary Journal*, and chapters 1 and 9 in *The Edgar Allan Poe Review*. Permission to reprint these essays has been kindly granted by the editors of those journals and by their authors.

The contributors to this volume deserve special recognition. Not only has their work made for engaging and stimulating reading, but their patience has probably stretched the bounds of credulity through what became an unusually long period of composition and production. I am sure they are glad to see their superb essays finally in print.

I am grateful to Winifred "Bo" Moore, Dean of the School of Humanities and Social Sciences at The Citadel, for funding for research assistance. A sabbatical leave, underwritten by The Citadel Foundation, also provided time to work on this book.

To these friends and colleagues in particular I owe thanks for help, ideas, and, when needed, an attentive ear: Scott Peeples, Ben Fisher, Wally Coberg, John Jebb, Peter Norberg, Rich Fusco, Barbara Cantalupo, Susan Donaldson, Kevin Hayes, Matthew Pearl, Richard Rust, and James L. W. West III. All Poe scholars are deeply saddened by the passing of Burton R. Pollin, Jr., but his vast and important writing on Poe will continue to aid the work of generations to come.

As always, thanks go to my wife, Rachel. She reminds me that peace and quiet are nice, but a little healthy chaos is a good thing too.

J. H.
January 2011

Introduction

James M. Hutchisson

When in 1941 Arthur Hobson Quinn published his authoritative *Edgar Allan Poe: A Critical Biography*, he inaugurated the serious scholarly study of Poe. Before Quinn, Poe's most well-known biographer was his erstwhile friend and literary executor, Rufus Griswold, who turned out to be his most malicious enemy. Griswold's lengthy obituary of Poe, published in the *New York Tribune* two days after the author's death, depicted Poe as a drug-crazed lunatic who closely—perhaps even exactly—resembled the bizarre characters in his stories of terror and the supernatural. In laying to rest Griswold's slanders, Quinn effectively opened up Poe's work as a legitimate subject of critical inquiry, and since then the author's poetry and fiction have been standard elements of American literature course syllabi, of critical monographs on a wide variety of topics, themes, and techniques in Poe's writing, of lecture series and keynote speeches, and of an oft-repeated, sad, but compelling story of someone whose life may now seem to have been doomed almost from the start.

In the ensuing seven decades since Quinn's biography, we have seen shelf after shelf of books, journal articles, and conference proceedings generated about Poe and his work, from deconstructionist readings and gender studies to psychoanalytic criticism and reader-response interpretations. One must in good conscience ask, is there room for more to be said?

I think most scholars would readily agree that there is, simply because of the inherent richness of Poe's multilayered texts—hence one reason for the publication of this collection of critical essays. Poe's fiction, poetry, and essays do truly fit the universal criterion of art, which is that we find something new or different or intriguing almost every time we read them. Continuing to write about Poe has expanded our portrait of arguably one of the most unique figures in American literature—a complex person working within an imaginative realm of complicated anxieties and high artistic ideals.

Another reason is that as a critical community, Poe scholars are still placing a perhaps disproportionate emphasis on the tales of psychic conflict and supernatural events—the so-called horror fiction with which Poe is most closely linked in the public mind. In other words, Poe studies to a degree continue to suffer from scholars' insistence on concentrating mostly on the tales of terror—"The Fall of the House of Usher," "The Black Cat," and "The Pit and the Pendulum," to name just a few—to the subordination of much other fiction. Poe's poetry and his extensive body of book reviews have also suffered (relatively) from disproportionate academic interest in the supernatural tales. And there remain in Poe's oeuvre a dozen or so complex and teasingly sophisticated stories that, because they defy easy categorization, have also been neglected. Yet these pieces, too—"Thou Art the Man," "The Thousand and Second Tale of Scheherazade," "The Imp of the Perverse," and others—present us with a duplicitous and beguiling fictive universe every bit as intriguing as the ones in Poe's more familiar works.[1] As Jorge Luis Borges said of Shakespeare, "No one was as many men as this man."[2] Editor, literary journalist, reviewer and critic, satirist, hoaxer, mystery writer and pioneer of science fiction, poet, even playwright—Poe was all of these artists. A simple tally of his published works confirms it: allowing for very generous definitions of genre, only fifteen of Poe's tales genuinely concern what we regard as "the supernatural," compared to the rest of the canon of his fictional writings, which numbers fifty-two.[3] That variance is wide, indeed. This volume is therefore also in part a collective effort to reassert the importance of some overlooked or critically undervalued texts.

But the most compelling reason for continued investigation of Poe's writing is apparent when one tracks the trends in Poe scholarship over the past twenty to twenty-five years. Removing Poe from the essentialist realm to which critics often assign him, scholars have come to see Poe in historical and contextual terms. Once deemed the odd man out in the American Renaissance, Poe has most recently been the subject of readings that show him enmeshed in the social fabric of the nineteenth century, his texts woven with finely filamented fibers that touch on and connect his works with the main currents of nineteenth-century American thought. We have seen, among other studies, books and articles linking Poe to science and technology, to wars and politics, to the cult of death and bereavement, and—probably most controversially—to slavery and stereotyped attitudes toward women.

We therefore now stand at a propitious moment in the evolution of Poe scholarship. We have witnessed much scholarly activity linking Poe's imaginative writings with the historical realities of nineteenth-century America. What we need now is a more systematic approach to that way of thinking about the author. This collection of essays, taken as a whole, is an argument for a new topical school of Poe criticism, whose scholarly and pedagogical implications could prove to be vast. If we study Poe in this manner, I believe that a portrait will emerge of a more coherent artist, someone who blended topics of intellectual and social importance and returned repeatedly to these ideas, in different works and using different aesthetic strategies, throughout his brief but highly productive career. Among the essays in this volume, readers will see many shared implications and critical conclusions. Taken as a whole, the collection should point readers to new ways of considering Poe's themes, techniques, and aesthetic preoccupations.

To begin with, we need to think more about Poe's relationship to environment. We can start by setting aside our critical tendency to define "environment" as the Gothic setting. We need to enlarge our definitions of Poe's thematic treatment of environment to include landscapes—urban, rural, and imaginative. Moving from the outside in, we also need to place our thinking about Poe's views on interior design, or "decorism," as it was called in the nineteenth century, within the rubric of environment. We need to pay particular attention to Poe's concepts of balance, symmetry, understatement, and effect.

Poe's sense of environment was unique. He did not necessarily separate interior and exterior, rural and urban, in his mind. One reason for this was the peculiar geographic trajectory that his life took. His first years were spent travelling with his actor-parents from one city to another, up and down the eastern seaboard, as they performed in different theaters. Poe was then taken in by the wealthy Allan family, lived in Scotland and England for five years as a child, and then grew up, through adolescence and young adulthood, in a capacious, rambling mansion, Moldavia, in Richmond, Virginia. Rejected by his foster father after an unimpressive stint as a student at the University of Virginia in Charlottesville, Poe then took up the life of a nomad, from his enlisting in the army in Boston to his final years as a kind of hermetic figure taking rambles in the woods while living in a cottage in Fordham, New York. More interesting, the pattern of Poe's attempts from year to year to establish some kind of permanent "home" was a pattern of diminishment rather than expansion. Each abode became smaller and sparser. How claustrophobic and tight Poe's own spare existence must have felt to him when imaginatively confronted with such profligate spaces as we see in the settings of the house of Usher, the castle of Metzengerstein, or the palace of Prince Prospero. This style of living may also suggest why the interior settings in most of his tales are so constricted and claustrophobic—quite in contrast to the wide open spaces exalted by Poe's peers and near-contemporaries like James Fenimore Cooper, Francis Parkman, and Washington Irving and as painted by Thomas Cole, Albert Bierstadt, and others of the Hudson River School.

Taking these principles to another level, we can link Poe's views of the importance of interior and exterior setting with his views on the foundations and structures of writing. In "Poe's 'Philosophy of Furniture' and the Aesthetics of Fictional Design," C. T. Walters shows how Poe, critical of America's lack of aesthetic taste, sought to combine the decorative with the aesthetic, a reflection of his interest in the "transformation of the aesthetic principles of painting into the specific necessities of furniture." This principle Poe also affirmed in "The Oval Portrait" and "The Oblong Box," as well as in the essays "The Domain of Arnheim" and "Landor's Cottage"—his final two published works. "The Philosophy of Furniture," however, is probably the best example of this view of art. In this essay, we can easily see Poe's aesthetic theory in play. Poe is particularly hostile to "the rage for glitter"—glass surfaces reflecting harsh, glaring light, "partly on account of [their] flashiness," but also because "the light proceeding from . . . these gaudy abominations is unequal, broken, and painful" (382).[4] In other words, Poe reacted against the disarrangement of parts in interior design: the lack of unity, symmetry, and order that were the hallmarks of his aesthetic theory. In "The Philosophy of Furniture," he was applying such ideas about literary creation—later made famous in his reviews of Hawthorne and in "The Philosophy of Composition"—to residential architecture. He was also staking out his own independent literary territory, with its dim and gloomy interiors. Further, Poe's two "Philosophy" essays should be seen as complementary. We should note that "The Philosophy of Composition," Poe's most famous critical pronouncement, was, in an analogue to his fiction, almost supernatural in its prescience and precision. The essay is ratiocinative in nature, with its emphasis on (or even obsession with) order, symmetry, and control. Both of these seminal essays suggest the stridency and singularity of Poe's critical strictures: both essays' titles suggest that there is a single way of thinking about art: "*the* philosophy," so to speak, according to Poe.

Another recent topic in Poe scholarship has been his fictive engagements with "the Other." This tendency can be seen to intersect with the topic of environment. In recent years, the critical conversation about Poe and the Other has focused largely on Poe's treatment of African American characters and, by implication, his perceived position on slavery. As Toni Morrison has said in her study of American writers, *Playing in the Dark*, a black or "Africanist" presence exists throughout the history of American literature and has always fueled notions of racial difference. "No early American writer is more important to the concept of American Africanism," than Poe, Morrison writes.[5]

Building on readings of *The Narrative of Arthur Gordon Pym* and "The Gold-Bug," some critics have constructed an image of Poe as supportive of antebellum slavery that may be more rhetorical than real.[6] In "Race, Pirates, and Intellect: A Reading of Poe's 'The Gold-Bug'" John F. Jebb takes up the continuing debate over Poe's racial views—one of the thorniest issues in Poe studies. Poe often uses African American characters to comic effect. Led by biographer Kenneth Silverman, many scholars have held that Poe's stories present African Americans as undignified, foolish, and unworthy of respect. Much recent criticism has tended not so much to rebut the charge as to deflect it. Norman Stafford, for instance, observes that the comic depiction of the black slave Jupiter in "The Gold-Bug" doesn't reveal Poe's racism, but rather the racism of the society which created the stereotype.[7] The recent collection *Romancing the Shadow: Poe and Race* tends to emphasize the social-racial context of antebellum Charleston (the setting of the story), perhaps overlooking some of what actually occurs in the story, which is much more of a disquisition on the nature and capacity of the human intellect than it is a tale that reveals racial conflict.[8] Jebb restores the context of the tale and re-invokes Poe's life, his writings, and his reading, especially his review of Robert Montgomery Bird's *Sheppard Lee*—a novel that, like Poe's tale, includes an African American who disciplines his white master. This role reversal cannot easily be dismissed.

As the academy broadens its understanding of the Other to include a wider range of outside or marginalized voices in society, we can perhaps more accurately come to terms with the complicated anxieties and contradictory stances that we have identified in Poe's treatment of race. Two complementary trends in Poe's work that come to mind are his interest in "Orientalism" and in Islam, including references to the culture of Egypt. (This was in part a nod to the widespread interest in archaeological findings that swept through America during Poe's time.) Taking my cue from numerous critical conversations in which Poe has been figured as a "postmodern" writer, delighting in wordplay, metafictionist constructions of tales within tales, and anti-Aristotelian notions of narrative, I attempt to show how in "The Thousand and Second Tale of Scheherazade," a slight but much neglected story, Poe plays with the predictability of teleological art. In the tale Poe anticipates much postmodernist fiction by Barth, Borges, Calvino, and others who spin endless stories, like modern Scheherazades. Poe's preoccupations with narrative authority ramify into other, very Poesque themes, most notably the reciprocal relationship between writing and death.

If we continue to broaden our understanding of Poe's relations with his various social, intellectual, and artistic communities, conceptions of "otherness" can also include figures marginalized not just by ethnicity but also by psychological makeup, behavioral nonconformity, or bodily disfigurement, illness, or dysfunction. Proceeding from Walter Benjamin's conceptualization of the *flaneur* in urban culture, scholars from a variety of disciplines have used several of Poe's tales as touchstones for understanding the modes of perception in urban settings.[9] In "The Man in the Text: Desire, Masculinity, and the Development of Poe's Detective Fiction," Peter Goodwin addresses both the Other and the question of how Poe used narrative modes and crossed generic boundaries. Goodwin argues that this tale, in its compulsive investigation of an irresistibly attractive gentleman, spotlights a crisis of sexual definition that lies at the heart of Poe's detective fiction. "The Man That Was Used Up" introduces the detective impulse as originating in the narrator's vexed, homoerotic desire for intimate knowledge of another man, an impulse that Poe pursues to surprising ends here and in two of the tales that follow, including "The Man of the Crowd" and "The Murders in the Rue Morgue." As Goodwin's essay suggests, the unsettling dependency of desire, and the unpredictable directions in which it flows, effectively fractures the Jacksonian ideal of unified, integral white manhood, opening the masculine subject to both violence and transformation. Poe was therefore also obliquely commenting on the societal trend toward muscular nationalism and patriarchy.

The body continues to be a compelling subject for inquiry in reading Poe's texts. New insights into a frequently seen concept in the tales, the dichotomy between the mind and body, may be drawn out if we investigate more extensively Poe's engagement with human physicality, notably his infirm, disfigured, or handicapped male characters. The body as both a mechanical and organic/chemical vessel intrigued Poe, and he frequently depicted deformity in its various physical states—for example, in "Berenice" or "Hop-Frog." The body as an independent entity also figures prominently into various of his plot paradigms, when one considers the degrees of sadism, masochism, and aberrant acts that are instruments of cruelty and/or revenge. Could we see the body as a version of the Other as well? It would seem so.

Poe also displaced, objectified, and transposed culture-specific environments and peoples. This in part explains why the settings of so many of his tales are deliberately vague. In terms of locale, Poe's characters journey through ancient Italy, the deserts of Egypt, colonial Virginia, central London, and—most fantastically in *The Narrative of Arthur Gordon Pym*—below the eighty-fourth parallel. A different destination is the American South, in which Poe was raised and about which he wrote frequently, albeit often in an allegorized or figurative mode. Amy Branam examines the fragmentary play, *Politian*, within the context of its own historical moment, building on the recent work of Terence Whalen and Meredith McGill.[10] During the early nineteenth century, American drama began to evolve into a distinctive national form, yet the older, European dramatic forms persisted, such as the sentimental drama, the melodrama, and the Gothic drama. In particular, the Gothic facilitated "the exercise, release, and containment of personal and social anxieties." By looking at Poe's drama within its theatrical context, as well as in conjunction with his sociohistorical position in American history, Branam uses *Politian* to redefine the Gothic impulse in Poe's work. She also sees the play as a veiled commentary on issues affecting the American South. Poe's primary displacement involves the vying of English and Italian characters within an Italian setting to address anxieties regarding the sensitive position of the antebellum South in its relations with the North. However, this play is not a straightforward allegory. In effect, Poe's management of the displacements reinforces the argument that his allegiance might have lain more with his aesthetics than with presenting an unequivocally pro-southern political stance.

Politian is as much an imaginary mind-scape as it is a verifiable setting. Yet sometimes Poe drew inspiration more directly from the historical record. In these cases, the issues of landscape and the Other seem to have become even more closely interwoven in his mind. It is interesting to note that the landscape of Poe's half-finished novel, for instance, "The Journal of Julius Rodman," comes close to approaching Poe's definition of an Arcadia like that found in "The Domain of Arnheim"—a land of aesthetic order and sublimity marred only by a displaced element—here, African Americans and Native Americans. In "Julius Rodman," Poe follows Lewis and Clark in historical revisionism by overlooking the violence of European-American colonization of the west in favor of the violence promulgated by the primitive natives that were encountered in the widening of America's so-called democratic vistas. Such is also the case with the underrated "A Tale of the Ragged Mountains." Daniel Philippon places this story in the context of the social and natural history of the countryside surrounding Charlottesville, Virginia, where Poe lived during the brief time he attended the University of Virginia. Philippon examines in detail Poe's Virginia heritage, making use of nineteenth-century novels that took the Virginia backwoods as their setting—classics of early American literature from Captain John Smith to Thomas Jefferson, local histories of Albemarle County, and nonprint sources, as well, especially local legends from the area. The locality and the people who inhabited the area at the time provide important contexts for appreciating the story's ironies and understanding Poe's analysis of the relationship in art between Orientalism and local resonances.

Moving from themes to techniques, we know that Poe's narrative strategies have long been of interest to scholars. There have been numerous studies of Poe's uses of traditional literary modes and artistic techniques: the allegory, the jeremiad, the journey motif, and much else. Yet an area that has yet to be plumbed deeply is Poe's mocking and/or self-consciously parodying the popular fiction genres of his time, most notably the Gothic. Indeed, writing in 1997, Kent P. Ljungquist noted the fact that much remained to be said about this side of Poe, especially his numerous early tales. "With generic categories blurred and aesthetic hierarchies challenged," Ljungquist argued, "Poe's early satires, once dismissed as inferior hackwork, now constitute an important foreground for Poe's fictional career, in which the serious and the comic, the grotesque and the arabesque, romantic transport and ironic detachment play complementary roles, even when categories are held in disequilibrium or tension."[11] The Gothic narrative mode was, of course, a staple of American, British, and Continental writing for more than half a century and filled the pages of such periodicals as *Blackwood's Edinburgh Magazine* and the *London Quarterly Review*. Taking his cue from Gothicism, Poe enriched its texture, embroidering it with philosophical speculation. Yet Poe seemed at times both to be modeling his fiction on such tales—using them as launching points for his own philosophical speculations about the nature of death and dying—and at other times them, as has been observed.[12]

The locus of this type of writing is Poe's early abortive collection, *Tales of the Folio Club*, a sophisticated satirical rendering of the world of American letters in the early 1830s. Benjamin Fisher casts new light on the context of that project by scrutinizing "King Pest," a plague story similar to "The Sphinx" and the better-known "The Masque of the Red Death." "King Pest," however, has long been regarded as one of Poe's lesser tales—perhaps because it seems on the surface to embody too little of the transcendental and too much of the "mere *physique* of the hor-rible"—the quality for which Poe himself would later chastise William Gilmore Simms in his review of *The Partisan* (901). Fisher, however, makes plausible a reading that would indicate that this tale may have played an important role in Poe's experimentation with *Tales of the Folio Club*. Specifically, Fisher argues that Poe may have thought of using this tale as the concluding piece in the Folio Club book—an alternative to Alexander Hammond's long-standing view that the so-called "expose" story in the proposed collection was probably the much different "Lioniz-ing."[13] Fisher also demonstrates why "King Pest" should not be relegated to "minor" status in the Poe canon. He in effect shows how this early tale predicts a strategy of varying, complex narrative expression found throughout much of the later Poe.

We have concluded that Poe was adept at crossing generic boundar-ies, pushing the aesthetic parameters of modes of writing and creating hybrid forms. There have also been discussions of the filmic aspects of his writing. These kinds of skills enabled Poe to redefine and refurbish con-ventional narrative forms, as is shown by his pervasive influence on such experimental writers as Borges, Nabokov, Robbe-Grillet, and many oth-ers. Now we might ask, how and where do these strategies intersect? Kevin J. Hayes analyzes a text that is among the most undervalued of all of Poe's fiction, the early tale entitled "Why the Little Frenchman Wears His Hand in a Sling." Here we see a story written while the nature of "tale writing" proper was still gestating in Poe's critical consciousness. Curiously, "The Little Frenchman" is as much an oral legend as it is a "tale." Like the comic monologue, "The Spectacles," this story suggests another lens through which to view Poe's narrative purposes, the oral rather than the written word. "The Little Frenchman" offers a mock biog-raphy of an Irish rustic named Patrick O'Grandison who has recently and unexpectedly been awarded a baronetcy. Poe explores the contrast be-tween the unsophisticated world that O'Grandison's words represent and the ostentatious world of sophisticated "society." Hayes explores the ways in which these contrasts are presented by Poe, and how they ramify into areas beyond mere humor. Hayes also sees similarities between this tale and both "The Murders in the Rue Morgue" and "The Man of the Crowd" in their reliance on the supremacy of visual evidence in establishing cognitive awareness. Such a view has important implications for understanding Poe's sensitivity to language, his view of the much-trumpeted "power of words," and his subtlety at using what an audience sees or reads versus what an audience "hears."

Much recent scholarship has also focused on Poe's interest in scientific advances in the nineteenth century and in technology. Such developments as the daguerreotype, improved optical lenses, and engines and machines for making daily life easier and more efficient, fascinated him. In "The Domain of Arnheim," Poe imagines a garden that creates the effect of transcendence by manipulating rather than suppressing "the eyes which were to behold it on earth." In her chapter on "Arnheim," Laura Saltz argues that Poe's interest in the science of human vision and his working knowledge of Scottish physicist Sir David Brewster's *Letters on Natural Magic* (1831) enabled him to conceive and represent the protagonist Ellison's garden in a way such that it would appeal optically to the hypothetical "visiter" [*sic*] who travels through it in the final pages of the tale. Elaborating on other scholars' investigations into Poe's uses of Brewster's volume, Saltz argues that *Natural Magic* was not simply a source of optical tricks that Poe imported into "Arnheim." Poe also shared with Brewster an understanding of how the eyes work: why a glance can be more effective than a direct view, how the eyes perceive depth, and how the physical eye and the mind's eye are related—drawing us back, once again, to Poe's critical insistence that a separation of mind and body must perforce result in human disharmony and discontent. Through his scientific understanding of vision, Poe simulates in "Arnheim" a set of optical effects that parallel the out-of-body states in which the poetic sentiment, in Poe's view, is best apprehended.

Another very rich area for further study is the new economic criticism as it might be applied to Poe. Poe provides a profoundly interesting model for this line of inquiry. In a commercial society driven by materialism and money-lust (the words "millionaire" and "businessman" were coined in Poe's time), Poe lived a marginalized existence because of lost opportunities, exploitation by others, and the choice of a career that was, except for a select few, not very remunerative. He was either destitute or living near the poverty level for most of his life. Poe was therefore envious of wealth, particularly when he saw it close up, as he had in the household of John Allan. When Allan died and left Poe no monetary legacy, Poe was furious.

When Poe wrote about money in his fiction, he therefore either inveighed against its evils or concocted wish-fulfillment fantasies in which wealth was abundant. His anger at Allan, for example, and at the whole mercantile society that Allan represented, came out viciously in "The Business Man," in which the protagonist, Peter Proffitt, is ridiculed. Another example is "The Philosophy of Furniture," in which Poe directs his invective against the rage for possessions that make people think they are of a higher social station than they really are. On the other hand, in texts like "The Domain of Arnheim," Poe created an ideal inheritor-figure for whom the supply of money is virtually unlimited. Likewise, "Metzengerstein" depicts a young man whose noble birth entitles him to riches; in "William Wilson," the title character is something of a sybarite, pursuing women, games, and good food and wine without, apparently, the worry of how to pay for such a life. Hordes of cash lie about the L'Espanaye's apartment in Paris in "The Murders in the Rue Morgue," and LeGrand searches for buried treasure on a remote barrier island outside Charleston, South Carolina in "The Gold-Bug."

Yet Poe saw possibilities for achieving both artistic acclaim as an erudite writer and purveyor of culture as well as wealth from his literary work. Poe would often fixate on those few literary figures in his milieu who had done both: most notably Longfellow, against whom he waged a well-known war of words that emanated mostly from Poe's feeling that Longfellow got more praise than he deserved, while he himself got little.[14] Poe had also seen firsthand how magazines could make their owners rich. With each magazine that Poe took editorial control of, subscriptions increased, making their publishers wealthy, while Poe was paid a pittance. In the pathetic last years of his life, Poe was exploited again by magazine owners who reduced him to accepting whatever they would hand out to freelancers who were at their mercy. The great ambition of Poe's life, of course, was to own a periodical, over which he would have full artistic control and use to wield power over the literary world, as well as make money from it (a dream never realized).

The point is that Poe not only saw literature as a business, but he saw his own skills in writing and editing as of immense value in earning the way to wealth. Reason, logic, order, and method—his constant mantras—were also the ways in which his characters triumphed over the ordinary masses of humanity, exhibited their intellectual prowess, and were rewarded with riches.[15] No one can overlook Poe's immersion in the subject matter and practices of the publishing world of his time, especially given the recent surge in scholarly interest in book history, literary journalism, and publishing. Few nineteenth-century literary figures other than Poe were involved so intimately in so many aspects of the competitive world of letters and, more importantly, perhaps none more fully dramatized the tensions inherent in literary competitiveness. In "'A Species of Literature Almost Beneath Contempt': Edgar Allan Poe and the World of Literary Competitions," Leon Jackson explores Poe's engagement in literary contests from his first prize as an academy student in Richmond through his late and controversial publication of the prize-winning "The Gold-Bug" in 1843 and after. Poe's social marginality as an author, Jackson argues, led him to challenge some of the most cherished assumptions on which competitions were predicated. This essay suggests a new lens through which to read Poe's biography; it offers fresh readings of Poe's works, including "Tamerlane," *Tales of the Folio Club*, and "The Gold-Bug"; and more generally it suggests the centrality of literary competitions to the history of antebellum culture. Drawing on archival sources, intellectual history, and the new economic criticism, it extends recent attempts to place Poe firmly in his milieu, both biographically and historically.

Related to Poe's position in literary society as a "magazinist"—editor, critic, and reviewer—is his literary criticism. Poe earned his living as a workaday journalist, book reviewer, and professional critic. In fact, he wrote more literary criticism than anything else: from 1835, when he became formally associated with the *Southern Literary Messenger*, until his death in 1849, when he was contributing regularly to several magazines in the northeast, Poe wrote close to one thousand essays, reviews, articles, columns, and critical notices. Some were no longer than a paragraph or two, some ran to as many as a half-dozen pages, but taken as a whole, they constitute, as Edmund Wilson said in 1955, "the most remarkable body of criticism ever produced in the United States."[16] Poe later took the criteria he laid down in these pieces and distilled them into a systematic series of critical precepts in such essays as "The Philosophy of Composition" and "The Poetic Principle."

Two final essays in this volume explore Poe's literary criticism as a lens through which to view his belletristic writing. First, Justin Wert examines the substantial body of reviewing that Poe did on the works of Robert Montgomery Bird, a fellow southerner and successful novelist and playwright of the 1830s and 1840s who had risen quickly to the status of having, in Poe's words, "a very enviable reputation." Wert places Poe's critiques of Bird in the context of Poe's other reviews of American literature to show how the Bird reviews advanced Poe's evolving aesthetic criteria. Wert also looks at Poe's critical stances regarding the role of genre in American literature and his role as a southern editor working at a southern magazine. Complementing Wert's chapter is a new examination of "The Philosophy of Composition" by Dennis W. Eddings. This essay contextualizes "The Philosophy" and "The Raven" in light of Poe's review of Elizabeth Barrett Browning's *The Drama of Exile*. The three works combine in a powerful critical statement about poetry and its uses and abuses. Most scholars conclude that Poe could be rhetorically extravagant in stating his poetic credo and aesthetic goals, but that he was comparatively orthodox in his practices. Eddings shows that this was not always so. He argues that the three texts together show Poe's most concerted attack on one of his frequent aesthetic targets: the Romantic sensibility that exalted intuition and feeling above poetic control. Eddings further develops some recent trends in scholarship on "The Raven" which view Poe's most famous poem as a kind of "anti-fairy tale," written against the idealism that produced that explosion of children's literature in the nineteenth century.[17]

In one of the "Marginalia," Poe claimed it was a "curse of a certain order of mind, that it can never rest satisfied with the consciousness of its ability to do a thing. Nor even is it content with doing it. It must both know and show how it was done."[18] In adopting this view of the artist, Poe became not only excessively self-analytical, but in so doing he gave new critical tools to those of his peers who read him with interest, later generations of writers who were influenced by him, and modern scholars interpreting his texts. In most things Poe was primarily an aesthetician, and aesthetic concerns simply cannot be separated from the historical realities of an author's era. Ever the doubter, ever the seeker, ever the incurable romantic who hoped against hope for what was sometimes the patently impossible, Poe both absorbed the spirit of his times and refracted it through the dark prism of his imagination.

Brazenly self-confident, full of expectant optimism, and never for a minute doubting in the divine sanction of its own manifest destiny, America in the 1830s and 1840s was vibrant and moving forward. In a world that had a sense of complacent stability, Poe continually questioned and interrogated the very nature of reality. If we are to understand Poe's mind even more profoundly than we have thus far, we must move back into his world more deeply, for the one cannot be separated from the other.

NOTES

1. This is despite the commercial availability, in paperback, of Poe's "other" writings, viz., *The Science Fiction of Edgar Allan Poe*, ed. Harold Beaver (New York: Penguin, 1975) and *The Other Poe: Comedies and Satires* (New York: Penguin, 1983). Recently, however, the Library of America began issuing paperback "College Editions" of most of the major authors in its series. The Poe volume includes a generous selection of the criticism, journalism, and satires.

2. Jorge Luis Borges, "Shakespeare's Memory" (1983), *Shakespeare's Memory* (New York: Penguin, 2007), 167.

3. In the order of publication, the fifteen "horror stories" would arguably include: "MS. Found in a Bottle," "Berenice," "Morella," "Ligeia," "The Fall of the House of Usher," "William Wilson," "Eleonora," "The Oval Portrait," "The Pit and the Pendulum," "The Tell-Tale Heart," "The Black Cat," "A Tale of the Ragged Mountains," "The Premature Burial," "Mesmeric Revelation," and "The Facts in the Case of M. Valdemar."

4. All references to Poe's published writings herein are to the Library of America volumes: *Poetry and Tales* (1984) and *Essays and Reviews* (1984).

5. Toni Morrison, *Playing in the Dark: Whiteness and the American Literary Imagination* (Cambridge, MA: Harvard University Press, 1992).

6. This conclusion is based on Poe's alleged authorship of a review-essay about two books on the slave question. For a full review of the debate, see William Doyle Hull, "A Canon of the Critical Works of Edgar Allan Poe with a Study of Poe as Editor and Reviewer," Diss., University of Virginia, 1941; Bernard Rosenthal, "Poe, Slavery and the *Southern Literary Messenger*: A Reexamination," *Poe Studies* 7 (Dec. 1974): 29–34; J. V. Ridgely, "The Authorship of the 'Paulding-Drayton' Review," *PSA Newsletter* 20, no. 2 (Fall 1992): 1–3, 6; and Terence Whalen, "Average Racism: Poe, Slavery, and the Wages of Literary Nationalism," in *Edgar Allan Poe and the Masses* (Princeton: Princeton University Press, 1999).

7. Norman Stafford, "Edgar Allan Poe's 'The Gold Bug,' the Trickster, and the 'Long-Tail'd Blue,'" *Thalia* 18 (1998): 72–83. See also Scott Peeples, "Love and Theft in the Carolina Lowcountry," *Arizona Quarterly* 60, no. 2 (2004): 33–56.

8. *Romancing the Shadow: Poe and Race*, ed. J. Gerald Kennedy and Liliane Weissberg (Baton Rouge: LSU Press, 2001).

9. Walter Benjamin, *Charles Baudelaire: A Lyric Poet in the Era of High Capitalism*, trans. Harry Zohn (New York: Verso, 1997). In literary studies, a good recent example is Kevin J. Hayes, "Visual Culture and the Word in Edgar Allan Poe's 'The Man of the Crowd,'" *Nineteenth-Century Literature* 56, no. 4 (Mar. 2002): 445–65 (later expanded within *Poe and the Printed Word* [Cambridge: Cambridge University Press, 2000]).

10. See Meredith McGill, *American Literature and the Culture of Reprinting, 1834–1853* (Philadelphia: University of Pennsylvania Press, 2003), 141–217; and Whalen, *Edgar Allan Poe and the Masses*. The trend was perhaps inaugurated by Joan Dayan's chapter in *The Columbia History of the American Novel* and by the same scholar's pivotal 1994 essay, "Amorous Bondage: Poe, Ladies, and Race," *The Columbia History of the American Novel*, ed. Emory Elliott [New York: Columbia University Press, 1991], 89–109, and Dayan, "Amorous Bondage: Poe, Ladies, and Slaves," *American Literature* 66 [1994]: 239–73.) See also J. Gerald Kennedy, ed., *A Historical Guide to Edgar Allan Poe* [Oxford: Oxford University Press, 2001]; and Kennedy and Weissberg, eds., *Romancing the Shadow*.

11. "Prospects for the Study of Edgar Allan Poe," in Richard J. Kopley, ed., *Prospects for the Study of American Literature* (New York: NYU Press, 1997), 45.

12. The definitive treatment of this idea is by David S. Reynolds, *Beneath the American Renaissance: The Subversive Imagination in the Age of Emerson and Melville* (New York: Knopf, 1988). In a different manner, the detective novelist Julian Symons's book on Poe, *The Tell-Tale Heart* (1984), presented Poe against the backdrop of a boisterous literary world in which generic distinctions were less rigid than they have since become. Symons's excellent book, sadly, is long out of print.

13. Alexander Hammond, "Poe's *'Lionizing'* and the Design of *Tales of the Folio Club*," *ESQ* 18 (1972): 154–65.

14. Other writers whom Poe criticized as having undeservedly high reputations include Charles Dickens and William Cullen Bryant. See his reviews of these authors, respectively, in *Southern Literary Messenger*, June 1836 and January 1837.

15. In the detective stories, for instance, intellect triumphs over greed and crass materialism. And, of course, in "The Philosophy of Composition," Poe points out that the successful poem will please both the "popular as well as the critical taste."

16. Edmund Wilson, "Edgar Allan Poe," *The Shock of Recognition*, vol. 1 (New York: Grosset and Dunlap, 1955), 79.

17. J. T. Barbarese, "Taking Poe Seriously," *Georgia Review* 58 (2004), 802–15.

18. Poe, "Marginalia [part II]" (B), *Democratic Review*, December 1844, 15:580.

ONE

Poe's "Philosophy of Furniture" and the Aesthetics of Fictional Design

C. T. Walters

> Glowing color, the illusion of great space, and splendors all the richer
> that they owe nothing to materials and everything to art, these are the
> hallmarks of an apartment that, appropriately, belongs to a painter. —
> *House and Garden*, November 1983

Preceded and followed in *Burton's Gentlemen's Magazine* for May 1840 by
the poems, "The Betrayed" and "The Pilgrim to His Staff," Poe's short
article "The Philosophy of Furniture" exerted and continues to exert an
influence far beyond its modest scale. In 1864, little more than fifteen
years after Poe's death, the article was reissued in an English periodical,
Cornhill Magazine, under the title "The Fashion of Furniture." Immediately thereafter, Clarence Cook (1828–1900), one of the most influential writers of Victorian life and decorum, annotated Poe's essay in the *New Path
Magazine* of 1865, a periodical inspired by John Ruskin. Brief, yet expansive in meaning, Poe's *impromptu* on design survives well into the twentieth century as a vital document of taste and culture. In 1959 the Brooklyn
Museum organized an exhibition of an actual room carefully reconstructed to visualize Poe's remarks. And in the 1980s, more than one
hundred and forty years after its initial publication, Poe's admonitions
were reissued in the chic *House and Garden* magazine, with the addendum
that the "American master of the macabre offered unconventional ideas
on the arrangements of houses."[1]

"The Philosophy of Furniture" is a study in both text and context. As a
summary of Poe's own interest in painting, music, and landscape gardening, his philosophy affirms the intent of his fiction. The contents of the

1

magazines in which Poe's article was published also establish a setting of popular pretense and intellectual ambition. In 1840, when Poe first published his "Philosophy of Furniture," *Burton's Gentleman's Magazine* expressed the cultural aspects of the moment. An article on "A Critical Notice of the Picture Galleries of the North of Europe" specifically suggests many of Poe's sources: a sunset by Salvator Rosa, "two fine Raphaels," a Psyche and Cupid, and a Guido. Notices also appeared on "Science and Art" and catalog entries ranging from "The Florist's Guide," to the Art Union, to improvements in the daguerreotype. The list is completed with a note provocative in its implication on "ridiculously large plate mirrors" imported from France—all the rage then in American homes.[2]

In its most recent reincarnation, in *House and Garden* magazine, Poe's ideas of taste and restraint seem ironically compromised by the mentality of a decade of consumption and misapplied wealth. In November 1983, we read of Poe's "macabre taste." Amid advertisements for Steinway pianos, modern collections of fine Saxony rugs and porcelain statuettes touted by the Franklin Mint, the reader encounters an excursion into the glitter of eclecticism worthy of Poe's satirical wit honed to its finest edge. A feature story on "Englishness of the English Country Style" alternates with a photo essay on a neo-Egyptian pied-à-terre; while a description of a Spanish colonial bungalow balances an artist's apartment decked out to resemble one of his splashy neo-abstract paintings.

Poe's ideas may have indeed differed radically from the taste of his time; however, "The Philosophy of Furniture" presents a logical response to the social conditions that emerged during the decades preceding the Civil War. With a degree of justification and a hint of paranoia, Poe was convinced that economic and social democracy would ultimately destroy the ethical soul of American society. Characterized by a wonderful sense of aesthetic sarcasm, the essay itself is neatly divided into halves: one half devoted to the disease of progress, the other to a cure. This is what Americans have done, Poe says somewhat facetiously, and this is what they should do. Stuffed with mirrors and with cut glass chandeliers, the American home, according to Poe, threatened to be little more than a poor museum stuffed with status symbols—the detritus of newly created wealth.

Poe challenges the spirit and the temperament of his age, an era characterized—as one writer lamented in *Godey's Magazine*—as "ostentatious, haughty, arid, [and] keenly analytical."[3] The structure of Poe's essay is carefully balanced. Fashionable convention, as Poe defines it, is nothing more than idolatry, a "display of wealth," the product of money and success. Taste, however, is acquired through the discipline of reason, through the study of history, and through the application of the principles of art. To distinguish between taste and the whims of fashion, Poe lists four styles of design that he integrates into a convincing personal aesthetic. From the Dutch to the French, to the Italian, to the English, he identifies the vanity of these fashions, analyzes them to the last detail, and exposes their facetiousness and pretense. The first on his list are the Dutch, who, Poe chides, "have not much else than an indeterminate idea that a curtain is not a cabbage." Dutch design was, indeed, stuffy and routine. Straight lines and sharp angles characterized it; chairs, for example, were composed on rigid vertical and horizontal axes and embellished only slightly with elements of ornament.[4] Dutch interiors were predictable, mathematically perfect, but ultimately boring. Poe satirizes this element of domestic predictability in "The Devil in the Belfry." Set in a Dutch village suggestive of a Girard Dow painting, the architectural setting consists of houses with symmetrical gables constructed in Dutch cross bond: alternating headers and stretches of colors arranged in diamond patterns to create an effect that Poe likens to "chessboards." The most important piece of furniture Poe mentions is a high backed, leather-bottom armchair with "crooked legs and puppy dog feet." The chair symbolically becomes a throne that declares masculine power and the righteousness of an ordered world; the thin legs and soft seat form an expression of self-satisfaction and domestic sentimentality.

In the 1840s, a mania for expensive French furniture and decoration swept America. Much to Poe's consternation, styles found in French royal palaces were imitated in American homes. Poe found the French to be "too much a race of gadabouts with more taste and fashion than artistic sense" and lamented that Americans felt compelled to fill their boudoirs with "ormolu'd cabinets."[5] In "Bon-Bon," a humorous tale in which a transcendental gourmand is crushed to death in a room furnished in the *style à la Grec*, Poe satirized this trend. Fashionable women of the time were advised to don dresses that were as diaphanous as the people who adored Greek revival states. The demoiselle was challenged to wear her hair *à la Grec*, with frizzled locks, bangs across her forehead, and a cap worn at the back.[6] Likewise, in interior design, the French style emphasized motifs adapted from Greek architecture (columns, acroteria flutes, and scrolls) that were combined with more intimate details of design—oval moldings, vases and medallions. Suddenly and inevitably, French names were appended to the simplest forms of furniture. Under the aegis of fashion, the flowerpot was elevated to the status of an exotic potpourri. New furniture for the hall, the parlor, the dining room, and the bedroom were invested with silhouettes derived from classicism and endowed with names derived from the French language: A bed was no longer a bed; it was a *lits droit*. A sofa was not simply a sofa; it became a *tête-à-tête*. A setting stool was no longer a settee; it was a *tabouret*.[7]

In "Duc de l'Omelette," Poe further satirizes French taste, pushing it to the edge of aesthetic and moral decay. Waiting in a chamber of cold marble furnished with dazzling brocades, the Duc of Pate faces purgatory in a room stylistically defined by the writings of Charles Le Brun, designer of the megalomania that characterizes the Palace of Versailles. The *style Louis Quatorze* sets in place a chain of fictional events. The room where the Duc fiddles and fidgets can best be described as a salon. Filled with Goblein tapestries, the salon is a room of passage (an interconnection between a hall and drawing room, between an entrance and a gallery) or in this case between heaven and hell, where the Duc awaits final judgment. Dramatically elongated from top to bottom, the chamber explodes into a fresco. The height of the room is exaggerated beyond human experience to encompass the scale of gargantuan ambition, lust and desire. To assemble the decor of the Duc's antechamber, Poe relies upon the most appropriate principle of design. Everything, he writes, is *"tout ensemble"*—that is, a unified whole or single stylistic entity. From plastered stucco to bombastic decorative motifs, to carpets, to ormolu clocks, such fragments express the design of the story and paraphrase the Duc's character. He is refined, yet brutal and vulgar—and so is the salon. The ensemble is detailed by a single piece of furniture, an ottoman. Although the *style Louis Quatorze* is rigidly prescribed, the decoration of individual pieces of furniture is more creative and inclusive. The furniture details classical emblems intermingled with grotesque ornaments like the Egyptian Sphinx. This arabesque allows the mind of the artist to wonder and dream within rooms whose shape and size are determined by courtly ritual.

The Duc's apartment, as Poe describes it, is a lost world altered by the experiences of life. The corners of the suite are worn away into four carved niches, two of which contain Greek statues (for Poe an indication of the immorality of beauty). The third niche displays an Egyptian image, the suggestion of death. The remaining corner is concealed. It contains either an image of Hermes with the sandaled foot of time or Venus de Milo, the supreme celebration of classical beauty. The sculptures that Poe selects are copies of the ancients. No matter how well-crafted they are, they are plasters, they are French, and they are fake. The single authentic element in the Duc's chamber is a series of paintings by Raphael whose work was transformed in the seventeenth and eighteenth centuries into Goblein tapestries that graced the walls of the Baroque chateau of Versailles. According to Poe's scenario, Raphael's paintings are piled one on top of the other so that the multitude of golden frames paraphrases the cold beauty of the stars in the ceiling paintings above. Poe's inclusion of the painter is pivotal to the meaning of the story. For Poe, Raphael is a painter of brilliant colors and special effects who possesses the ability to penetrate the veil of sensuality and sin, and to express the ultimate beauty beneath the conceit of external appearances.

The glamorous surface of detail that Poe renders conceals the greater shadows of hidden sin and ultimate terror. The Duc has spent his entire life struggling to make his room. His salon is a biography. He has collected statues of voluptuous women; he has even obtained a red ruby, indicative of the desires of a Persian harem. His ambitions, however, are to no avail, for the Duc is wrinkled and repugnant. Through the chambers of his purgatory, he sees only the hopeless and the damned. He utters one last epitaph that unites him with the room: *"que s'il n'eût pas été De L'Omelette il n'aurait point d'objection d'être le Diable."*[8] Translated, the epigram means: Had he not been *De l'Omelette*, he would have had no objection to being the Devil. In a philosophical sense, the Duc has stepped into a cooler climate, the frigid salon of old age. He has become rational, balanced, and indifferent. Yet remembering the physical joys of youth, the Duc would like to be young again. But he cannot. The flame of life Poe imagines is threatened with extinction. The ravages of time have left only the moral exhaustion of a softened egg; the Duc's ambitions remain as a piece of worn-out furniture.

As a remedy for the encroachment of materialism, Poe proposes in "The Philosophy of Furniture" an ideal room constructed according to the principles of art, wherein sight, sound, smell, and touch combine to form the perfect painting. Poe's canvas of effects is carefully rendered. The sides of his parlor, a room some thirty by twenty-five feet, are blank with openings cut into both ends: a door at one end and a window at the other. The door is relatively nondescript, while the windows, which are carefully delineated, are set deeply within a recess opening onto a veranda. The full-length windows are filled with crimson panes that filter the quality of the light, thus subverting the forces of nature to conform to the principles of artistic composition. The windows are also carefully padded with two levels of curtains, one set on the inside and one on the outside. The covering on the inside consists of cloth tissues, while the exterior is covered with a thick cloth that has been tinted gold, crimson, and silver. The outside edges of the box that Poe reveals have been softened. The corners of the wall and the ceiling have been covered with a broad entablature of gilt work that surrounds the upper extremities. The floor is covered with Saxony carpeting (a carpet with inscribed patterns) one-half inch thick, which extends from wall to wall. Both color and light brighten Poe's pallet. Crimson and gold in the shape of cords, festoons, and arabesques contrast with the silver-gray tint of the wall surfaces.[9]

Because of the soft lighting, the furnishings that Poe selects are somewhat difficult to visualize. Poe chooses a kaleidoscope, an octagonal table with gold threaded marble, four large Sevres vases, a mirror, two sofas, two chairs, and a rosewood piano guarded with a coverlet. Each item suggests its own philosophy. The piano is a parlor instrument, a form of middle-class amusement. For Poe the piano becomes a specific instrument of consolation: it combines the voice with the harp and the harp with the lute to form a rainbow of sound. The four Sevres vases, one anchoring each corner of Poe's parlor, originated in eighteenth-century France. These Rococo porcelains embellished with pastel colors were considered middle-class status symbols.

The piano, the vases, and the curtains all exist within a conceptual framework, a picture that confines and isolates human incident. In Poe's essay, a single character, a poet who resembles a hero from a Donizetti opera (Donizetti's *Somnabula* was one of Poe's favorites), sleeps and dreams. And in his dreams he conjures a psychic landscape in which individual objects assume lives of their own. The furnishings are also philosophically suggestive. Even a lamp or a modest chair can illuminate the history of civilization or initiate the melancholy of human experience. As a repository of culture and art, Poe's room exhibits a double edge. The windows in Poe's study are covered by curtains—layers of cloth, muslin beneath damask. In the world of nineteenth-century domestic economy, which Poe mimics and burlesques, curtains kept out the cold, the heat, the dust, and the insects. To create an ensemble, curtains also provided a vital principle of composition. The colors and textures matched carpets, wallpaper, and upholstery. In Poe's philosophy, a curtain casts a shadow, like the wing of death over the process of writing; while a closed window draws itself around the psyche. Lulled by a composition recently improvised on a piano, the poet in the essay, perhaps Poe himself, falls asleep on a settee. Gazing at the corners of his studio, the poet-musician becomes imprisoned in a corner of punishment, trapped beyond poetic imagination in his own inspiration and self-doubt.

Against a wall of silver gray, spotted with arabesques of crimson, Poe hangs the fairy grottos of Clarkson Stanfield and *The Dismal Swamp* of J. G. Chapman. Each of the painters Poe selects adds still another dimension to his aesthetic repertoire. Stanfield (1793–1867) made his reputation as a painter of seascapes and as a popular illustrator. His search for the picturesque led him to paint a virtual dictionary of romantic icons: ruins, stormy seas, glaciers, and wrecked ships destroyed by the sublime powers of nature.[10] Stanfield made his reputation as an illustrator of travel books (such as *Heath's Picturesque Annual*, 1832; *Traveling Sketches*, 1832; and *Stanfield's Coast Scenery*, 1836) and popular novels like Frederick Marryat's *Poor Jack* (1840). Particularly noteworthy are Stanfield's illustrations for the poems of George Crabbe (1834). Filled with Tudor castles inscribed against the bucolic English landscape, such images evoke the misty villages and ancient houses that detail much of Poe's fiction. The second artist, John Gadsby Chapman (1805–1889), was a painter and a gifted draftsman whose most accessible work, *The Baptism of Pocahontas*, is still displayed in the Rotunda of the United States Capitol. Chapman was praised for his inventiveness and his talent for making the arts of design accessible to popular taste. When he lived in Italy, for example, Chapman made copies of Guido Reni's paintings *Aurora* and *Flora* for display in the American parlor.[11] He also provided materials for American annuals. He contributed an entire portfolio of engravings to one of the masterpieces of illustrated books, James K. Paulding's *Christmas Gift from Fairyland* (1838). Typical of the finely detailed engravings, the frontispiece abounds with flourishes, festoons, Indians, and stalks of corn: a buckskin interpretation of the courtly style of late eighteenth-century France. Chapman painted *The Dismal Swamp* in 1831, nearly a decade before Poe wrote "The Philosophy of Furniture." Although the painting itself, based upon a poem by the Irish poet Thomas Moore, has never been recovered, it was engraved for display in the parlors of American homes. *The Dismal Swamp* was such a popular image that it became a conversational idiom. In a short story, "A Day in a Railway Car," a little old lady lives alone in a boarding house. When questioned about her kith and kin, she responds with tears in her eyes that even her favorite nieces have grown up and left home. Her days of vanities and triumph have vanished, she responds. But even with dwindling income and diminished expectations, she replies that "I have not yet got into the Dismal Swamp." She is not yet ready to die. [12]

Poe laments that the typical American apartment was an artistic failure. Its most usual defect, he writes, is its "want of keeping." This term Poe borrowed from eighteenth- and early nineteenth-century aesthetic theory; keeping simple meant harmony. To establish a sense of compositional integrity for his apartment, Poe studies painting. Using Chapman and Stanfield as his examples, Poe addresses one of the most important issues of his age: the usefulness and pragmatism of art. The mission of the artist, Poe realized, was to combine the decorative with the aesthetic, the results being the artful delineation of the American home. Poe's essay argues for the transformation of the aesthetic principles of painting into the specific necessities of furniture. Chapman's *Dismal Swamp*, with its landscape of the dark sublime (like the tarn in "The Fall of the House of Usher") anticipates the thick, black curtains that line the windows. Poe modulates the color of Stanfield's exotic Venetian setting into an arabesque. The golds and purples of Venice find their equivalents in the carpets and the picture frames suspended from the ceiling. Poe disassembles specific works of art for his own purposes. He reconfigures painting to paraphrase the rhythms of nature. With the eye of an artist, he abstracts the pastoral landscape, transforming it into a parlor where skies become ceilings, where meadows and forests form the equivalent of rugs and tapestries.

Poe had done this before in "The Island of the Fay." With the aid of his friend John Sartain (1808–1897), a Philadelphia engraver noted for his gift books, Poe took an engraving by the English landscape painter John Martin (1789–1854) and poeticized it in the piece. Martin's landscapes were notable for achieving a balance between the chaos of the sublime and the repose of the beautiful. [13] From this source material, Poe crafted a subtle essay on the ethics of art, an essay visualized through landscape painting and anesthetized through the power of music. In it, he maintained that the only way to be conscious of life is to be conscious of art, because art— through its graphic structure—reveals the beautiful and the good.

To transcribe his thoughts, Poe relies upon a consistent tradition in poetry and music: the charmed Arcadia of sprites, fairies, and nymphs. Karl Maria von Weber, Poe's favorite composer, used the themes in his work, *Oberon*. And contemporary resources abound with references to flowers and fairies, fountains and enchanted isles, all of which picture rainbows of color shaded with elements of melancholy.[14] Poe's depiction of the familiar is both philosophical and symbolic. His version of the Garden of Eden, a place of artful delight within the mind of the poet, is built to exist for only a moment. The island emerges between light and dark, where the sun breaks the shadows, where the moon interrupts the darkness of night, where the light of the mind enters the darkness of the subconscious. Poe very carefully paints his images. A waterfall provides the elixir of life; while a river of time isolates the island that, in turn, suggests a canvas that consolidates the minutest details of nature. Hidden in pastoral solitude, a color-winged fay dances back and forth. The fairy, Poe's version of Psyche, plays a tune that echoes through valleys, hills, and mirrored lakes. As she flutters in and out of light and dark, she illustrates the two sides of the universe. She emerges from joy and sunshine, from spring and winter, and finally she dies. The fay frolics so that the aesthetic spirit may live in creative freedom. But when she vanishes, the poet, Poe discloses, relinquishes the conscious recognition of his artistic identity; the creative spirit dies as well.

In "The Island of the Fay," Poe defines all the creative possibilities of artistic process and the eclectic probabilities of style. His idealized parlor creates its own sense of reality based upon the simplest rudiments of artistic experience. Poe manipulates artistic vocabulary to create a perfectly ordered world. He identifies line, shape, form, and color to render the intangible tangible, and to complete a sense of logic that is purposely left incomplete. The layout is a group of circles confined by a square, a combination suggestive of the forces of nature: the sun above and the earth beneath. The circle placed within the corners of a room also indicates cause and effect. As the intense colors of the room induce a state of aesthetic languor, the poet sees the consummate room filled with the appropriate furniture.

Poe also suggests a precise method of classification for his philosophies of furniture. He reduces the most complicated of intellectual puzzles or the most frightening of emotional predicaments to rudimentary principles of design. Poe uses a repertoire of shape and form. He deploys circles, squares, parallelograms, and triangles. In "The Oval Portrait," for example, Poe describes an artistic dilemma confined to an ornamental frame. He casts an entire story within a sophisticated symbol: a shape that is pragmatic, imaginative, and traditional. From Poe's perspective, which represented the transposition of classical taste into the modern world of the nineteenth century, the oval was reserved for library tables and designed for the back of Adamesque chairs. As a symbol favored by the Romantics, it also indicated the perpetual circle of life: the beginning and the end, birth, and death. The form Poe selects delineates the universe: the sun and the moon confined within an elliptical cycle of movement.

For Poe, the ideal room is longer than it is wide, a configuration most appropriate for an internalized landscape where furniture can be artfully arranged. Poe compresses his apartment into a container, a repository of style, that measures the panorama of history. In "The Oblong Box" Poe's creative geometry functions both as subject and subject matter. Mr. Wyatt, inebriated by the spirit of the pure ideal, engages a suite of staterooms on board a ship. In one of the staterooms he cries and moans and sleeps with the oblong box, which we later learn contains the corpse of his late wife. The container occupies the entire floor of Wyatt's stateroom. It paraphrases the restrictions of the room and the beds assigned to the berths. As a piece of furniture, the crate suggests the shape of a settee: two chairs combined upon which to be seated and when no one is looking, to stretch upon and gaze at the corners of the ceiling and walls. In Poe's philosophy, shape determines meaning. The contours of the box are historically suggestive and aesthetically proper. The shape indicates the permanence and restriction of death. Poe also develops the box as a historic symbol. The dimensions suggest the ground plan of a Greek temple or a Gothic cathedral. The altar is the head of the box; the west work or the foot provides an entrance into a religious ceremony where the artist is being sacrificed.

Through the voice of the narrator, Poe tells us that the oblong box is much too large to be simply a coffin. It contains, we are informed, artistic secrets, or more specifically, the reproduction of Leonardo's *Last Supper*, a fresco that rivals the size of any room. Poe, we assume, considers Leonardo to be a genius who contributed a beautiful moment; his art, however, no longer survives, lingering only as a myth that has disintegrated. With four sides, a top and a bottom nailed into place, this piece of furniture is transformed into an image for a wish and for a dream. This fixture contains the artist's hopes for eternity. It circumscribes the world of poetry that begins with the image of Grecian idealism to encompass the Renaissance, an epoch best characterized by the splendor of the *Last Supper*, a painting in which Judas, acting the role of the critic, pushes and prods the artist to redefine his beliefs. And because Poe is repulsed by the desperate sorrows of the human condition, the box stinks. It emits the smell of turpentine: the decay of putrid literalism, the smells of self-indulgence—the odor of progress without conscience or morality.

The oblong box also circumscribes the achievements of painting accepted by history. Poe uses these passions to illustrate the meaning of his story. He intimates that this world has been debased by material progress. Even the dream of classical perfection and the spirituality of the Renaissance have been corrupted. Nothing remains but the ashes from civilizations past, contained in a cheap pine box.

Poe's destination as an artist, so delightfully schematized in "The Philosophy of Furniture," was determined by the collective aesthetic. When Poe philosophized, all of the arts were woven into the same related fabric. A painting was conceived as a musical composition; music was described as a picture. (According to the rubric of the age, Michelangelo was compared to the inventiveness of a Bach fugue, Raphael to the grace of a Mozart, Guilio Romano to the passions of Beethoven, or Haydn to the innocence of Corregio.) As a piece of furniture, the piano located in Poe's salon evoked the potential for landscape painting. The concertgoer encountered a fantasy piece of brilliant pianistic effect that prompted the sounds and color of a romantic landscape complete with clouds and brooding forests. Designers and decorators of the time studied paintings by Claude Lorraine, transforming his compositions into staged settings for intimate cottages.[15]

In his last two publications, "The Domain of Arnheim" and "Landor's Cottage," Poe divides his artistic testament into equal halves of music and furniture—a landscape balanced by the interior of a house. In "The Domain of Arnheim," Poe orchestrates a tone poem. From a world of dreams and despair, Poe crafts a ballad carefully modeled after his own investigation of contemporary practice in landscape gardening. The text is a paraphrase of one of the most popular paintings of the 1830s, Thomas Cole's *Voyage of Life*.[16] The pilgrim path depicted in it leads into "Landor's Cottage," a fictionalized description of Poe's own home in Fordham. Poe structures the essays through the vision of Ellison, whose ideas have been empowered by four basic principles: confidence, love, spiritual and physical energy, and the pursuit of the ideal. In his search for the spiritual world beyond mere appearance, Ellison opens the window of his soul and, forsaking the collection of false virtue (plaster casts of dead art and the potpourris of dead plants), seeks the most complete form of art—landscape gardening.

The perfect form of unification was, indeed, landscape gardening. The pictorial garden was unsurpassed because it reflected the artistic ideals of the romantic movement, providing Poe with the imperative to retrieve and unify the spirits of music, poetry, and metaphysics. As an intellectual discipline, landscape gardening transformed aesthetic ideals that existed as images on a canvass or notes on a musical staff into something that was real: a room with a rug or an Arcadian environment, simultaneously sublime, beautiful and picturesque. Landscape gardening also best illustrates Poe's concept of time, a concept set by artistic opinion, by taste, and by style. In music, time lingers as a memory; in painting, it is affixed to a flat surface. The dynamics of time in the garden, however, are infinite. Poe's sense of landscape is never finished. It is affected by the time of day (dawn to dusk); the time of the seasons (spring to winter); and the epochs of life (from infancy to old age). Poe's view of the garden, which supersedes the simplicity of painting, is fluid and mobile. We do not look through a frame. Instead we are led into the landscape where we experience paths, meadows, and mountains that characterize the spiritual essence of nature.

For "The Domain of Arnheim," Poe meticulously read and incorporated insights from the most important book on landscape gardening of his age, Sir Uvedale Price's *On the Picturesque*. Published in many different editions, illustrated and annotated, Price's treatise on the adaptation of paintings to the picturesque garden addresses the conflict and final resolution between two styles of gardening design: the formal, more absolute order of the late seventeenth century and early eighteenth century, and the pictorial format of the late eighteenth and early nineteenth centuries. Poe labels the styles "the artificial" and "the natural." The first style was based on the rule and the order of line, the example of the English landscapist Capability Brown, whom Poe mentions by name. Nature was subjected to a geometric plan whereby the gardener improved the environment. This hierarchy of artistic ritual found its highest achievement in the style of Versailles, Poe informs his reader, or the Italian symmetrical parterres, boxes of shrubs and trees that open and close to reveal calculated panoramas with hidden niches and secret compartments (much like we see also in the schoolgrounds in the tale "William Wilson"). In the more formal style, gardens were conceived as houses, rooms without ceilings, designed for polite discourse or to initiate conversation. The second style was the picturesque garden, a landscape crafted from studying three particular painters. Claude, noted by Poe, was cherished for his softness, his glowing colors, and his vivid effects. Poussin, mentioned by Price in his essay and suggested by Poe in the text, was valued for his architectonic space. Completing the trilogy was Salvator Rosa, an artist of the sublime whose dramatically lit landscapes were filled with passion, his paintings charged with terror and fear.

To illustrate "The Domain of Arnheim," Poe selected Thomas Cole's *Voyage of Life*. Cherished by a generation of Americans for its moral sensibility, Cole's painting is a theme with variations consisting of four matched canvasses. These can be interpreted through the poems that Cole wrote to accompany the work. In the first poem, subtitled "Infancy," Cole creates a gentle river accompanied by a fantastic landscape. The river is a leitmotif in each section of the poem. On the stream floats a golden vessel bearing a baby who is protected by a guardian angel. On this "Stream of Life," a boy, to the accompaniment of an ever-changing landscape garden, grows into manhood. In his barque, the pilgrim encounters trials and tribulations—the storms of life—and finally, at the end of the river, confronts death. The angel who protects the child descends from an autumnal gale; a trumpet's crystal voice sounds and the old man rises from his barque borne aloft by dazzling wings, as his spirit soars to heaven. Cole's soliloquy ends with a sigh, as the poet remembers the four seasons of life, each event consolidated by the power of nature, by the river of life.

It is the second verse, "Adolescence," that is the most important for Poe. A youth on the edge of manhood emerges from a storm to confront his ambitions. The landscape vista widens, reflecting through a purple haze, the sky, the clouds, and a mountain peak. With his hand firmly planted on the tiller, the youth sees an enchanting structure on the horizon—a white building that floats, symbolizing the delirious expectations and ambitions of youth. This edifice is a tantalizing piece of eclecticism. As a study in style, the "Gorgeous Palace" categorizes the pinnacles and peaks of the Gothic Revival; the columns and shafts of an "antique song" and the exoticism of the Near East. Cole's compendium of architectural elements measures the rhythms of nature, while illuminating the power of a higher world of ethical perfection.

In Poe's piece, the approach to Arnheim is opened by a river upon which floats an enchanted vessel of gold and ivory. Philosophically, the river functions both as a mirror and a clock. The stream sinks into a maze that Poe compares to a room. Without floor and ceiling, the basin reflects the sky, recreating the impression of a gigantic curtain filled with beautiful flowers. The river measures time. It winds its way from east to west, from the rising and setting of the sun, from light to dark, the triumphs and tragedies of life. Through a landscape in which everything is concealed and nothing is as obvious as it seems, we arrive at the end of an intricate path designed by a silver rivulet. The buildings found in Cole's painting punctuate the passage. With tiller in hand the youth turns toward the horizon, and hearing a strange melody, he beholds in Poe's words, "a mass of semi-Gothic, semi-Saracenic architecture, sustaining itself as if by miracle in mid-air, glittering in the red sunlight with a hundred oriels, minarets, and pinnacles; and seeming the phantom handiwork, conjointly, of the Sylphs, of the Fairies, of the Genii, and of the Gnomes."[17] Poe and Cole create their landscapes from an aesthetic palette of carefully defined symbols. In Poe's garden, trees and shrubs represent much more than simple compositional motifs. Cole's paintings and mountains likewise supersede simple geological study. Paths, rivers, clouds, and skies—the elements of landscape painting—all assume the dimensions of allegory. Hidden paths that plunge and ascend suggest despair and hope; rivers indicate the transience of nature; clouds signify the tenderness of human passion. Through color and image, Poe and Cole expropriate the same poetic visions. They transform the present worldliness of America into a potential Garden of Eden filled with enchantment and intrigue.

At the end of the path lies a modest cottage inhabited by Landor and his beautiful daughter, who steps from the vestibule and introduces us to the interior: three rooms behind three doors enclosed within a piazza. To a certain extent, "Landor's Cottage" is modeled after Poe's own house at Fordham, which still survives and has been recently refurbished. Like Poe's cottage, Landor's home consists of a modified English-Dutch style with three rooms on the first floor; a kitchen, a sitting room and a hall which connects one of the doors to an adjacent staircase and a bedroom at the back of the house. Initially, Poe fills Landor's cottage with flowers, the residues of nature, which symbolize the transitory nature of life. Violets (always considered symbols of death) and geraniums occupy vases placed on the edges of windows and on shelves built into the corners of the parlor. Curiously, Poe also places bouquets in the fireplace. But the fireplace, the first element of civilization (providing cooking, light, and heat) does not have a fire. Because it functions as a symbol, it is cold, silent and mechanically inert. The hearth in Poe's design becomes a domestic sanctuary of hope, faith, and lost memories where flowers bloom (and quickly die) and where man is momentarily reunited with nature.

The bookshelves in Landor's cottage indicate the academic world. The function of the books is to assist the poet in reconstructing and intellectualizing a return to nature. The round table Poe adapts for the smaller objects of civilization: bottles, lamps, perhaps portfolios, and notebooks. This collection of *virtu*, simulating life itself, grows layer upon layer, and finally disintegrates into dust. Poe's catalog continues with a rocking chair, perhaps the truest form of Americana, in which men and women loll away the hours. A settee, a doubled chair, is painted white to cover the cheap wood grain. The white color indicates the white of a winding cloth, the white of purity, the white of snow. Two people can be seated, but the settee is so constrictive that it is uncomfortable. Matching the four corners of the room are four empty chairs. The chairs indicate the transformation of the wilderness—the trunks and branches of trees—into tamed functional objects. Because not all share in the process of civilization, some chairs are empty, some chairs are occupied. A floor covered with woven mats (a common practice in the American cottage when rugs were too impractical or expensive) completes the ensemble. Finally, windows unify the domestic stage. They frame a view of nature that can no longer be retrieved. The windows are covered with curtains, Poe writes, made from Jaconnet, a "lawn" cloth: a type of muslin used for handkerchiefs, caps, and skirts sometimes in the style of Louis XlV.[18] From top to bottom and from side to side, Poe carefully measures the curtains so that every pleat falls into place. Perfect folds evoke the flutes inscribed in the circumference of Greek columns.

Poe completes the interior of the cottage with three illustrations, prints of paintings adapted from Bernard-Romian Julian's exquisite lithographs, "*a trois crayons.*" Julian (1802–1871) was a popular illustrator for the contemporary French political journal, *Charivari*.[19] Of all the items in Landor's cottage, these prints indicate Poe's intent as an artist. They illustrate the history of western civilization from the time of the ancient Greeks to the present. The first picture is an illustration of oriental luxury, the splendors and luxury of Venice; the second, a carnival piece, the Bacchanalian rituals of a decaying Rome; the third, an adaptation of a classical head, the visage of Greek myth, the dream of ancient perfection. Poe's choice of pictures represents values that have been either lost or discarded in favor of the aesthetics of the present moment. As the tale unfolds, the artist walks away from nature into the subterfuge of middle-class American life. Poe suggests that once the path has been set, the room furnished, the house built, man can never return to the perfect garden. After he has relinquished the primal forest, the most that he can do is mimic to transcribe and transpose. Nature, Poe concludes, can only be enjoyed and experienced through art.

According to Poe's "Philosophy of Furniture," what was wrong with the American home was that it was "unpicturesque." Lacking both discipline and graphic definition, the typical parlor in the typical house was simply bad still life. Poe suggests that the most effective principle of design is the painting. With his art—his landscapes of the soul—Poe proposes a brilliant solution to the encroachment of materialism: make a room look like a picture that reflects personality and social consequence. In a world compromised by the glitter of mirrors and the glare of candelabra, Poe speaks an eloquent language of art, furniture, and aesthetic commitment.

NOTES

1. *House and Garden* 155 (November 1983): 158; Cook, "Our Furniture: What It Is and What It Should Be," *New Path* 2 (April, May 1865): 55–62; 65–72. Cook was one of the most important figures of the Gilded Age; he published such books as *The House Beautiful* (1880), *The Tsar and His People* (1891), and *A Description of the New York Central Park* (1869).

2. Poe, "The Philosophy of Furniture," *Burton's Gentleman's Magazine* 5 (April 1840): 185–89; 5 (May 1840): 246–50.

3. "Hints for an Essay on Presents," *Godey's* 30 (January 1845): 27 .

4. J. C. Loudon, *Cottage, Farm and Villa Architecture* (London: F. Warne & Co., 1869).

5. According to contemporary carpentry manuals an "or-moulu [is] a species of guilding by means of mercury, to which French furniture owes its effect." Peter Nicholson, *The New and Improved Practical Builder* (London: T. Kelley, 1848), Book III, 35.

6. "A Sketch of the History of Female Costume," *Godey's* 38 (January 1849): 196.

7. "New Furniture," *Godey's* 40 (January 1850): 152–53.

8. Poe, *Complete Works, Tales*, Vol. 1, ed. James Harrison (New York: AMS Press, 1965), 202.

9. Loudon devotes an entire section to Monsieur Argand and his miraculous invention of 1780. Note "Artificial Illumination," 179–80.

10. For contemporary references note the following: "M. Stanfield," *The Crayon* 1 (June 1865): 361; "Art News from England," *The Crayon* 3 (July 1856): 209; *Gentleman's Magazine* 4 (July 1867): 108–10, contains an obituary of the artist.

11. *Godey's* 33 (July 1846): 117–20, contains a complete contemporary biography. It was also noted in *The Crayon* 7 (January 1840): 45, that Chapman illustrated *Hayden's Bible*, Schmidt's *Tales*, and Whittier's *Songs of Labor*.

12. "A Day in a Railway Car," *Godey's* 25 (July 1842): 54.

13. Sartain was a prolific writer and artist. *The Crayon* 3 (September 1856): 376, includes references to "Martin's Pictures."

14. Among the innumerable poems, articles, and books dealing with the Fairyland as a sentimental image, we might note Joseph Rodman Drake's *The Culprit Fay* (New York: G. Dearborn, 1836), which Poe reviewed, along with the poems of Fitz-Greene Halleck, for the *Southern Literary Messenger* in 1836; J. K. Paulding's article on "Fairyland Folklore," *Godey's* 34 (June 1847): 302; and Harriet F. Read's "Fairy Teachings," *The Crayon* 3 (September 1856): 325. One of the most provocative allusions is that of a Victorian garden cemetery. The poem "An Enchanted Island" ends with a reference to Greenwood Cemetery in Brooklyn: "When the evening comes with its beautiful smile, and our eyes are closing to slumber awhile / May that "Greenwood" of Souls be in sight." *The Crayon* 2 (December 1858): 388.

15. "German Music," *The Crayon* 1 (March 1855): 183; J. S. Dwight, "The Concerts of the Past Winter," *The Dial* 1 (July 1840): 124–34; J. Loudon, "Principles of Designing Villas," 778.

16. *Thomas Cole's Poetry,* ed. Marshall Tymme (York, PA: George Shumway, 1972), 145–61. Note particularly 150–53.

17. Poe, *Complete Works, Tales*, vol. V, ed. Harrison (New York: AMS Press, 1965), 196.

18. Pierre Verlet, *The Eighteenth Century in France*, trans. George Savage (Rutland, VT: Charles E. Tuttle, Co., 1967), 258. This notation forms part of an inventory from a French nobleman's elegant townhouse.

19. Ulrich Thieme and Felix Becker, *Allgemeines Lexikol!* Vol. 19 (Leipzig: W. Engelmann, 1907), 305–6.

TWO

Race, Pirates, and Intellect: A Reading of Poe's "The Gold-Bug"

John F. Jebb

In 1843 and 1844, advertisements for public lectures by Edgar A. Poe prominently mentioned him as author of "The Gold-Bug." In a famous letter to James Russell Lowell, Poe boasted, "Of the `Gold-Bug' (my most successful tale) more than 300,000 copies have been circulated."[1] The popularity of this story probably derives in large part from its appropriation of the popular legend of the hunt for pirate treasure, mixed with Poe's literary innovations in mystery and detection. Whereas other treasure hunt stories of his era tend to highlight the irrationality of the hunters, Poe invests his character William Legrand with the ratiocinative skill of a master detective, indeed, skill similar to Poe's earlier creation, the detective C. Auguste Dupin. That is, Poe narrates a treasure hunt whose success derives from the intellectual power of the hero. A quick survey of other specimens of the treasure hunt genre will attest that Poe takes this traditional plot line in a new direction.

Yet the vast popularity of the story is also curious because Poe portrays a rough equivalence between the white and black characters, that is, between the main character Legrand and his black servant (not a slave) Jupiter. His dialect, lack of basic knowledge such as right vs. left, and some very exaggerated reactions do indeed render Jupiter as a comic figure. Yet Jupiter also has the inclination to beat Legrand, engages in verbal sparring, and works as an equal partner in the treasure hunt. The 1840s seems an odd period for the popularity of a story in which a black

man threatens to beat a white man. While not being overtly revolutionary, Poe manages to be subversive and surprising in his portrayal of race,
especially given the antebellum Southern setting.

But Poe gets little credit for being so subversive in writing the story.
Instead, critics tend to cite that Poe was raised in Virginia by a man, John
Allan, who held (eventually) over 200 slaves. And Poe does use black
servant characters to humorous effect through confusing dialect, unusual
physical appearance, and bewildered reactions in such tales as "A Predicament" (1838), "The Man That Was Used Up" (1839), and "The Journal of
Julius Rodman" (1840). Biographer Kenneth Silverman offers this acerbic
appraisal: "Poe opposed abolition, and identified with slaveholding
interests in the South, whom he felt Northern writers misrepresented.
Although in no way consumed with racial hatred, he considered blacks
less than human—as did many other Americans in the 1840s. . . . His
friend Mary Starr later remarked that he 'didn't like dark-skinned people.'"[2] Silverman cites Jupiter and "The Gold-Bug" as evidence of Poe's
racial attitudes.

This easily accepted notion that Poe had racist tendencies has infected
Poe scholarship for years and perhaps has discouraged others from sift-
ing the evidence, both biographic and literary. Three examples can suffice—though a fourth, Toni Morrison, will appear later in this essay. Scott
Peeples writes that the stories mentioned above do "little to subvert racist
hierarchies, and much to reinforce them."[3] Craig Werner begins his discussion of allusions to Poe in fiction by black authors, notably Ishmael
Reed and Richard Wright, by acknowledging "Poe's somewhat deserved
but often overstated reputation as a man who shared the racial attitudes
of his time and place."[4] David Leverenz accepts that "Poe subverts various discourses shoring up white male supremacy, even as his writings
display recurrent racism." Regarding "The Man That Was Used Up,"
Leverenz admits that it describes a "racial crossing" that "unsettles," but
the evidence of the story does not lead him to reconsider Poe's alleged
racism.[5]

Such a preconception of Poe and his work is similar to the attitudes of
the Parisian police in "The Murders in the Rue Morgue." Confronted
with the gruesome, bloody room and with two hacked-up corpses, the
police focus on a detail that makes sense to them: that the victims had
withdrawn a large portion of their money and had their wealth in the
room with them when they were attacked. Deciding that robbery was the
motive only because it is a motive that they understand, the police arrest
the banker's clerk Adolphe Le Bon because he knew about the money.
But as the detective hero Dupin establishes, the theory that Le Bon is the
killer accounts for too little of the evidence, especially as the money remains at the scene after the killings. Dupin admits that his eventual conclusion does not account for each detail—some mysteries remain and can

receive only speculation—yet is a much fuller analysis than that done by the police. Similarly, seeing Jupiter as confirmation of Poe's supposed Southern racial mindset ignores some significant evidence.

This essay seeks to restore that evidence to discussion of the story and perhaps even to the discussion of Poe's racial outlook. On the way to the analysis of Jupiter and race, the essay offers a reading of the story involving its use of popular legend and its treatments of Legrand's grand intellect. Indeed, the chief value within the story is rationality: rational analysis and experimentation can resolve almost any mystery. The hyper-rational hero also happens to have an oddly equivalent relationship with his manumitted slave.

Published in 1843, "The Gold-Bug" uses the technique that Poe pioneered in the earlier tales of Dupin, "The Murders in the Rue Morgue" (1841) and "The Mystery of Marie Roget" (1842–1843). (The third Dupin story, "The Purloined Letter," came in 1844, the year after "The Gold-Bug.") Dupin confronts mysterious circumstances, acts on a bizarre-seeming theory which proves to be true, and then delivers a lengthy explanation of how he inducted the theory from the facts before him. The hero of "The Gold-Bug" is William Legrand, a fallen New Orleans aristocrat who lives in seclusion with his black servant Jupiter on Sullivan's Island near Charleston, South Carolina. On the beach, they find a large gold-colored beetle. Because it snaps and bites, Legrand wraps it in a scrap of parchment that Jupiter found nearby, partly buried in sand. The parchment soon attracts Legrand's attention. Days later, he summons his friend the narrator, and with Jupiter the three, close to nightfall, go into the nearby woods on the main land[6] and dig a deep hole, wherein they find the vast treasures of the pirate Captain William Kidd. After they secure the loot at his hut, Legrand explains how he knew to look for the treasure. The parchment revealed a cipher, coded writing, which Legrand decoded and interpreted as instructions to locate the treasure.

This plot outline sets up discussion of the three key aspects of the story: Poe's use of the legends of Captain Kidd, Poe's continued exploration and variation on the themes of ratiocination, and Poe's portrayal of equivalence between white and black. In each of the these elements, Poe demonstrates his originality as a writer. First, Poe unites the treasure hunt story, usually a tale of irrational behaviors, with the hyper-rational detective story. Next, Poe innovates within his own new genre: for example, Legrand and the narrator behave and relate to each other very differently than the similar pair in the Dupin stories. And finally, Poe surprises us about race in ways that Silverman and others do not lead readers to expect.

PIRATES

> The name of Captain Kidd was like a talisman in those times, and was
> associated with a thousand marvellous stories. —Washington Irving,
> "The Money-Diggers"

So says the narrator of Washington Irving's "The Money-Diggers," setting up a tale in which several denizens of old New York will become
convinced that Kidd's treasure is out there for the finding and taking.[7]
The lure of Kidd's treasure appears in stories by several nineteenth-century authors, notably Washington Irving in 1824, Robert Montgomery
Bird in 1836, Poe in 1843, and Harriet Beecher Stowe in 1871.

Of these four, only Irving is historically accurate, sort of, in placing the
presumed treasure in New York, but one of Irving's characters, a seaman
who should be a good source, scoffs at the treasure seekers, "I tell you
Kidd was never up the Hudson. What a plague do you know of Kidd and
his haunts?"[8] The other authors place Kidd inaccurately in New Jersey,
South Carolina, and the coast of Maine. Yet their uses of Kidd, across a
period of almost fifty years, attest to the strength and popularity of the
legend. Kidd and treasure seem to be easy devices, familiar and interesting to nineteenth-century readers. If readers knew of Kidd's career in
only the vaguest terms—that he was a pirate whose treasure went largely
unaccounted for at his death—all the better; such readers would not object to characters hunting the treasure in South Carolina or Maine.

Although buried treasure has been a favorite theme in the pirate stories of fiction, there are very few documented examples of real pirates
burying their loot. Most pirates preferred to spend their plunder in an
orgy of drinking, gambling, and whoring when they returned to port.[9]
Thus, according to David Cordingly in *Under the Black Flag: The Romance
and the Reality of Life Among the Pirates* (1995), the legends are more fantasy than history (perhaps similar to the beliefs that aliens landed in Ros-
well or other fantastic conspiracy theories that often appear in current
popular fiction). But in his account of Kidd's career, Cordingly admits
that the history tantalizes. Born about 1645, Kidd took up pirating later in
life, roughly at age fifty. Having signed on as a leader of an expedition to
capture pirates, Kidd turned criminal and seized ships off the eastern
coast of Africa and eventually sailed to the West Indies. Perhaps thinking
that his former business partner who had become governor of New York
and Massachusetts Bay would help him, or perhaps missing his wife and
daughters in New York, Kidd sailed to Long Island.

Kidd gave his former associate, Lord Bellomont, an extensive statement on the vastness of his plunder. And Kidd had time to roam the
Long Island coast in his ship. Kidd was indeed a wanted man, and Bellomont scrupled to help him and thus arrested him and sent him to England for trial. Kidd suffered execution by hanging in 1701. But the testi-

mony of witnesses on how much booty Kidd had along with Kidd's own statements to Bellomont did not square with the loot in his possession when he was finally taken. Thus the legend arose. Did he secret the treasure to his family and friends? Did he bury some of it during his prowling off Long Island? Cordingly writes that Kidd's arrest in the Colonies and his demise in England excited great interest, and "over the years people have tried to find the remnants of Kidd's treasure and carried out searches on Gardiners Island [New York] and many other locations, but without success."[10] One hundred and seventy years earlier, Washington Irving's narrator said much the same: "Such is the main outline of Kidd's history; but it has given birth to an innumerable progeny of traditions. The report of his having buried great treasures of gold and jewels before his arrest, set the brains of all the good people along the coast in a ferment."[11]

Poe's use of Kidd as the source of the treasure thus appeals to popular legend. And Poe crafted the name into a brilliant clue: Legrand decides that a drawing of a goat on the parchment is a pun on "Kidd." He thus decides further that the cipher refers to Captain Kidd and that the language of the cipher is English. Having spent time there during his brief stint as a soldier, November 1827 to December 1828, Poe also likely knew that Charleston, South Carolina, endured a bloody history with pirates.

In June of 1718, Edward Teach, aka Blackbeard, commander of a four-ship pirate fleet, attacked vessels near Charleston and took prominent people hostage, including a four-year-old boy. He offered them in trade for medical supplies, or he would behead them. Charleston's royal governor accepted the terrorist's demands, and the hostages went free. But in August of that year, Stede Bonnet, who had been with Blackbeard, returned to menace the coast. The local authorities this time raised ships that embattled Bonnet's crew near Cape Fear, North Carolina. Thirty-five pirates were captured and brought to Charleston, including Bonnet. But Bonnet managed to escape and hid on Sullivan's Island for roughly three weeks. His sojourn there attached pirate lore to the island. After his recapture, he was tried and executed. That fall, in November, Blackbeard himself died in battle off Ocracoke Island, where according to reports he had planned to establish a haven for pirate ships. The fondness of pirates for lingering at islands near the coasts gave such islands a mystique. Perhaps the pirates buried treasure there.[12] Poe thus merges the more northern legends of Kidd's treasure with the local history of pirates' violent raids near Charleston.

Here are annotations for the previously mentioned tales about hunting Kidd's treasure. Irving's "The Money-Diggers" from *Tales of a Traveller*, published in 1824, features two treasure hunters. The first digs for Kidd's treasure near Boston and while doing so encounters the Devil, who offers to reveal the booty only if the man puts the money to certain uses; deals with the Devil cannot go well for the human. The story shifts to New York, where a band of hunters finds the buried chest but are scared off by a ghostly visitation. The main character instead finds fortune through real estate sales.[13] Robert Montgomery Bird embedded references to Kidd near the opening of his two-volume novel, *Sheppard Lee*, published in 1836. The eponymous New Jersey landowner becomes inspired by his slave's insistence that Kidd's treasure lies nearby. But while digging for it, Lee plunges his mattock into his foot and falls into a trance. His soul separates from his body and wanders the Middle Atlantic states inhabiting recently deceased bodies: he stays in a body until danger necessitates that his soul must find another host. The errant soul experiences seven migrations.[14]

Poe approvingly references both of these texts in his critical writings. Poe writes (in 1842 and 1847 reviews of Hawthorne's *Twice-Told Tales*) that *Tales of a Traveller* are "graceful and impressive narratives" and "rare" examples of an American fiction "of high merit." Poe's review of *Sheppard Lee* comprises mostly lengthy plot summary with brief comments on the humorous tone and the use of metempsychosis, a concept Poe himself would employ in "A Tale of the Ragged Mountains" (1844).[15] Several scholars, notably Liliane Weissberg and Nancy Buffington, find the influence of Irving and Bird in "The Gold-Bug"; I will return to this matter and to Weissberg and Buffington when I discuss Jupiter.

Stowe's "Captain Kidd's Money" appears in *Sam Lawson's Oldtown Fireside Stories*, published in 1871. An audience of children listens to Sam narrate how he and other residents of his Maine town dislodged and almost hoisted a buried treasure, only to be scared off by cracking sounds and the breaking of their rope. Poe obviously did not know of this tale, since he died in 1849. However, the story is relevant for our discussion because one of the diggers is black, and how the others treat him contrasts significantly with how Poe's characters treat Jupiter.

The point is not that these authors influenced each other, but that they drew from similar popular legends. The four tales share (sort of) the following aspects. They include characters who make fun of the random alleged locations of Kidd's treasure. Quotations from Irving's characters appear above. Sheppard Lee is especially satiric: "Some called the place Captain Kid's [*sic*] Hole, after that famous pirate who was supposed to have buried his money there, as he is supposed to have buried it in a hundred thousand other dismal spots along the different rivers of America."[16] Legrand does not speak so satirically, because unlike the other characters, he actually has evidence: the drawing of the goat on the parchment and the directions on the decoded cipher. The characters in the other three stories have no firm evidence; they rely on rumors and the vague memories of others. They act in hope, whereas Legrand acts with rational certainty.

All four authors include a black character in their stories, usually as one of the diggers. Bird presents Sheppard Lee's slave Jim Jumble as the character who believes in the legend and inspires his master to seek the fortune, though Lee seeks it alone and in secret.

Irving and Stowe refer to faded carvings and lines on rocks as markers of the location. Poe's aggrandized version of these faint indications is the directions on the parchment. The other three authors, Poe excepted, include supernatural elements: spectral visitations during the digging, spirits guarding the site, a cameo appearance by the Devil. Sheppard Lee's slave believes that "midnight was, in his opinion, the only true time to delve for charmed treasure."[17] Poe, an author of tales frequently friendly to supernatural elements, banishes them from "The Gold-Bug." Poe innovates the treasure hunt story by insisting that the hunter employ only rational evidence.

Stowe's Sam tells the children: Kidd "'allers used to kill one or two men or women or children of his prisoners, and bury with it [the treasure], so that their sperits might keep watch on it ef anybody was to dig arter it.'"[18] Here is a detail that Stowe may have borrowed from Poe, as Poe's diggers unearth two skeletons with the loot. Poe ends the story with Legrand's theory that Kidd, needing help to bury his bounty, killed his helpers lest they betray him. Readers surely realize that Legrand needed two helpers to unearth the treasure, and he left them alive—one of them is telling the story. But the skeletons offer a subtle threat—what if Legrand were more greedy, more violent, less willing to share with his two helpers.

HYPER-RATIONALITY

What chiefly separates "The Gold-Bug" from these other treasure stories is the exercise of intellect by Legrand. Irving's character becomes demented and obsessed after hearing vague stories about Kidd and so destroys his fertile vegetable garden in his fruitless treasure hunt. Stowe offers an impoverished character who avoids paying his debts by underhanded scams and who sees Kidd's money as easy money. Stowe's characters are so lazy that they hire a black man to do their digging: they truly want something for nothing. Legrand exerts effort, both mental and physical, and claims his reward.

Legrand is a variation on the character Dupin, and the variations demonstrate that Poe the writer did not let himself get stuck following a formula, even when he invented the formula. Legrand and Dupin are character types who probably appealed to Poe: brainy guys who win acclaim for their intellectual powers. They are fallen aristocrats, facing reduced circumstances through financial reversals. The stories are vague on what happened and if the men were at fault: Dupin suffered "untoward events," Legrand endured "a series of misfortunes." They respond with retreat. Rather than get jobs and earn their money, they subsist in seclusion, relying on the minimal income still available to them. Their behaviors hint of embarrassment over their situations. In the tales, they will win back the esteem of others. Dupin, in "The Murders in the Rue Morgue," solves the case not for money but for his own intellectual exercise and to do a good deed for the man whom the police have wrongly arrested. At the tale's conclusion, he enjoys knowing that the police know that he outworked them. Legrand seeks a more tangible reward. (In "The Purloined Letter," published after "Bug," Dupin claims a substantial fee from the police for recovering the letter; perhaps Poe decided that intellect should pay off, literally, for both his intellectual heroes.)

Dupin loves books and searches after rare ones. Legrand also collects books, but does not read his. (Seeing this detail as Poe's playing his characters off against each other is not far-fetched.) Instead, Legrand enjoys the outdoors, as his selection of a coastal island as his home would suggest. He hunts game, wanders on the beach, and gathers specimens of shells and insects. He has a network of friends and fellow collectors, including the narrator.

The relations of the narrators to the two heroes also differ. Dupin's friend writes from hero-worship. He presents Dupin as an exemplum of human "analytical power." He even tells us, "I was permitted to be at the expense of renting, and furnishing" the house in which they lived.[19] Another, less charitable way to interpret this relationship is that Dupin latches on to the narrator as a loyal audience for his intellectual showing-off and as a needed source of funds, allowing Dupin to live in better circumstances than before.

The speaker in "The Gold-Bug" shows much more realism about Legrand's faults. He admits that Legrand can be moody, angry, sulky.[20] Legrand seems insulted when he thinks the narrator has questioned his drawing ability. When Legrand has figured out the cipher and asks the narrator to accompany him on an adventure to the main land, he gives too few clues of what the task will involve and tries the narrator's patience. The speaker decides that Legrand must have delusions and asks that Legrand come under his care when the adventure is over. Legrand is not only cagey with his secret, but playful. As they walk to the place where Legrand is sure that the treasure lies, he twirls the gold bug on a string. He explains later, "'I felt somewhat annoyed by your evident suspicions touching my sanity, and so resolved to punish you quietly, in my own way, by a little bit of sober mystification. For this reason I swung the beetle.'"[21]

Despite these artful differences, Dupin and Legrand share the same mindset. Each man confidently expects to resolve any mystery. If the mental powers attend to an issue with open observation and no preconceptions, those powers will find an answer. Dupin boasts that the very confounding aspects of the killings on the Rue Morgue will make them easier to explain.[22] A relentless curiosity accompanies this self-confidence. Thus Dupin expects to find "amusement" by viewing the death scene to look for clues, and Legrand drives himself to explain why a death's head appeared when the parchment—on which he had drawn the gold bug, the drawing which he thinks the narrator criticizes—was held near fire.

COINCIDENCE AND PRECISION

The drawing that becomes conflated with a death's head is but one of a clever network of coincidences that Poe embeds in "The Gold-Bug." (We might imagine Poe amusing himself by inserting the significant details as he wrote.) Unless particular chance events had occurred in their particular sequence, the clue of the death's head would never have surfaced. Legrand says, during his final speech of explanation, "'I say the singularity of this coincidence [the death's head] absolutely stupified me for a time. Thus is the usual effect of such coincidences. The mind struggles to establish a connexion—a sequence of cause and effect—and being unable to do so, suffers a species of temporary paralysis.'"[23] Rather than remain confused and so surrender, Legrand seeks the explanation.

The events when Jupiter and Legrand found the bug had to happen precisely as they did. Indeed, the bug itself may have set off the chain of events, but it is not a clue. The story's very title is a red herring. Jupiter—not Legrand, a wonderful ironic detail—spies the parchment and uses it to encase the snapping beetle. They encounter a fellow collector who wants to keep the bug overnight. So to describe the bug to the narrator, Legrand must draw it, and pulls from his pocket the parchment. Legrand continues, "'The weather was chilly (oh rare and happy accident! [for October in Charleston]), and a fire was blazing on the hearth.'"[24] For warmth, the narrator huddles near the fire and so almost lets the parchment burn when Legrand's dog leaps on him. The heat releases the death's head. All of these actions and circumstances are accidental; their exposure of the clue is completely random.

But the *analysis* of the clue cannot be random. To contrast this string of coincidences, Poe writes that Legrand must investigate with careful precision. Deciding that the parchment might have more invisible drawings, he heats it, exposing the goat and the cipher. He explains how he decoded the cipher using what he knew of the frequency of letters in English, common letter combinations, and some psychologizing about how the cipher's author may have over-compensated—that is, crowding characters at passages where the translated version would have sentence breaks.[25]

Precision becomes especially important when Legrand goes onto the mainland to follow the clues on the cipher. The references to a "good glass," the "Bishop's hostel," and the "Devil's seat" lead him, with a telescope, to a ledge of rock. He must sit in precise position to remain on the ledge, and must hold the telescope exactly as the clues direct—"twenty-one degrees and thirteen minutes northeast and by north." Only by doing these things, he sights the skull on the high tree branch.

At the base of the tree, Legrand cajoles Jupiter to climb and drop a weight, actually the gold bug itself, through an eye socket of the skull. Legrand decides where to dig by measuring out from the tree trunk, past where the bug fell. But the first digging turns up nothing. Dejected, preparing to leave for home, Legrand cannot accept that he misread the cipher or calculated incorrectly. His pride forbids that he doubt his own rational powers. He correctly inducts that Jupiter dropped the bug through the wrong eye of the skull. That difference, which Legrand figures was under three inches, became magnified as he completed the line from the trunk out to the perimeter. Recalculation and re-digging disclose the treasure. The story again asserts the need for exact precision.

Detective and mystery stories require intricate clues; such is a given of the genre. Yet seldom in the genre do we find the artfulness of Poe's construction: accidental clues must be followed-up in the most deliberate manner. "The Gold-Bug" displays the shift from a group of coincidences to a precise series of causes and effects.

RACE

The Southern setting suggests slavery, as perhaps does Legrand's status as a former New Orleans aristocrat. Yet Poe emphasizes that Jupiter has been manumitted, but has remained with Legrand out of ingrained loyalty. Why would Poe not do what was expected and write Jupiter as a slave? Terence Whalen offers an answer in his theory of "average racism," a view that reflects the often overlooked point that authors and editors want lots of people to buy their books and journals. Before the Civil War, authors and editors seeking a national readership needed to negotiate how they treated the great issue of the time: slavery. Whalen pithily defines "average racism" as "a strategic construction designed to overcome political dissension in the emerging mass audience." Put another way, as an editor and a writer, Poe would slant aspects to appeal to (or at least not to offend) both North and South. Regarding Jupiter, Whalen writes:

> Poe shrewdly tries to have it both ways. On the one hand, he exploits conventions about the intimate, loyal bonds between white masters and black servants. On the other hand, he attempts to evade any outcry

over such a portrayal by making Jupiter free, and although Legrand is referred to as "master" on several occasions, never once in the entire story does Poe use the word "slave." . . . Through a crucial yet subtle change in Jupiter's legal status, Poe attempted to create a sanitized South that could circulate freely in the national literary market.[26]

Whalen's analysis explains a couple of other noteworthy details. To find out about the "Bishop's Hostel" and if it actually refers to the ancient Bessop family (it does—Legrand scores again), Legrand visits a plantation and talks to "older negroes." Surely, they are slaves, but he does not use the term. Another term he never uses is the epithet "nigger," even when Jupiter makes him angry, but Jupiter three times uses the term in reference to himself.[27]

The story presents some other aspects that "average racism" may not fully explain. For the sake of completeness, all the story's quizzical racial aspects appear below in list form.

1. Jupiter is a manumitted slave.
2. Legrand treats the slaves at the nearby plantation with some respect. He realizes that they are good sources of local history, and so taps them instead of white people. He offers to pay the old woman who directs him to the high rock that is *Bessop's Castle*. But she declines his money.
3. Legrand never uses the epithet, but Jupiter does.
4. When Legrand becomes impatient and yells because Jupiter resists climbing out on the tree limb with the bug, Jupiter shouts back, "'Yes, massa, needn't hollo at poor nigger dat style.'"[28] That is, Jupiter talks back to Legrand, is not docile nor submissive, even if he does finally do what Legrand wants.
5. Indeed, an indication that he is far from docile is what he plans to do when Legrand, whom he thinks is sick, goes missing for a day. Jupiter tells the narrator: "'I had a big stick ready to gib him d—d good beating when he did come—but Ise sich a fool that I hadn't de heart arter all—he looked so berry poorly.'" And a letter from Legrand to the narrator verifies the incident: "'I verily believe that my ill looks alone saved me a flogging.'" The narrator does not express horror at the possibility, instead cautioning that Legrand must be unwell and Jupiter should "not be too severe." The relationship of Jupiter and Legrand is one in which Legrand does not have unmitigated power; indeed, Jupiter has the authority not only to talk back, but to punish physically.

   Poe's modern editor Thomas Ollive Mabbott writes in an endnote, "The question is sometimes asked if a Negro's threat to beat a white man would have been accepted in the old South. It should be observed that if not malicious it could have been approved. A beating was popularly regarded as excellent treatment for incipient madness."[29] Well . . . Thomas D. Morris in *Southern Slavery and the Law, 1619–1860* (1996) reports that in 1819, "Virginia amended its law on persons of color lifting a hand against whites, adding the phrase '[or] use provoking and abusive language to [*sic*].'" Morris continues by describing South Carolina court cases in which insolent slaves suffered lashes, in one case even after Whites testified that the slave had been provoked by an assault from a drunken man, who was not the slave's master. According to South Carolina law, "If a slave presumed to strike a white person at all, he or she would be punished at the court's discretion for the first and second offenses and executed for the third." As early as 1740, South Carolina required "the death penalty for any slave who 'shall grievously wound, maim, or bruise any white person.'"[30] Morris' survey of legal statutes and cases suggests that Jupiter—a person of color and a former slave who now functions as a servant—comes close to committing a crime. Given these facts, one wonders what Poe's original readers thought of this surprising aspect of the story, especially given that the story was so very popular.

6. Here is Jupiter's reaction when the trio finally uncovers the treasure: "He seemed stupified—thunderstricken. Presently he fell upon his knees in the pit, and, burying his naked arms up to the elbows in gold, let them there remain, as if enjoying the luxury of a bath."[31] This lusty embrace suggests that Jupiter will share in the reward, that the treasure is his to embrace.

Stowe's "Captain Kidd's Money" especially contrasts here. The lazy seekers hire a black well digger to do the heavy labor for them. In contrast, Poe's narrator tells us, "we all fell to work with a zeal worthy a more rational cause" (an ironic use of "rational").[32] But one of Stowe's characters objects to sharing what they find with a "nigger." More wise than his hirers, the black well digger insists on payment up front and later reasons that he was paid only to dig a hole, not refill it, and leaves the white guys to finish the job. No such exclusion appears in Poe's story, and Jupiter's hugging of the gold suggests mutual sharing.[33]

How to explain these six indications from the story of deference and equivalence between black and white? The fairest response is that Poe chooses to be more subversive in his treatment of Jupiter than even "average racism" would suggest.

Regarding Jupiter as an equal partner with Legrand is not a popular reading of the story. Rather, critics point to traits that make Jupiter seem quite dense. When in the tree facing the skull, he cannot tell which is the skull's left or right eye; indeed, he barely knows right from left. He is very literal-minded: he cannot separate the gold color of the bug from the illogical idea that the bug is made of gold, and he refers to himself in the third person (always a troubling sign). And his dialect, samples of which appear above, can be difficult to decipher. The dialect seems not to be geographically nor anthropologically accurate; it is not Charleston Gullah, and would not be, as Jupiter comes from New Orleans. Liliane Weissberg summarizes the efforts to place the accent and decides: "In short, Jupiter's dialect designates him as different, but it does not ground its speaker in a specific geographic and cultural setting."[34]

Indeed, the standard line on Jupiter, adopted by Weissberg and by the novelist Toni Morrison, is that Jupiter's traits separate him, make him an "other," rather than bring him into equivalence. In an influential passage from *Playing in the Dark: Whiteness and the Literary Imagination* (1992), Morrison asserts, "No early American Writer is more important to the concept of American Africanism than Poe." She cites "The Gold-Bug" and "A Predicament" as "samples of the desperate need of this writer with pretensions to the planter class for the literary techniques of 'othering,'" such as dialect, stereotype, fetish. She admits that "Jupiter is said to whip his master," which is not exactly accurate as Jupiter only threatens to do so, and explains this aspect as an "unmanageable slip." Morrison slips herself by twice referring to Jupiter as a "slave."[35] This passage suggests that Morrison reads the tale through the author's alleged attitudes. She does not try to integrate the switched power relationship between Jupiter and Legrand into her reading. And she does not address the persisting question of the sharing of the treasure.

Nancy Buffington, in an article from 2004, does confront Jupiter's insolent traits and merges them with a Southern literary motif of the slave who defends slavery, a motif which appears *Sheppard Lee*. In *The Yemassee* by William Gilmore Simms (1835), a slave refuses manumission, insists that his owner accept responsibility for him. Similarly, the slave Jim Jumble refuses freedom from Sheppard Lee. Buffington describes Jim as "saucy" and "tyrannical"; she continues that Jupiter is a similar example of an assertive black man who wants to preserve his subservient status, although Jim does not go so far as threaten to beat Sheppard Lee. The story, according to Buffington, keeps Jupiter in that status: "Jupiter is tyrannical, but ultimately incompetent in this tale, and Poe's narrator credits the venture's success to Legrand. 'The Gold-Bug' thus begins with a destabilized master-slave relationship [and] restores a conventional power dynamic by the end."[36] This reading leaves out that Jupiter's last scene, aside from helping to carry the treasure to Sullivan's Island, is to embrace the gold. Especially when contrasted to Buffington's examples from Simms and Bird, Jupiter seems not to defend subservience so much as to exercise his own power and sense of responsibility for Legrand's welfare. And Poe's story does not include scenes that tame or chastise Jupiter. If in the successful treasure hunt Jupiter learns to trust Legrand's insights, so does the narrator.

These readings from Weissberg, Morrison, and Buffington suggest an inability to tolerate internal irony. Poe's supernatural stories suggest that he possessed a high level of such tolerance. Some of his most famous tales, "Ligeia," "The Black Cat," even "A Tale of the Ragged Mountains" imply both supernatural agencies and explainable psychological causes for what befalls the characters. Does the dead Ligeia return to life, or does her grieving, drug-addled husband hallucinate? Is the vision of Bedloe in "Ragged Mountains" the result of reincarnation or of psychological influence (even a mesmeric spell) from a shadowy doctor? Contradictory evidences come together in these stories, without neat resolutions. Jupiter may be a similar case. Poe creates a rather dense former slave who, despite his loyalty to his master, also achieves equivalence with that master. Poe allows the contradictory elements to come together in the story. Perhaps, Poe wanted a version of race relations acceptable to North and South, as Whalen suggests, and at the same time sought to shake up his readers' racial expectations.[37]

Like this discussion of Jupiter, fresh looks at Poe's other portrayals of blacks suggest that the stories contain more than racist comedy. In "A Predicament," for example, Signora Psyche Zenobia both praises and chastises her black servant Pompey. Though he is a corpulent dwarf, she relies on him to assist her up the stairs of a clock tower. She refers to him as "sweet" and "gallant," yet when he trips while guiding her, she seizes his head and pulls out clumps of hair. Later she will refer to him by the epithet. She regrets her anger and pledges to be considerate as she stands on his shoulders so that she can see out of an opening in the clock-face. Then when the clock's minute-hand traps her by the neck and she screams for help, he refuses because she earlier disdained his request for her to dismount. The story's comedy comes—in addition to Zenobia's description of her gradual decapitation—from the exaggerated extremes in her treatment of Pompey.[38]

A black valet named Pompey also appears in "The Man That Was Used Up." His function is to re-assemble, in front of the startled narrator, the body of General John A. B. C. Smith, who had been mutilated by Indians. Dis-assembled, the General appears as "a large and exceedingly odd-looking bundle of something which lay close by my feet on the floor" and which the narrator kicks out of the way. Pompey screws in limbs, applies a wig and torso, affixes an eye, and speaks only to apologize when he forgets to insert the palate. During this process, the General verbally abuses Pompey, calling him "nigger," "scamp," and "black rascal." These epithets do not start until the assembly is well under way; that is, when he is just a bundle, the General is not so insulting. The General gains assertiveness as he becomes whole, so taking these terms as ironically affectionate does not seem to fit the scene.[39]

This story is usually read as a satire about war heroes, especially war heroes who publicize their military exploits to become politicians, perhaps even of General and later President William Henry Harrison.[40] (For twenty-first century readers, the science fiction aspect of the story attracts attention; Poe foretells the substitution of working, lifelike parts for damaged parts of the human form.) Yet embedded in the story is a striking contrast: the General abuses the person on whom he is totally dependent. In neither this tale nor in "A Predicament" is the black character simply a comic servant: he is the recipient of ironic abuse despite his necessary status with his abuser. In both stories, the white person, each of whom employs the epithet, is a helpless ingrate. The stories, even with their comedy, do not reinforce the Southern antebellum racial ideology.[41]

Nor can Whalen's concept "average racism" quite account for the ironies in these tales and in "The Gold-Bug." Poe places the servant in some position of power over the master: Pompey has complete control over the General, and Jupiter can beat Legrand. Jupiter seems to share equally in the treasure. To claim that Poe advocates or foretells the social equality of black and white would be too extreme, yet the stories present relationships of give and take and power switching between the races. Whatever Poe, who was raised in a slaveholding household, thought of blacks, these stories' portrayals are subversive rather than conservative. As D. H. Lawrence warned in 1923 in *Studies in Classic America Literature*, readers should trust the tale, not the author.[42] The New Critics issue the same warning.

An 1845 essay indicates that Poe was proud of his creation of Jupiter. Scholars debate whether Poe wrote this review of his own collected *Tales*. *The Poe Log* reports that the author is Thomas Dunn English, "who repeats some things Poe has told him."[43] G. R. Thompson in the Library of America collection of Poe's criticism bluntly attributes it to Poe himself. The consensus seems to be that Poe was at least complicit in the contents, and those contents include these lines regarding "The Gold-Bug": "The negro is a perfect picture. He is drawn accurately—no feature overshaded, or distorted. Most of such delineations are caricatures."[44] Ironic humor may be in evidence here, as this allegedly accurate picture includes the elements discussed above, which readers then and now would find surprising.

The thesis of the review is that Poe is valuable for his originality, for his willingness to "escap[e] the shackles of imitation" of other previous renowned authors. (It is fun to imagine that Poe did write this stuff about himself.) "The Gold-Bug" is indeed startling original: in its variation on the treasure hunt story, in its variation within a genre that Poe himself created, and in its conception of how Jupiter and Legrand should interact. This effort to craft an original tale provides readers with a view of race relations designed to provoke reactions, and the provocations still carry force in our day.

NOTES

1. *The Poe Log: A Documentary Life of Edgar Allan Poe, 1809–1849,* by Dwight Thomas and David K. Jackson (Boston: G. K. Hall & Co., 1987), 441, 449, 463.

2. Kenneth Silverman, *Edgar A. Poe: Mournful and Never-Ending Remembrance* (New York: HarperCollins, 1991), 207. The number of John Allan's slaves comes from Silverman, 98. Regarding Allan's slaves, see also *Poe Log,* 24, 64.

3. Scott Peeples, "Love and Theft in the Carolina Lowcountry," *Arizona Quarterly* 60, no. 2 (2004): 39.

4. Craig Werner, *Gold Bugs and the Powers of Blackness: Re-Reading Poe* (Baltimore: Edgar Allan Poe Society and the Library of the University of Baltimore, 1995), 4.

5. David Leverenz, "Spanking the Master: Mind-Body Crossings in Poe's Sensationalism," in *A Historical Guide to Edgar Allan Poe,* ed. J. Gerald Kennedy (New York: Oxford, 2001), 96, 116.

6. Many readers accept that Legrand and the others found Captain Kidd's treasure on Sullivan's Island. For example, Willard Hallam Bonner in *Pirate Laureate: The Life and Legends of Captain Kidd* (New Brunswick: Rutgers University Press, 1947) writes, "Poe airily disregarded geography and located the cache of treasure on Sullivan's Island off the South Carolina coast" (190).
And Liliane Weissberg, in her article about Poe's use (actually non-use) of the Island's history, writes of "the white pirate who used the island as his temporary landing spot and hiding place for stolen treasure, a place presumably valued for its desolation" (in "Black, White, and Gold," in *Romancing the Shadow: Poe and Race,* ed. J. Gerald Kennedy and Liliane Weissberg [New York: Oxford, 2001], 141). She also notes that the Island "acquires . . . a peculiarly hilly landscape" for Legrand to visit (140), though Poe earlier describes the Island as largely beach, without trees, dominated by thick myrtle shrubs (Thomas Ollive Mabbott, editor, *Collected Works of Edgar Allan Poe,* vol. III [Cambridge: Belknap Press of Harvard University Press, 1978], 807).
The treasure is probably found on the coast, not on Sullivan's Island. Poe describes the Island as "about three miles long . . . separated from the mainland by a scarcely perceptible creek." (806–7). Legrand says to the narrator, "Jupiter and myself are going on an expedition into the hills, *upon the main land* [italics added], and, in this expedition, we shall need the aid of some person in whom we can confide" (816). If we need further proofs, here they are. The treasure hunters cross the "creek" in a skiff (817). The tree Jupiter climbs is a majestic tulip rising over "sixty or seventy feet from the ground" (818–19), whereas the Island has no trees, only shrubs no higher than twenty feet (807). Legrand later explains that a clue in the cipher refers to "Bishop's Hostel," that he can find no memory of it among people near the Island, so that he traveled "about four miles to the northward of the Island" (840–41) to pursue his idea that "Bishop" refers to the manor-house of the old "Bessop" family. Recall that the island is only three miles long. This area four miles away is the "hilly landscape" Weissberg references. Legrand's idea proves to be accurate, siting the treasure in a desolate, now abandoned sector of the mainland.

7. Washington Irving, "The Money-Diggers," in *The Complete Tales of Washington Irving,* ed. Charles Neider (Garden City, NY: Doubleday, 1975), 456.

8. Irving, "The Money-Diggers," 464.

9. David Cordingly, *Under the Black Flag: The Romance and the Reality of Life Among the Pirates* (New York: Random House, 1995), 179.

10. Cordingly, *Under the Black Flag,* 190. Bonner in *Pirate Laureate* cites a document that cites Bellomont directly: Bellomont "bad the Gaoler to try if he could to prevaile with Captain Kidd to discover where his treasure was hid . . . but he said nobody could find it but himself and would not tell any further." Bonner continues, "Real or fictitious, it set off what might be called the buried-treasure period in American history" (113).

11. Irving, 434. Kidd's modern biographer, Robert C. Ritchie, describes Joseph Ingraham's two novels about Kidd, published in 1844 and 1859. The first records that Kidd sank with his ship in the Hudson River. Ritchie sounds like Cordingly and like Irving's characters as he describes the resultant mania: "Although the story is quite fantastic, there were enough realistic elements to cause investors to rush forward and fund a number of companies that had as their sole purpose finding the sunken ship and salvaging Kidd's treasure" (in *Captain Kidd and the War Against the Pirates*, [Cambridge: Harvard University Press, 1986], 238).

12. Liliane Weissberg complains in "Black, White, and Gold" that Poe ignores the racial and social history of the Island, which was a transit point for the slave trade and the location of a pest house, a place of quarantine for diseased blacks and whites. See also Walter J. Fraser, Jr., *Charleston! Charleston! The History of a Southern City* (Columbia: University of South Carolina Press, 1989), 31, 78, and 82 for this history. Weissberg does not mention, nor does Poe, the eponymous Florence Sullivan, who in 1670 according to Robert Rosen in *A Short History of Charleston* (Charleston: Peninsula Press, 1992), 14, "was sent to the island to man the signal gun" and who was popularly castigated as "'an ill-natured buggerer of children.'" For more on Blackbeard and Bonnet and Charleston, see Cordingly 194–201, Fraser 33–37, and Rosen 15–17.

13. Bonner in *Pirate Laureate* highly compliments this tale: "However much such trappings as ghosts haunting pirate spoil, treasure spots curiously marked, or sinister pirate-strangers bragging in seaside inns may have gathered from common fireside gossip with spore-like fecundity about the head of Kidd, they never had been worked into any previous artistic shape. Some may deny this achievement to Irving, but it is beyond doubt that the dreaming author-folklorist was the first person of genius to attempt to fashion the story now recognized as the buried treasure tale" (161). Bonner spends eleven pages in analysis of Irving, and gives "The Gold-Bug" but four pages.

14. Bird gives the novel a droll tone, as in this early line: "My father was a farmer in very good circumstances, respectable in his degree, but perhaps more famous for the excellent sausages he used to manufacture for the Philadelphia market, than for any other quality of mind or body that can distinguish one man from his fellows" (*Sheppard Lee* [New York: Harper and Brothers, 1836], 7). The satiric humor, fast-paced action, and diverse locales make this novel fun to read. It is a buried treasure of American antebellum fiction.

15. For Poe's reviews, see *Essays and Reviews*, ed. G. R. Thompson (New York: The Library of America, 1984), 568 and 586 about Irving, 389–403 for the review of *Sheppard Lee*.

16. Bird, 36.

17. Bird, 36.

18. Harriet Beecher Stowe, "Captain Kidd's Money," in *Sam Lawson's Oldtown Fireside Stories* (1871, rpt. Boston: Houghton, Mifflin, 1884), 108.

19. Thomas Ollive Mabbott, editor, *Collected Works of Edgar Allan Poe*, volume II, *Tales and Sketches, 1831–1842* (Cambridge: Belknap Press of Harvard University Press, 1978), 523.

20. Michael Williams reads the narrator's attitude toward Legrand as "the condescension of a socially secure urbanite for a displaced peer" ("'The *language* of the cipher': Interpretation in 'The Gold-Bug,'" in *On Poe: The Best from American Literature*, ed. Louis J. Budd and Edwin H. Cady [Durham: Duke University Press, 1993], 213).

21. Thomas Ollive Mabbott, editor, "The Gold-Bug," in *Collected Works of Edgar Allan Poe*, volume III, *Tales and Sketches, 1843–1849* (Cambridge: Belknap Press of Harvard University Press, 1978), 844.

22. Mabbott, II, 548.

23. Mabbott, III, 829.

24. Mabbott, III, 832.

25. Arthur Conan Doyle obviously adopted the structure of Poe's tales to create the Sherlock Holmes stories. Doyle may offer tribute to "The Gold-Bug" in his own story "The Adventure of the Dancing Men" (1905), in which Holmes also decodes a cipher

using theories about the frequency of English letters and some psychologizing about the word choices. Doyle and Poe do differ in their lists of frequent letters. Doyle's "The Musgrave Ritual" (1893) may be another tribute. It features a buried treasure; the clues to its whereabouts involve figuring distances from tree trunks. And a body is encased with the buried treasure.

26. Terence Whalen, *Edgar Allan Poe and the Masses: The Political Economy of Literature in Antebellum America* (Princeton: Princeton University Press, 1999), 112, 142.

27. For "older negroes" see Mabbott, III, 841. For Jupiter's uses of the epithet, see 818, 820, 826.

28. Mabbott, III, 820.

29. For the lines from Jupiter and Legrand about the beating, see Mabbott, III, 812, 813. For Mabbott's note, see 846.

30. Thomas D. Morris, *Southern Slavery and the Law, 1619–1860* (Chapel Hill: University of North Carolina Press, 1996), 296–98.

31. Mabbott, III, 826.

32. Mabbott, III, 823.

33. Richard Hull disagrees: "Will Jupiter get to keep his third [of the treasure]? Of course not. This manumitted slave is not really free and far from getting a share commensurate with his contribution" ("Puns in 'The Gold-Bug': You Gotta Be Kidding," *Arizona Quarterly* 58, no. 2 [2002]: 15). But Hull cites no evidence from the story that Jupiter will not share. This line from Hull, I contend, is yet another example of preconceptions being allowed to negate the evidence.

34. Weissberg, "Black, White, and Gold," 140.

35. Toni Morrison, *Playing in the Dark: Whiteness and the Literary Imagination* (Cambridge: Harvard University Press, 1992), 32, 58, 83.

36. Nancy Buffington, "Fictions of the South: Southern Portraits of Slavery," in *A Companion to American Fiction, 1780–1865*, ed. Shirley Samuels (Malden, MA: Blackwell, 2004), 378–87. The quotation about Jupiter is from 380.

37. This same internal irony regarding race appears in *Sheppard Lee*. Lee describes Jim as "crabbed, self-willed" and decides that Jim does not want freedom because he is lazy. Yet Lee also admits, without seeming to get the irony, that Jim is an industrious worker who along with his wife, a free woman, raises and sells crops. Indeed, if anyone keeps the land going, it is Jim, as Lee takes no interest in his own affairs and allows bad financial deals to take much of the land away. Jim may say that he wants his master to take care of him, but in actuality he takes care of his master. And if that master does act peevishly, Jim lets him go without dinner. Jim declines freedom, perhaps, not because he is lazy, but because he realizes that as Lee's slave, he has an ironic self-sufficiency.

Later in the novel, Lee's soul inhabits the body of a black slave, and Bird writes of the contentment on the plantation and how the slaves take advantage of their master. An Abolitionist pamphlet falls into their hands and incites them to riot. Some casuistry may be necessary to unite the subversive portrayal of Jim with these more stereotypical plantation scenes.

Bird (1806–1854), a native of Delaware who also lived and worked in Pennsylvania and Maryland, presents his own curious disconnect between his stated views and his art. His biographer, Curtis Dahl, writes of Bird, "The author of the antislavery play *The Gladiator* [about Spartacus, and we might add, the creator of *Sheppard Lee* and Jim Jumble], it should be remembered, was also the man who wished to move out of Pennsylvania if Negroes were given the franchise there!" (Dahl, *Robert Montgomery Bird* [New York: Twayne, 1963], 109).

38. Mabbott reflects the original publication of the story by including it as a tale within a tale, that is, within "How To Write a Blackwood Article," II, 347–57.

39. The re-assembly scene is the last in the story. Mabbott, II, 386–89.

40. See especially the discussion in Jeffrey Meyers, *Edgar Allan Poe: His Life and Legacy* (London: John Murray, 1992), 109–110. Meyers also mentions the revered English hero Admiral Horatio Nelson, who lost body parts in combat.

41. David Leverenz strongly disagrees: he sees these two stories as satires about "an unnatural social order" and judges the last line of "A Predicament," in which Zenobia uses the epithet, to be the "most racist finale in any of Poe's stories." See 115–16. More willing to explore the surprising implications of the status reversal is Robert A. Beuka, whose "The Jacksonian Man in Parts: Dismemberment, Manhood, and Race in 'The Man That Was Used Up'" (*Edgar Allan Poe Review* 3, no. 1 [2002]: 27–44) examines the story's historical context and finds Poe to be quite willing to critique the prevailing racial ideologies.

42. See D. H. Lawrence, *Studies in Classic American Literature* (1923, rpt. New York: Penguin, 1977), 8.

43. *The Poe Log*, 586.

44. *Essays and Reviews*, 869.

THREE

Storytelling, Narrative Authority, and Death in "The Thousand and Second Tale of Scheherazade"

James M. Hutchisson

It is a critical commonplace that Edgar Allan Poe's tales are usually set in an indeterminate time and place. In striving for universality of theme and effect, Poe rarely grounds his work in a specific social, political, or geographic context. This is true even in those cases where he veers into allegory, or what he called in an 1839 review of Baron de la Motte Foque's *Undine* "undercurrents of meaning"—for example, the southern gothic elements of "The Fall of the House of Usher" or the symbolic plague-ravaged country of "The Masque of the Red Death." Even when Poe seems to want readers to apprehend a text allegorically, in other words, the landscapes of those texts remain otherworldly.

One setting, however, that Poe turned to time and again over the course of his tale-writing career, from his early stories and hoaxes to his late, enigmatic fables and "prose poems," was that of the Middle East. Many of these tales, among them "Four Beasts in One—the Homo Cameleopard," "The Sphinx," and "Some Words with a Mummy," are read as light satire, poking fun at the crude materialism of Jacksonian America, spoofing popular journalism, and mocking cultural boosterism and America's infatuation with technology. To be sure, a strong satiric element does infuse these tales, yet I think they go beyond indictments of empiricism, industrialization, and even New England literary arrogance. The most compelling element of Middle Eastern culture that drew Poe was storytelling and the corollary power of narrative. This concept animates "Some Words with a Mummy," "Silence," "Shadow," and several other texts, including the most complex of these Eastern stories, "The Thousand and Second Tale of Scheherazade."

Looking at these tales through the lens of Eastern culture allows us as well to explore ancillary thematic concerns that run through all of Poe's work, such as the deliberately blurred distinction between fact and fiction, the reciprocal acts of death and storytelling, and the production of a fabulist type of writing that was a nineteenth-century forerunner of the postmodernist notion of metafiction. Poe also places importance on the implied contract between reader and writer—between storyteller and audience—that presents fiction as a self-generating process, akin to the work of those postmodernists like Jorge Luis Borges, John Barth, and others, whom Poe profoundly influenced.

Poe reflects on and seems to depict the hazards of the European fascination with the imaginative geography of the Orient in the nineteenth century. Unlike the late theorist Edward Said, however, who described and critiqued "Orientalism" as a constellation of false assumptions underlying Western attitudes toward the East, Poe does not aim to show how such representations serve hegemonic ends. Instead, Poe connects these particular and infrequent "Eastern" representations in his tales to the authority of storytelling and its reciprocal relationship with death.

Poe's interest in the culture of the Middle East was wide-ranging. Saracenic, Arabian, Mongolian, and Islamic motifs saturate many of the stories. Such motifs can be seen even from the start of Poe's career: the title of his first proposed story collection, after all, was "Eleven Tales of the Arabesque." Although Poe was later to modify the title and to explain in Schlegelien terms how he used both the words "arabesque" and "grotesque," the modifying genitive case of the word that connects "tales" with the Eastern, or Arabian, character of storytelling points to the generative nature that Middle Eastern culture assumes in his art.

This should not seem unusual, given the interest in the Middle East in nineteenth-century America. Reports from expeditions to the region filled the newspapers and captured Americans' imaginative hunger for exploration and discovery. Antoine Galland's translation of the massive *Arabian Nights* in 1704 was hugely popular. Jean-Francois Champollion deciphered the Egyptian hieroglyphs in the early 1800s. There were several translations of Persian and Arabic texts by such scholars as William Jones and Abrhama Hyancinthe Anquetil-Duperron. Such men of letters as Byron, Moore, Scott, and Goethe produced "Oriental" texts, and dozens of Oriental Societies were founded in the early to mid 1800s.

One might even argue, as Malini Johar Schuller does, that "The Arabesque is the engendering force that gave birth to [Poe's] fiction."[1] Certainly there are early tales that confirm this point. Poe's first published story was "Metzengerstein," the tale of a rivalry between a count and "the Saracen Berlifitzing." Poe created this story as one of the proposed

Tales of the Folio Club, with its framing device seemingly borrowed from Washington Irving's format of a comic literary club in *Salmagundi*, which appeared in 1807–1808. In *Salmagundi,* Irving, like Poe, uses the Middle East to spin satires on the American scene, through the letters of his character Mustapha. "MS. Found in a Bottle," another early tale, might also be considered an "Oriental" narrative. Its narrator seems to be an Orientalist who "imbibed the shadows of fallen columns at Balbec [Lebanon], and Tadmore [Syria], and Persepolis [Persia]."[2] Similarly, the narrator of "Ligeia" acts in the manner of an Orientalist, as John C. Gruesser notes, in transforming his English abbey into a place of "imaginary geography" that sets the stage for a peculiarly Oriental process of reincarnation.[3] Numerous Orientalist motifs pervade the story, from the description of the rooms to the description of Ligeia herself, a dark woman with "raven-black" hair (263) and an exquisite beauty, "the beauty of the fabulous Houri of the Turk" (264). Finally, the poems "Tamerlane," "Al Aaraaf," and "Israfel" also employ Eastern themes and use Mongolian, Indian, and Islamic motifs, respectively.

"Four Beasts in One—the Homo Cameleopard" derives from ancient Syrian history. It presents, in mock-heroic fashion, the homecoming of Antiochus IV, monarch of the Seleucid Kingdom of Syria in the second century BC. This story of a tyrant king who so abuses his subjects that they turn on him is a biting critique of mob rule and a denunciation of President Andrew Jackson, whom Poe felt to be a tyrant leading a rabble. Two other humorous stories, "The Sphinx" and "Some Words with a Mummy," both refer to ancient Egypt. In the former a bespectacled scholar thinks he sees a monster but his myopic perspective has taken a harmless insect and swollen its image into something gargantuan and ugly. In the latter the fad of American Egyptology is lampooned when a revived mummy shows that nineteenth-century American achievements were actually employed by the ancient Egyptians.

By far, the most fictively intriguing of these Eastern stories is "The Thousand and Second Tale of Scheherazade." Poe derived the idea for this 1845 tale by reading an English translation of *The Thousand and One Nights*. The mouthpiece of the stories is Scheherazade, daughter of the grand Vizier of the Indies. The sultan Schahriah, having discovered the infidelity of his sultana, resolved to have a fresh wife every night and have her strangled at daybreak. Scheherazade entreated to become his next wife, and so amused him with tales for a thousand and one nights that he revoked his decree, and bestowed his affection on her. By arousing the king's curiosity through storytelling, Scheherazade prolongs her life.

In Poe's version of the legend, however, the narrator notes that this conclusion is "more pleasant than true." In consulting a heretofore unknown Oriental text, the *Tellmenow Isitsoornot* (a punning reference to truth "or not"), he is "not a little astonished to discover" that the fate of

Scheherazade, as told in *The Thousand and One Nights*, is inaccurate. He discovers that Scheherazade had actually withheld from her sovereign the "full conclusion" of the story of Sinbad the sailor and, wishing to remedy the situation, goes on to tell another tale, a thousand and second story, which recounts the natural and technological wonders encountered by Sinbad on his most recent voyage. Scheherazade's new narrative series combines modern wonders—such as battleships and hydrogen balloons—with decidedly "unnatural" natural history—such as bees displaying mathematical abilities and distances measured in light years. At one point, she comes to the most unnatural and incredible wonder of all, the bustle worn by women in the nineteenth century. Ironically, the sultan simply cannot accept this to be true, and, after querying the veracity of what Scheherazade has been telling him throughout the tale, he loses patience and orders her execution. As Poe does in *The Narrative of Arthur Gordon Pym*, perhaps the most postmodern of all his work, in "Scheherazade" Poe both establishes and blurs the boundary between fact and fiction. When he announces that the commonly received ending of *The Thousand and One Nights* is "like a great many pleasant things, more pleasant than true" (789), Poe establishes a dichotomy between fancy and truth that corresponds closely to the division between fiction and fact. Poe alerts us to how this strategy may be a dominant element of his version of *The Thousand and One Nights* in the epigraph to the tale, which warns that "Truth is stranger than fiction." The epigraph is deliberately misleading since the opposite is the basis for Scheherazade's storytelling and her survival. In order for her to survive, fiction must be made to be stranger than fact. This adage is similar to the hoaxing framework with which Poe surrounded *Arthur Gordon Pym*, cloaking a tale that is a fiction in the garb of a reportedly objective scientific report of an actual polar expedition.[4] In "The Thousand and Second Tale of Scheherazade," the fabricated *Isitsoornot* is presented as an actual published book by contextualizing it with reference to the *Zohar of Simeon Jochiades* and the *Curiosities of American Literature*, an anthology produced by Poe's erstwhile friend, Rufus W. Griswold. On the other hand, the adventures of Sinbad related in the ersatz Oriental text, although filled with descriptions of natural and technological realities, are imaginary. As Jerome D. Denuccio says, then, "the 'true' functions to correct the pleasant 'error' of the original story that is itself an error, a fiction in the garb of truth."[5] Thus the original perceived opposition between fact and fiction is really not an opposition at all, but a mutually nourishing, generative dynamic. Fact and fiction partake of each other and depend on each other for survival.

Yet another layer of meaning is interleaved in the tale as Poe appends a multiplicity of footnotes to the story of Sinbad's various adventures—thirty-two footnotes, in fact, to a tale that itself occupies only eighteen to twenty pages in a conventionally printed text. These footnotes elaborate on, gloss, and reference the list of marvels described in the story. They seem to confirm the authenticity of the details that Scheherazade is telling the sultan. Yet there is a disconnect here between oral and verbal discourse. We as readers, reading Poe's version of the original tale and the fabricated overlayer of the thousand and second tale, know the facts to be true because we can read the footnotes and accept their authority. Scheherazade, on the other hand, has no recourse to footnotes and the sultan no ability to receive the documentary information. Thus the storyteller must rely on persuasive ability and rhetorical credibility to convince her audience of the veracity of her assertions and thus save her own life. The use of citation embroils the narrator in an interpenetration of texts that results in dispersed meaning. Scheherazade seems to cite multiple texts to validate her credibility as a storyteller. Yet she instead opens herself up to an intertextuality that confuses fact (the footnotes) and fiction (the imaginary wanderings of Sinbad). In the tale, Poe also presents fiction as a self-generating process. Part of Poe's theory of fiction, as we might envision it in "Scheherazade," is a rejection of complete textual closure. Scheherazade originally escapes her fate by telling a story about "a rat and a black cat" (perhaps a joking reference by Poe to one of his own tales) but does not finish it by the time morning comes. The king's curiosity, however, prevails over his "sound religious principles" and he postpones her execution until the next morning, "for the purpose and with the hope of hearing that night how it fared in the end with the black cat . . . and the rat" (788). Poe emphasizes that the king is left with "no resource" but to defer his next act—Scheherazade's execution—just as the storyteller Scheherazade must put off the end of the tale until evening comes again.

The aesthetic strategy here articulated is nothing more elaborate, really, than the techniques employed by the great serial novelists of the Victorian age such as Dickens and Thackeray: postponed endings and virtually endless beginnings. Once opened and denied closure, the fictional process continues unabated. As the narrator notes, "The next night there happened a similar accident with a similar result; and then the next—and then the next; so that, in the end, the good monarch, having been unavoidably deprived of all opportunity to keep his vow during a period of no less than one thousand and one nights, either forgets it altogether by the expiration of this outright, or gets himself absolved of it in the regular way, or, (what is more probable) breaks it outright" (789). And so on—an imaginative enterprise that pursues its own logic and creates the conditions for its own survival on into perpetuity.

Even the structure of Poe's story affirms this logic. We have at the very least four separate but interrelated levels of storytelling—perhaps five if we count Poe's actual text, the tale he entitled "The Thousand and Second Tale of Scheherazade" as one of those levels: a narrator quotes the fictional *Isitsoornot*, which quotes Scheherazade, the fictional character, who quotes Sinbad, another fictional character, relating the account of his voyages. Each level springs from its predecessor. It is recursive, and therefore theoretically limitless. What Poe creates, in effect, is a kind of tapestry text.

But most important of all, to Poe, is the reciprocal relationship between storytelling and life, or between textual closure and death. After all, Poe's abiding concern throughout his life and literary career was to understand the nature of death. His characters perpetually devise ways of experiencing death yet not dying, of losing loved ones yet somehow reclaiming them from the hereafter. Storytelling is an interminable, never-to-be-completed project that invisibly alters the author's relationship to death. It is in some senses a strategy of denial. The boundlessness of narrative replaces the anxiety that comes with storytelling, for to reach the end of the story is to reach the end of existing. No one lives happily ever after, except in storytelling, and more specifically in stories that posit endless permutations. As Pascal is reputed to have once said, life is like living in a prison from which every day different prisoners are taken away to be executed and do not return. We are all, like Scheherazade, under sentence of death, and we think of our lives as narratives, with beginnings, middles, and ends. Storytelling is, at bottom, consolatory, for it promises us new beginnings. Paradoxically, it may also signify ultimate endings—that is, finitude. For Poe, the fear of dying is often linked metaphorically with reaching the end of a narrative. A good example is "MS. Found in a Bottle." In that tale, death and the loss of language are inextricably intertwined. As the narrator moves toward death, he sustains himself through writing, much as Scheherazade preserves herself through the telling of tales. Each sentence is a deferral of the end of writing, a strategy of denial.[6] In "The Thousand and Second Tale of Scheherazade," Poe stresses the positive side of this life-equation: at the end of the text, Scheherazade, the narrator says, "derived . . . great consolation, (during the tightening of the bowstring,) from the reflection that much of the history remained still untold, and that the petulance of her brute of a husband had reaped for him a most righteous reward, in depriving him of many inconceivable adventures" (804). Death might usually force the end of storytelling, but storytelling itself might be in danger of extinction, too, if fiction were not aesthetically engineered to be self-perpetuating.

It is interesting that in at least two other of Poe's Eastern tales, this theme of trying to escape the reality of death pervades. "Shadow" and its companion piece, "Silence," are set, respectively, in ancient Egypt and along the shoreline of the River Zaire. While Poe is usually purposefully vague in reference to historic or geographic setting, in "Shadow" he is deliberately specific, perhaps because the plague that is referred to in that work actually occurred in the Nile Delta region during the reign of Justinian (527–565). Poe perhaps selected Egypt, moreover, since it was a death-denying culture, the very idea that he is dramatizing in the text. In "Silence," we find a common motif in ancient cultures: words engraved on rock. Amid the bleak landscape, the narrator, with the aid of the red light from the moon, sees the word "DESOLATION," inscribed on the rock. We intuit that the word refers not to the landscape, which has already been identified as desolate, but to the relationship between language and the world.[7]

In "Scheherazade" Poe also layers the text-within-texts with self-reflexive nods to his own fiction, creating another level of interimplication in the story's narrative authority. Examples abound, beginning with the reference to a "black cat" in Scheherazade's first tale. Poe then embarks on a comic riff that seems a reference to the color symbolism in "The Masque of the Red Death": "The night having arrived, however, the lady Scheherazade not only put the finishing stroke to the black cat and the rat, (the rat was blue,) but before she well knew what she was about, found herself deep in the intricacies of a narration, having reference (if I am not altogether mistaken) to a pink horse (with green wings) that went, in a violent manner, by clockwork, and was wound up with an indigo key" (788–89). Scheherazade's "beautiful black eyes" recall Ligeia's, and the sultan himself is very similar to Poe's own earlier King Pest. In speaking of one of the more outlandish modern miracles, Sinbad/Scheherazade echoes Poe's earlier "Maelzel's Chess-Player": "One of this nation of mighty conjurors created a man out of brass and wood, and, leather, and endowed him with such ingenuity that he would have beaten at chess, all the race of mankind with the exception of the great Caliph, Haroun Alraschid" (801). A later paragraph begins with the Voltaic motion of corpses ("The Facts in the Case of M. Valdemar")[8] and continues through other miracles to a different "magician" whose procedure of directing the sun "to paint his portrait" (803) alludes to the daguerreotype, about which Poe wrote a series of short pieces published in 1840.[9] It is as if Poe is perpetuating his own sense of the fiction-making process through Scheherazade's thousand and second tale.

Lastly, in the tale Poe asserts that an implicit contract binds storyteller and audience. He suggests that there is a dialectical relationship between the imagination and the rational mechanism of the brain. The "calculating" faculty and the "ideal," Poe once said, do not oppose each other but "are never to be found in perfection apart."[10] The alchemy of the two produces a kind of magic that a storyteller exploits for fictive effect. This is what Scheherazade does in order to egg the sultan on to one more tale and thus one more twenty-four-hour period of life. She coaxes his threshold for believability to one more level, then another, and so on. Scheherazade expertly takes images from the king's experience—things he already knows and thus believes to be true—and applies them to the modern marvels that Sinbad is said to have encountered—a rough parallel to the artist's skills at filtering everyday perceptions of reality through the alembic of the imagination and then re-presenting them to an audience.[11]

For example, Scheherazade begins the story with bird imagery, presenting a kind of beast fable. She speaks of Sinbad reaching a land in which "the bees and birds are mathematicians . . . of genius and erudition" (799). She then shifts to describing a massive flight of birds that sounds equally unreal but actually is not: "We had scarcely lost sight of this empire when we found ourselves close upon another, from whose shores there flew over our heads a flock of fowls a mile in breadth, and two hundred and forty miles long; so that, although they flew a mile during every minute, it required no less than four hours for the whole flock to pass over us—in which there were several millions of millions of fowls" (799). She then portrays "a fowl of another kind": "we were terrified by the appearance of a fowl of another kind, and infinitely larger than even the rocks which I met in my former voyages; for it was bigger than the biggest of the domes on your seraglio, oh, most Munificent of Caliphs" (800). The beast, "fashioned entirely out of belly," turns out to be nothing more unusual than a hot air balloon (recalling another Poe text, "The Unparalleled Adventures of One Hans Pfaall"). The point here is that like the king, we as the audience fabricate images based closely on real experience. Taking that a step further in the arena of narrative authority, the king only trusts Scheherazade to the extent that he believes the "facts" related in the Sinbad text might possibly, marginally be true, given their connection—however tenuous—to his own experience. When his mind cannot perceive this possibility—as in the female bustle—he suspends the fantasy and orders the storyteller's death.

Poe's tale investigates the relationship between the author and the reader of a text. Recent contributions to reader-response theory suggest that the reader is relatively passive.[12] Poe suggests that the relationship is more complex: readers enter into complicity with writers and create the illusion of the writer's mastery over meaning in order that they might also see themselves as masters and become writers in their own place. The king does not exactly usurp Scheherazade's role as storyteller/author, but Scheherazade does lose her life because she violates the delicate interdependency of the author-reader contract.

All of these aesthetic ideas, of course, are quite postmodern ones, and it should come as no surprise to speculate that Poe's textual manipulations in "Scheherazade" may have profoundly influenced later writers. As we know, Poe's contributions to American literature were vast. He was arguably the first literary theorist in the United States. He helped invent and popularize both detective fiction and science fiction. He made short fiction the finely modulated art form that it is today. And he ranged freely among a variety of literary forms and moods—comedies, hoaxes, plays, poems, philosophical essays, satires—and, of course, literary criticism. As such, Poe was among the most influential of all American writers. His impact on later writers and thinkers, as many scholars have shown, runs the gamut from Nietzsche to Nabokov.[13]

But Poe's posthumous influence can perhaps most strongly be seen in the work of those novelists whose narrative methods dominated the late 1960s and early 1970s—and continue to influence millennial writing—the so-called metafictionists, creators of books within books and puzzles within puzzles. In this sense Poe's influence on the Argentine writer Jorge Luis Borges is obvious, particularly in the story "Pierre Menard, Author of *Don Quixote,*" as well on the writings of the Italian author Italo Calvino (*If On a Winter's Night a Traveller*), on the Russian author Vladimir Nabokov's *Pale Fire*, on South Africa's J. M. Coetzee (*Foe*) and on such contemporary American writers as John Barth, Robert Coover, and Paul Auster, whose 1985 novel, *City of Glass*, features a detective protagonist named William Wilson. An even more recent example is the British poet James Lasdun's first novel, *The Horned Man* (2002), a tale of paranoia and imagined persecution to rival both Poe and Kafka. Among postmodern detective novelists, the French writer Alain Robbe-Grillet's indebtedness to the verbal trickery and shifting narrative identity that Poe experimented with is probably the most prominent, especially in his thriller *The Erasers*.

In a sense, the work of John Barth is a touchstone for this view of the role of art in the postmodern age. In such novels as *The Floating Opera* and *Letters*, as well as the short story collection, *Lost in the Funhouse*, Barth consistently illustrated the limits of traditional storytelling by commenting, through the fiction itself, on that very topic. In 1967, Barth published a manifesto of sorts in the *Atlantic Monthly* that articulated his principles of postmodern writing and served as a rallying cry for his generation of novelists. In this essay, "The Literature of Exhaustion," Barth proposed that the conventional modes of literary representation had been "used up," their possibilities consumed through overuse. The essay was soon vilified as another dirge bemoaning the death of the author—a misreading that Barth addressed in a follow-up piece called "The Literature of Replenishment." "By 'exhaustion,'" Barth wrote in the first essay, "I don't mean anything so tired as the subject of physical, moral, or intellectual decadence, only the used-upness of certain forms or the felt exhaustion of certain possibilities—by no means necessarily a cause for despair."[14] Both essays became exhortations for narratological experimentalism. Barth felt that novelists should, in a sense, thwart readers' expectations of what a novel should be—for example, defying the traditional chronological ordering of a narrative and directly addressing the audience at times in order to remind them that the events being depicted were wholly fictitious and thus amenable to being shaped, by the author, into an almost infinite number of iterations. This same conclusion is the implied theoretical premise of Poe's "The Thousand and Second Tale of Scheherazade," which posits an intellectual realm of myriad possibilities in storytelling. Poe illustrates how an artist may paradoxically turn the felt ultimacies of our time into material and means for his work while at the same time refuting them.[15]

Storytelling, the novelist and critic A. S. Byatt has written, is intrinsic to biological time, which we cannot escape.[16] Narration is as much a part of human nature as breath and the circulation of the blood, and we need stories like we need genes. They keep part of us alive after the end of our story. Poe's version of the master storytelling character Scheherazade dies and enters the hereafter not after one thousand and one tales but after one thousand and two. Poe extends her time, promises her a kind of false eternity which in his own life he must have known to be so much illusion. Yet he could console himself with what storytelling could promise: endings that created endless new beginnings and a chance for something to live on past death.

NOTES

1. Schueller, *U. S. Orientalisms: Race, Nation, and Gender in Literature, 1790–1890* (Ann Arbor: University of Michigan Press, 1998), 34.

2. Page references are to *Poe: Poetry and Tales,* ed. Patrick F. Quinn (New York: Library of America, 1984), 198. Future references to this and other Poe tales within the essay will be to this edition and will be noted parenthetically.

3. See John C. Gruesser, "'Ligeia' and Orientalism," *Studies in Short Fiction* 26, no. 2 (Spring 1989): 145–49

4. See, for example, see J. Gerald Kennedy, "The Preface as a Key to the Satire in *Pym*," *Studies in the Novel* 5 (1973): 191–96, and Kennedy, "'The Infernal Twoness' in *Arthur Gordon Pym*," *Topic* 30 (1976): 41–53.

5. Jerome D. DeNuccio, "Fact, Fiction, Fatality," *Studies in Short Fiction* 27, no. 3 (Summer 1990): 365–70.

6. See J. Gerald Kennedy, *Poe, Death, and the Life of Writing* (New Haven: Yale University Press, 1987), 23–29, for an elaboration of this view.

7. This is similar to the moment in "MS. Found in a Bottle" where the narrator draws the word "DISCOVERY," an act that is closely related to the act of narrative.

8. Both "Scheherazade" and "Valdemar' were published in 1845, but there is no precise dating for the composition of either text. Poe may have been writing "Valdemar" at the same time as "Scheherazade," or even before.

9. "The Daguerreotype" (1840), reprinted in *Classic Essays on Photography*, ed. Alan Trachtenberg (New Haven: Leete's Island Books, 1980).

10. *Complete Works of Edgar Allan Poe,* ed. James A. Harrison, vol. 11, 148. Much of Poe's criticism argues this idea — as do his tales of ratiocination, in particular the problem-solving processes described in "The Murders in the Rue Morgue" and "The Purloined Letter."

11. See Barbara Cantalupo, "Poe's Female Narrators," *Southern Quarterly* 39, no. 4 (Summer 2001): 49–57.

12. A notable exception is Dennis A. Foster, *Confession and Complicity in Narrative* (Cambridge: Cambridge University Press, 2003).

13. For the most comprehensive overview of this topic, see Jeffrey Meyers, *Poe: His Life and Legacy* (New York: Scribner's, 1992), chapter 15.

14. Rpt. in Barth, *The Friday Book* (New York: Putnam, 1984), 64.

15.   This is also the type of fiction described in Borges's "The Garden of Forking Paths." In all fictional works, each time a man is confronted with several alternatives, he chooses one and eliminates the others; in the fiction of Ts'ui Pên, he chooses *simultaneously* all of them. He creates, in this way, diverse futures, diverse times which themselves also proliferate and "fork."

16.   Byatt, *Passions of the Mind: Selected Essays* (New York: Random House, 1992), 22.

FOUR

The Man in the Text: Desire, Masculinity, and the Development of Poe's Detective Fiction

Peter Goodwin

In June of 1839, after two very lean years of freelancing following his break with the *Southern Literary Messenger*, Edgar Allan Poe found a welcome if not exactly comfortable landing place at *Burton's Gentleman's Magazine*. Founded in 1837 by the popular Philadelphia character actor William Burton, *Gentleman's* was the original American men's magazine—the predecessor of today's *GQ, Esquire, Details*, and the like. Redefining gentlemanliness as a distinction between minds rather than between estates, *Gentleman's* cultivated and addressed an ideal reading public for itself: a new, distinctively American class of young men who aspired to make themselves into gentlemen not only by their professional success, but also by refining their tastes, manners, and intellect.[1] Not surprisingly, Poe bridled against the bourgeois aims of the magazine, proving himself, as usual, a headstrong and quarrelsome editor; but despite his disagreements with Burton, writing for *Gentleman's* provided Poe a stimulating context for exploring the contours of Jacksonian-American manhood. In addition to his many reviews, Poe contributed seven tales and sketches to the magazine, most of which systematically purge the word "gentleman" of its familiar meanings. From "The Fall of the House of Usher," which depicts the intellectual aristocrat as an emasculated invalid, to "Peter Pendulum (The Businessman)," which exposes the self-made man as a petty con artist, Poe seems to be searching in vain for the robust, integral, wholesome gentleman that was supposed to grace the pages of the magazine.[2] In the place of this idealized but elusive figure, Poe posits a fractured masculine subject whose potency derives not from self-sufficiency, but from desire.

Poe's first contribution to *Gentleman's*, "The Man That Was Used Up," is not only a sharp satire of Jacksonian-American ideals of manhood; it also contains the kernel of Poe's celebrated "invention" of the detective story. In its investigation of an irresistibly attractive gentleman, the tale places a mystery of sexual definition at the heart of Poe's detective fiction in its formative stages. "The Man That Was Used Up" introduces the detective impulse as originating in the narrator's vexed, homoerotic desire for intimate knowledge of another man—an impulse that will be pursued to dissatisfying ends both here and in Poe's last contribution to *Gentleman's*, "The Man of the Crowd." The governing metaphor of these tales, however, has as much to do with textuality as with sexuality: the pursued men are figured as inscrutable texts that the narrators, with much difficulty, are endeavoring to read and transcribe. We might therefore read the work of detection as an instance of what Lee Edelman calls "homographesis," a literary practice that "textualizes male identity as such, subjecting it to the alienating requirement that it be 'read,' and threatening, in consequence, to strip 'masculinity' of its privileged status as the self-authenticating paradigm of the natural or the self-evident itself."[3] But Edelman's "homographesis" hinges on the historical emergence, late in the nineteenth century, of "homosexuality" as a minoritizing signifier of personal identity. These tales were all written between 1839 and 1841, at least a generation before questions of "sexual orientation" began to be articulated in terms that are familiar today, but right in the midst of a vigorous public dialogue about gender roles and sexual purity, without which the medical and social categories of homosexuality and "sexual inversion" that emerged a few decades later would have been inconceivable. Whereas the ideology of "separate spheres" and the scientific and literary discourse on sexuality was beginning to place inordinate trust in the direction of one's desire as a decisive marker of identity, these tales show desire leading in divergent and unpredictable directions, opening rather than closing the covers of the masculine text.

As precursors to Poe's tales of ratiocination, "The Man in the Text" and "The Man of the Crowd" train the reader not to expect a satisfying solution to the mystery the author has woven. The desire for a cohesive narrative subject leads to one moment of frustration after another, as Poe employs an array of devices that fracture and divert the narrative. Poe thus veers from a philosophy of composition based on "totality, or unity, of effect"; at the same time, he undermines a corresponding American ideal of masculinity as unified, integral, impenetrable, and fraternal. In so doing, Poe helps to create new discursive conditions for representing masculinity and desire in multiple, queerly shifting configurations.

THE DISMEMBERED TEXT: "THE MAN THAT WAS USED UP"

In "The Man That Was Used Up," Poe burlesques a popular figure of nationalist masculine heroics—exposing a renowned war hero in the wars against the Indians as a false image, propped up by slave labor and the latest technology. The narrator, a "constitutionally nervous" socialite, is initially aroused by the *"entire individuality"* of General John A. B. C. Smith, by his "presence singularly commanding," and by the distinct air of aristocracy "pervading the *whole man*" (378, my italics). Poe's emphasis on the General's singularity and wholeness is striking in the opening paragraphs of the tale, evoking an image of the "purified, unified, 'vigorous,' brotherly, national manhood" that Dana Nelson delineates as the ideal held up (but never realized) in American political and literary discourse from the Constitution to the Emancipation Proclamation. According to Nelson, in the early years of the republic, Federalist rhetoric promoted a homogenized, unified vision of white, American manhood "as a corrective to a whole range of frictions and anxieties men were experiencing as a result of postwar political, economic, and social dislocation."[4] Although such a unified subject position is impossible to achieve or maintain in practice, the ideology of white manhood nonetheless "has worked powerfully to naturalize 'white' men as essentially unified subjects" (27). In her discussion of Poe's "Some Words with a Mummy," Nelson argues that Poe exposes national (white) manhood as "a state of melancholy, a false and unhealthy nostalgia for a uniform, brotherly state of unity and wholeness that never in fact did or even could exist" (204). For Nelson, the revivified mummy in the tale represents a whole range of "democracy's 'others'"—"supplementary bodies" marked by race, gender, and class, which must remain contained (or dead) within the abstracted, homogenous space of U.S. democracy.

In "The Man That Was Used Up" it is not any "supplementary body" that exposes the tenuous foundations of white manhood; rather, the conventional ways of knowing (or not knowing) public figures effectively shield these foundations from view, and it takes the persistent detective work of our narrator—who seems not at all sure of his own "purified, unified, 'vigorous,' brotherly, national manhood"—to reveal them. At first glance, the Brevet Brigadier General John A. B. C. Smith appears to embody one of his era's most popular and legible stories: the tale of the valorous and ingenious white man who triumphs over a set of bloody, wretched savages. General Smith may have been a satirical stab at a number of American military heroes, including Andrew Jackson himself, who, like Smith, was well renowned for his "valor" in fighting Indians and his dedication to progress and innovation.[5] As Robert Beuka writes, "the Jacksonian mystique of masculinity posited a unifying image in the figure of the robust common man, committed to diligent labor and na-

tional progress," and importantly, Indian removal (35). Poe's tale systematically deconstructs this "unifying image," complicating the simplistic
text of masculine nationalist heroism by the fetishistic dissection of the
General into a catalogue of body parts, by the intersection of his story of
manhood with a series of other texts, and finally by his exposure as a
mere jumble of prosthetic devices.

With the first sentence, Poe invites the reader into an elaborate exercise in intertextuality, tying this burlesque tale to one of his most solemn
arabesques. "I cannot remember when or where I made the acquaintance
of that truly fine-looking fellow, Brevet Brigadier General John A. B. C.
Smith," the narrator begins. Compare the opening sentence of "Ligeia":
"I cannot, for my soul, remember how, or even precisely where, I first
became acquainted with the lady Ligeia" (378; 310). As the narrator continues, the tale begins to look like a lively self-parody. Just as Ligeia's
narrator-husband describes her physical beauty in minute detail, the narrator of "The Man That Was Used Up" renders the General's body into a
veritable catalogue of fetish objects. Having verbally dissected their respective objects of desire, both narrators proceed to reassemble and res-
urrect them through the process of narration. In an illuminating side-by-
side reading of the two tales, Ortwin de Graef argues that Poe's "transformation of the other into literature . . . involves a considerable deployment
of totalizing violence, a recuperation of that reality into an order which is
alien to it and consequently negates it."[6] According to de Graef, "The
Man That Was Used Up" depicts a "narcissistic dead-end at the heart of
literature." In contrast to Ligeia, whose narrator "sustains the unbearable
tension of the possibility of literature to the very end," General Smith is
stuck with a narrator who is too easily satisfied with language's ability to
"use up" the identity of the other—and who "thereby reveal[s] himself to
be a very poor reader" (1114).

Reading the text of the General's body with conventional expectations
of linearity, climax, and conclusion, the narrator is looking for what Roland Barthes might call a *masterpiece*. In Barthes's revision of the term, a
masterpiece is a pronouncement, necessarily false but nonetheless appealing, of wholeness, originality, immediacy. To comprehend a masterpiece is "to put an end to the infinity of codes, to find at last the origin
(the original) of the copies, to ascertain the cultural starting point."[7] In
contrast to the masterpiece, which effectively jams the mobile play of
linguistic codes in order to present the reader with the illusion of a stable
and graspable meaning, Barthes posits the *plural text*, which reveals the
plurality of its reader as well:

> The more plural the text, the less it is written before I read it . . . and *I* is
> not an innocent subject, anterior to the text, one which will subsequent-
> ly deal with the text as it would an object to dismantle or a site to

occupy. This "I" which approaches the text is already itself a plurality of other texts, of codes which are infinite or, more precisely, lost. (Barthes, *S/Z* 10)

Seeking in the object of desire a sense of wholeness he lacks in himself, the narrator of "The Man That Was Used Up" strenuously resists the fragmentation and plurality with which his desires confront him. His text, however, remains dynamically open and plural, inimical to the monolithic language of the masterpiece. In its place Poe offers a narrative style characterized by play, self-parody, comic hyperbole, innuendo, double-entendre, and eroticism.

Taking the homoerotics of envy and admiration to comic extremes, the narrator confesses, "Upon . . . the topic of Smith's personal appearance—I have a kind of melancholy satisfaction in being minute," and then proceeds to describe General Smith's "richly flowing . . . jetty black" hair, his "unimaginable whiskers . . . a mouth utterly unequalled . . . the most entirely even, and the most brilliantly white of all conceivable teeth . . . a voice of surpassing clearness . . . the finest bust you ever saw . . . the *ne plus ultra* of good legs" (379).[8] Superlatives pile up on each other, measuring the distance between the narrator and this seeming paragon of "national manhood." Face to face with the General's charming *"air distingue,"* the narrator is reduced to a state of "anxious embarrassment" (378), driven by a compulsive need to penetrate what he immediately perceives as a mystery surrounding the General.

As Barthes writes of Balzac's "Sarrasine," the subject knows the object of desire "only as a division and dissemination of partial objects: leg, breast, shoulder, neck, hands. . . . This sundered, dissected body . . . is reassembled by the artist (and this is the meaning of his vocation) into a whole body, the body of love descended from the heaven of art, in which fetishism is abolished and by which Sarrasine is cured" (*S/Z* 112). Like Sarrasine's pursuit of La Zambinella, Poe's narrator's pursuit of General Smith is an effort to reassemble the body that his own fetishization has sundered, and thus to rewrite his disjointed story as a single coherent narrative—a closed text, the text as a property that may be grasped and enjoyed, and which may thereby reify the reading subject's unitary, phallic wholeness. But just as Sarrasine's pursuit of La Zambinella culminates in "her" exposure as a castrato and thus Sarrasine's own symbolic castration, Poe's narrator's pursuit of General Smith culminates in Smith's exposure as "used up," divested not simply of his sexual organ (which goes unmentioned), but of his arms and legs, his shoulders and bosom, his hair, eyes, and teeth, even his palate.

Long before this climactic discovery, the emasculating effects of both reading and desire operate heavily on the narrator, as his detective impulse projects him into distinctively feminine social circles. Unsatisfied by "delightfully luminous conversation" with Smith himself—for the

General is evasive on the subject of his personal history—the narrator fishes for gossip with a series of ladies. In these scenes, Poe depicts gossip as an indirect and insinuating language, practiced mostly by women, discretely winding its way between the mainstreams of masculine public discourse. The narrator tries to insinuate himself into the network of gossip, beginning with a whispered *"tete-a-tete"* with Miss Tabitha T. at church one Sunday morning. Her long response to his inquiry demands careful attention, as it sets the pattern for all the responses that will follow.

First, she repeats the surname and verifies that the narrator is really asking about the General: "Smith! . . . Smith!—why, not General John A.B.C.?" Such an absurdly common name demands the addition of an official title if it is to signify the particular person in question. Second, she expresses her surprise that the narrator does not already know "all about *him*!" The implication that the secrets she is about to reveal are already common knowledge serves both to excuse her indiscretion and to delimit a social circle that includes only those who already know "all about" the General. Her revelations, therefore, would grant the narrator entry into this exclusive society, with herself as his patron. Third, she rattles off a string of fragmentary and glancing allusions to this "wonderfully inventive age," the General's "immortal renown," and his opponents' savagery. Taken together, these snippets of information demonstrate the speaker's casual familiarity with facts that are painfully out of the narrator's reach, suggesting a kinship between herself and the renowned General, and reiterating the narrator's distance from such "prodigies of valor." As the other ladies the narrator questions repeat these elements of Tabitha's speech, in almost the same terms, the repetition comprises a mounting chorus of innuendo, tantalizing the narrator with worthless common knowledge before leading up to the secret heart of the matter with the phrase, "Why, he's the man—" (382, 384, 385).

Just at this crucial moment in her speech, each woman is rudely interrupted when someone picks up that syllable, *man*, and diverts it from the referent toward which she was presumably leading. Each interruption, moreover, drowns out the subtle arts of gossip with the domineering language of decidedly masculine texts—the Bible, Shakespeare, *Robinson Crusoe, Manfred*. For example, Tabitha T.'s monologue is interrupted by a verse of scripture, bellowed from the mouth of the humorless Reverend Doctor Drummummupp: "Man . . . that is born of a woman hath but a short time to live; he cometh up and is cut down like a flower" (383; Job 14:1–2). With a thunderous thump on the pulpit, he unleashes language in its sternest Lacanian sense: the law of the father, drumming up a threat of universal castration. The imagery of coming up and being cut down is echoed in the next interruption, at the theater, when an actor by the telling name of Climax cuts off the near ecstatic shrieking of Arabella Cognoscenti with some lines from Shakespeare: "_____ mandragora /

Nor all the drowsy syrups of the world / Shall ever medicine thee to that sweet sleep / Which thou ow'dst yesterday!" (384; *Othello* III.3.330–33). The climax of cognition is thus preempted by a literary warning about the heavy cost that knowledge exacts upon its bearer. Next, in the tale's sharpest mockery of the notion of a masterpiece, the utterance of the word *man* at the Widow O'Trump's soirée elicits an argument over the title of Byron's poetical drama: Man-*Fred* or Man-*Friday*? The interchangeability of Manfred (Byron's iconic romantic hero, and the embodiment of defiant self-determination) and Man Friday (Defoe's figure of the affectionately submissive black slave) not only demonstrates the slipperiness of textuality as a foundation for white male subjectivity, but also prepares the reader for the anticlimactic end to the narrator's efforts to master the fragmented text of General Smith's body. As we shall soon see, this romantic American hero depends on his own "Man Friday" for the air of self-possession he so convincingly exudes.[9]

But first, we must attend to one more deferral. In a last resort before returning to the General himself, the narrator turns from the female gossips to his "particular friend, Mr. Theodore Sinivate." This conversation brings gossip's role in detective work into sharper focus. As Eve Kosofsky Sedgwick notes, "the precious, devalued arts of gossip, immemorially associated in European thought with servants, with effeminate and gay men, with all women . . . have to do not even so much with the transmission of necessary news as with the refinement of necessary skills for making, testing, and using unrationalized and provisional hypotheses about what *kinds of people* there are to be found in one's world."[10] With the peculiar character of Sinivate, Poe registers this crucial connection between the indeterminacy of language and the mystery of sexual identification. "Sinivate," as Thomas Mabbott explains, echoes a Cockney pronunciation of "insinuate," as rendered in Dickens's *Pickwick Papers* and a *Gentleman's* article by William Burton, for example ("Used Up," 390–91, note 2). This "particular friend" is certainly full of insinuations— stating nothing, implying everything. Particularly maddening to the narrator is the way Sinivate recasts the practice of insinuation back onto the narrator himself: "You don't mean to insinuate, now, really, and truly, and conscientiously, that you don't know all about that affair of Smith's, as well as I do, eh?" (196). Not only does this perpetuate the mystery surrounding the General; more importantly, it refocuses the investigative lens on the narrator himself, causing him to question the nature of his interest in the General and the nature of his friendship with Sinivate. The narrator now finds the language of gossip and innuendo confronting him with the cultural irregularity of his own desires. Storming away from his "particular friend" in a state of indignation and painfully heightened curiosity about the object of his investigation, he appears to be suffering an episode of homosexual panic.

Anachronistic though such a reading may be, Sinivate strongly resembles a character type that will become more familiar in the decades following the publication of this tale: the effete and *au fait* homosexual man. His appearance as the last in a series of feminine socialites, his identification as the narrator's "particular friend," his insinuating speech patterns (drawling vowels and breezy cosmopolitan affectations), and the narrator's sensitivity to his insinuations all contribute to the impression. But is this, as Valerie Rohy suggests of her lesbian reading of "Ligeia," merely "an optical illusion, visible only from one historical vantage point"?[11] Or should this apparently anachronistic character challenge our historical understanding of homosexuality's emergence as a marker of personal identity much later in the nineteenth century? What I am suggesting lies somewhere between these two alternatives. If Sinivate looks and sounds a bit queer to a modern reader, this perception results from a reading practice that is enabled, indeed required, by Poe's own style of composition. In Poe's rendering, insinuation is allied with an effeminate desire for the integral masculine subject, while a denotative textuality is allied with that elusive subject. Like connotation, insinuation and innuendo proliferate and disperse meanings, foiling the narrator's attempts to read the text of the General's body. In contrast to connotation, as Barthes demonstrates, denotation establishes "the closure of Western discourse" by tidily arranging "all the meanings of a text in a circle" around itself (*S/Z* 7). The narrator's desire for General Smith is both an intellectual desire to read the text of manhood itself, and an erotic desire to see the General's body as a beautiful whole; but the denotative language of the masterpiece encircles and protects the object of desire from the narrator's view. Thus depicting the detective impulse as a problem both of language and of sexual identification, the tale's prolonged deferrals and digressions suggest not only the eternal insatiability of desire, but also the linguistically constructed nature of white manhood.

Finally giving up on the language of gossip and insinuation, the narrator resolves to "go to the fountain-head . . . and demand, *in explicit terms*, a solution to this abominable piece of mystery" (386; my italics). For all his determination, however, the narrator proves inadequate to the task of reassembling the body that his own fetishization has sundered. It is not the narrator, but a maligned black servant, who restores the General to the wholeness of a master(piece).

Discovered in his bedchamber early in the morning, the General is nothing more than "a large and exceedingly odd-looking bundle of something," which gradually takes the shape of a man only with the assistance of an elderly Negro valet by the name of Pompey.[12] His "own" body having been decimated in his battles against the Indians, General Smith now consists of a set of expertly crafted prostheses, which Pompey dutifully reassembles each day. Among Poe's sporadic appropriations of racist stereotypes and ideologies, Pompey occupies a somewhat anomalous position. Neither a minstrel buffoon nor a menacing savage, Pompey silently reconstructs the disheveled model of white manhood, one prosthetic device at a time. For today's critic, this is a problem of historical dimensions: Pompey further dramatizes the way in which "whiteness" and "manhood" rely on each other for their discursive power in antebellum constructions of civic personhood. For Poe it is the perfect gag: without Pompey's assistance, the General has "one of the smallest, and altogether the funniest little voices" the narrator has ever heard (197). Yet with a barrage of racist epithets, this emasculated voice commands Pompey's service: "Now, you dog, slip on my shoulders and bosom! . . . Now, you nigger, my teeth! . . . Pompey, you black rascal . . . my palate" (198). Not only is the General's body a fake; his *air distingué* is a cover for his common, uncouth racism. Pathetic as these commands sound coming from this whistling, squeaking voice, they achieve their purpose. Inserting "a somewhat singular looking machine" into the General's mouth, Pompey re-embodies the General's voice, which immediately resumes its "rich melody and strength" (388). Thus the General regains the power to articulate and perform his white manhood, and the narrator receives his text, from the hands of the black servant.

At last, the unmanned, nervous, compulsively curious narrator is able to read his text—and hence able to tell his tale. Yet along with the solution to the mystery comes a deflation of desire. The eroticized image of masculine nationalist heroics has been reduced to a closed text—an amusing tale, but one that doesn't bear much scrutiny. Freed of the unsettling dependency of desire, the narrator-detective closes his investigation with a feeling of satisfaction—"a perfect understanding . . . a full comprehension of the mystery which had troubled me for so long" (389). For the reader, however, the effect of this anticlimax is quite different. If the tale has succeeded in mobilizing a desire that it never explicitly articulates, this bizarre yet tidy conclusion will only leave us yearning for further elaboration. Unlike this easily satisfied narrator, we remain unwilling to close the text.

THE CLOSED TEXT: "THE MAN OF THE CROWD"

The smug satisfaction with which this narrator closes his text seems to have struck Poe himself as too easy a response to the complicated questions the text had raised; fortunately, in his steady position at *Burton's*, Poe had the opportunity to pursue these questions in subsequent articles. Magazine work, as Margaret Beetham and James Werner have noted, does not engender the expectations of formal closure that readers and writers bring to a novel: "As a serial entity, coming out over time, the periodical is 'open' and resists formal closure; its boundaries are fluid, with articles referring to or continuing earlier pieces."[13] This is especially clear in Poe's development of the detective impulse, from its inception in "The Man That Was Used Up" to its fuller elaboration in the first proper detective story, "The Murders in the Rue Morgue." So before turning to that first Dupin tale, I would like to take a brief look at an intervening tale that picks up where "Used Up" leaves off.

No sense of satisfaction awaits the narrator of "The Man of the Crowd"—for the subject of this narrator's investigation is a book that "does not permit itself to be read" (511). This reader-narrator begins the tale sitting in a London coffeehouse, looking for something to read. He describes his mood as one "of the keenest appetency," a feeling of "calm but inquisitive interest in everything" (511). The word "appetency" again highlights the element of desire in Poe's development of the detective impulse: it means "the state of longing for, desiring, craving; appetite, passion," and it is usually used in conjunction with a preposition like *of*, *for*, or *after* (*OED*). So one may have an appetency *for* coffee and cigars, for example, or an appetency *after* an intriguing bit of news, or an appetency *of* a particularly fascinating person. But at the tale's opening the narrator's desire has no object. His attention wanders from the advertisements in the newspaper in his lap, to the "promiscuous company" in the coffeehouse, to the passersby on the street outside, as if searching for an object to which he may attach his free floating desire. His observations of the passersby gradually sharpen—first "abstract and generalizing," then "descend[ing] to details," and finally fixing upon the face of a "decrepid old man" (507–8). At last, his desire has found an object, which he quickly renders in terms of textuality: "How wild a history . . . is written in that bosom" he remarks to himself, as he is gripped by "a craving desire to keep him in view" (511).

Up to this point, the narrator has portrayed himself as a skillful reader of human texts. By carefully observing "the innumerable varieties of figure, dress, air, gait, visage, and expression of countenance," he is able to divide the crowd into types and classes; but the old man will confound his abilities as a reader. Poe habitually provides minute physiognomies of his major characters; even his critical articles typically include a detailed physical description of the author under review. As James Werner has shown in his study of Poe's "cosmic physiognomy," Poe's interest in phrenology and autography indicates his belief that outward appearances have much to say about inward character. But while Poe's physiognomic analysis comes with a "promise of legibility," this promise is always thwarted by "a nagging indeterminacy. . . . Each face Poe describes has at its essential core a cipher, something that ultimately defies being read" (Werner, 101–2). What first blocks comprehension in this case is the heterogeneousness of the old man's expression. Far from the admirable unity of effect that General Smith exudes in "The Man That Was Used Up," the old man's expression suggests a jumble of foreboding and contradictory impressions: "ideas of vast mental power, of caution, of penuriousness, of avarice, of coolness, of malice, of blood-thirstiness, of triumph, of merriment, of excessive terror, of intense—of supreme despair" (511). Even more explicitly than in "The Man That Was Used Up," this narrator's detective work will be figured as an attempt to read and transcribe an encrypted text—to stitch these confused and paradoxical signifiers into a single cohesive narrative.

In a famous essay from his biography of Baudelaire, Walter Benjamin identifies the old man of the crowd as a prime example of that consummate reader of the urban landscape, the flaneur. Benjamin's discussion of the flaneur is indeed integral to understanding this tale, but (as Werner also notes) the narrator is also a flaneur, and in some ways a better example of the type than is the old man. A flaneur is not a vagrant or an aimless wanderer; rather, "the street becomes a dwelling for the flaneur; he is as much at home among the facades of houses as a citizen is in his four walls."[14] Unlike the flaneur, who is perfectly at home on the crowded streets of the nineteenth-century metropolis, the old man moves restlessly among the crowd with an air of extreme discomfort, "his eyes roll[ing] wildly from under his knit brows in every direction, upon those who hemmed him in" (512). The more he is crowded, the keener his agitation; he gasps for breath, twisting his face into expressions of "intense agony," evincing no particular interest in anything, failing even to notice when the narrator "gaze[s] at him steadfastly in the face" (515). By contrast, the narrator is a calm but eager observer of everything he sees. The street is his library, and the old man is (to borrow a phrase from "The Murders in the Rue Morgue") a "very rare and very remarkable volume."

The flaneur is not only a reader, but also a detective; as Benjamin writes, "no matter what trail the flaneur may follow, every one of them will lead him to a crime" (Benjamin, 41). Indeed, the old man in this tale appears to be guilty of nothing more than walking, yet the narrator concludes that he is "the type and genius of deep crime" (515). So what is the crime in this tale? I argue that it is a type of illicit solicitation: he provokes in the narrator an unwholesome desire that he cannot fulfill. This is the real respect in which, as Benjamin writes of the flaneur, "he shares the position of the commodity" (Benjamin, 55). Benjamin notes that the flaneur circulates in the department stores and shopping arcades of nineteenth-century Paris without buying or selling, thus approximating a type of empathetic relationship with the objects for sale there: "The intoxication to which the flaneur surrenders is the intoxication of the commodity around which surges the stream of customers"; and "empathy is the nature of [this] intoxication" (55). The commodity in the window seems to speak to passersby, inspiring and promising to fulfill their desire at the same time: "You want me, you can have me." But the old man of the crowd blocks any such empathetic exchange. Never buying, never selling, never offering himself in any relation of exchange, the old man breaks the laws that structure the economy in which he endlessly circulates.

To provoke a desire that cannot be satisfied is to demand of the desiring subject a reevaluation of his desire. Perhaps there is something wrong with a subject who is drawn to such an unappealing object. The narrator resists this implication by seeking satisfaction: "[I] firmly resolved that we should not part until I had satisfied myself in some measure respecting him" (513). Gustavus Stadler notes a sexual valence of the phrase, suggesting that the narrator's language "slides into, and puns on, the meaning of 'satisfying myself' that signifies physical action, sexual climax."[15] Whereas Stadler argues that the tale narrates the inability to know the object of one's desire "while simultaneously allowing the narrators merger with a figure of 'deep crime'" (21), I maintain that this merger is keenly desired but never achieved, because the textualized body of the old man proves to be impenetrable, forbidding any form of intercourse.

To "demand satisfaction" was also a conventional way of challenging an offender to a duel in Poe's day—another mode by which men defended their honor and competed for sexual dominance. But if this is a duel, it ends in a standoff. Having followed the old man for nearly twenty-four hours—along the thronged streets of London, through the marketplace and the theater district, into scenes of "deplorable poverty," and back into the teeming streets in the morning—the narrator finally concedes, "It will be in vain to follow; for I shall learn no more of him, nor of his deeds." Unsatisfied, he consoles himself with pious speculation: "perhaps it is but one of the great mercies of God that '*er lasst sich nicht lessen*'" (515; "it does not permit itself to be read"). But if the narrator fails to "satisfy himself" regarding this man-who-is-a-book, it is not for lack of trying. As Werner notes, "the secret writing *itself* refuses to be read; its recalcitrance is not an indictment of the flaneur's method, but a testament to the city's (and humanity's) tendency to retain mystery" (142). Given the great pride and satisfaction Poe took in solving cryptograms, reading autographs, and performing physiognomic analysis, one must surmise that nothing would be more maddening to him than such a recalcitrant textual body. The detective impulse is thus further developed here as a desire to read and thereby master a consolidated textual subject. But here as in "The Man That Was Used Up," the erotic detective impulse is thwarted. The illegibility that frustrates desire in these two tales provides the impetus for the development of the detective story, wherein the desire for a consolidated textual subject—the desire to read, to write, to know, to *be* such a subject—is radically reconceived.

THE OPEN TEXT: "THE MURDERS IN THE RUE MORGUE"

When William Burton sold *Gentleman's* to George Graham, Poe carried on as an editor at the new venture; "The Murders in the Rue Morgue" was his first contribution to *Graham's Magazine* (March 1841). Though innovative and hugely influential, Poe's first Dupin tale is not a "masterpiece" in either the conventional or the Barthesian sense of the term. Like the escaped orangutan who perpetrates the murders, the tale itself refuses to be mastered. Few stories elicit greater resistance to the sense of an ending than what is widely acknowledged as the first modern detective story. An *orangutan* did it? It's an absurd and even maddening solution—designed to amaze and astound rather than to *satisfy* the reader. Many readers even feel cheated by the ending, as if victims of a cruel hoax. As John Bryant complains, "Poe never plays fair." [16] According to Bryant, Poe's narrative manipulation leaves readers feeling "intellectually deflated . . . forced to discard our deeper ratiocinations for something that is anticlimactically artificial" (34). John Irwin represents the opposite reaction, contending that the genius of Poe's detective fiction derives from his creation of "a repeatable solution, a solution that conserves (because it endlessly refigures) the sense of the mysterious." [17] Shawn Rosenheim helps explain these two opposite reactions by identifying decapitation as the tale's "structuring metaphor" [18]: in forcing us to "discard our deeper ratiocinations" for a solution that depends wholly on the apprehension of brute physical force, Rosenheim argues, the tale duplicates within the reader the split the narrator imagines within Dupin.

Much as the narrator of "The Man That Was Used Up" imaginatively dismembers the object of his desire through elaborate narrative fetishization, Dupin's narrator-admirer begins his tale by dividing Dupin in two: "Observing him in these [analytic] moods, I often dwelt meditatively upon the old philosophy of the Bi-Part Soul, and amused myself with the fancy of a double Dupin—the creative and the resolvent" (533). But "Murders" complicates the tidy closure of the masculine textual body that we see in the comedic conclusion of "Used Up." In the more psychologically unsettling conclusion of "Murders," Poe reintegrates the sundered text of the masculine body by imagining it as a penetrable space. Boasting to the narrator "that most men, in respect to himself, wore windows in their bosoms" (533), Dupin introduces a second structuring metaphor for the tale: that of the open window. The metaphors of textual and sexual penetration in the "Man" tales take on more menacing and violent implications in "Murders," as Dupin "throws himself into the spirit of his opponent" (529)—a ferocious orangutan who leaps through barred windows with "almost praeternatural . . . agility" (555). In the process of his investigation, Dupin will reenact the violent penetration of the L'Espanayes' private domestic scene, satisfying his detective impulse with a vicarious experience of the orangutan's "prodigious power." At the same time, however, the narrative will stealthily pry open the window in Dupin's own bosom, reintegrating him into a personal economy of circulation and exchange. The reintegrated masculine body is thus figured as a penetrable body, and the masterpiece is reimagined as an open text.

When the narrator first meets him, Dupin is a fallen aristocrat, "reduced to such poverty that the energy of his character succumbed beneath it, and he ceased to bestir himself in the world, or to care for the retrieval of his fortunes" (531). The detective plot will transform this listless aesthete into a model of self-possession and mental virility by ejecting him from his mental isolation and into purposeful engagement with the world outside. Indeed, the narrator is the tale's first detective, investigating the personal and family history of his fascinating new friend; but the two characters will merge in both formal and thematic ways over the course of the tale, with the roles of narrator and detective shifting back and forth between them.

As in the "Man" tales, the work of detection begins as a search for a text, with Dupin and the narrator happening to meet in the library in the Rue Montmarte, both "in search of the same very rare and very remarkable volume" (531–32). The text is soon forgotten, however, as the narrator transfers his interest onto Dupin himself. The two set up housekeeping together, with the narrator playing the role of the solicitous husband by paying the rent "and furnishing in a style which suited the rather fantastic gloom of our common temper, a time-eaten and grotesque mansion, long deserted through superstitions into which we did not inquire, and tottering to its fall in a retired and desolate portion of the Faubourg St. Germain" (532). This secluded locale resembles a familiar type of domestic situation for Poe's male-female couples, who live in retirement from society and crave only each other's company.[19] Like Roderick and Madeline Usher in their crumbling ancestral mansion, these two bachelors carry on a suspiciously private and unproductive textual intercourse in a house that is "tottering to its fall."

The literary bachelor occupied a liminal position in the nineteenth-century bourgeois discourse of separate spheres and domesticity. In Katherine Snyder's concise summation, "Although home and marriage were not literally synonymous, their ideologies were so intricately interwoven that they were virtually interchangeable."[20] According to these ideologies, the wife and mother was the producer and guardian of family virtue; a house was not a home without its "angel of the hearth." Insofar as married home life was essential to the cultivation of full civic personhood, bachelors were half-formed men. In popular literature by and about bachelors, books were often figured as the bachelor's surrogate family, and the bachelor's relationship to his book was construed as both problematic and redemptive. Unencumbered by family or national attachments, the bachelor is all the more attached to his *text*. For Washington Irving, as Bryce Traister argues, textuality is the bachelor's unique mode of productive citizenship. "Whatever I have written has been written with the feelings and published as the writing of an American," Irving writes in a letter to Henry Breevport—"How else am I to serve my country—by coming home and begging an office of it? . . . If I can do any good in this world it is with my pen."[21] Irving's fictional bachelors are both producers and consumers of narrative, and as such they both create and meet the demand for a distinctively American literary product.

The bachelors in residence in the decrepit mansion in the Faubourg St. Germain, though great lovers of books, do not initially take part in Irving's rhetoric of textual circulation and exchange. As an aristocrat of intellect, Dupin is a connoisseur and a collector, not a producer, of texts. "Books, indeed, were his sole luxuries," the narrator informs us (242)—desirable not for their utility or market value, but as self-edifying intellectual property. Textuality for him represents not the circulation of ideas, but the acquisition of a property that he takes out of circulation, shutting it up with him behind the "massy shutters" of his mansion. It takes a form of textuality quite different from the rarefied volumes they so treasure to draw this pair into more productive engagement in the public sphere: it is a headline in the evening newspaper that draws their attention to the "Extraordinary Murders" in the Rue Morgue. As Benedict Anderson has demonstrated, newspapers and other inexpensive, popular print media played an important role in the creation of a national imagination. Newspapers fostered an awareness among their readers that they were part of a public—a readership.[22] The *Gazette des Tribunaux* has an even more direct effect on Dupin and the narrator, as it draws them into public circulation. They begin their investigation with a minute reading of the papers, but in order to solve the mystery, they will have to venture out of their claustrophobic gothic mansion in the light of day; they will have to call on a favor from the Prefect of Police; and Dupin will even be able to repay a favor to his acquaintance Adolphe le Bon, who has been wrongly implicated in the murders.

It must be said that this is a particularly troubling manifestation of the homosocial structure in which the exploitation of a passive female object facilitates the abstraction of the bonds between men. The brutal murder of two women prompts Dupin and the narrator to redirect their erotic energy into the socially useful task of narration, thus enabling the abstraction of their relationship necessary to their formation as citizens in the imagined community. Without minimizing the significance of these shocking scenes of violence against women, however, I want to draw attention to the lines of affinity the tale draws between the victims, perpetrators, and investigators of this crime. First, the remote situation of Dupin and the narrator is mirrored by that of the murder victims and the criminal pair. Having captured an exotic orangutan during an excursion in Borneo with the intention of selling it for a profit, the sailor tries to keep his property secluded in a closet in his own residence—in order to avoid "the unpleasant curiosity of his neighbors" (564). The L'Espanayes, an elderly mother and her unmarried daughter, are said to have lived "an exceedingly retired life" on the lonely bystreet called the Rue Morgue. According to the newspaper account, "no one was spoken of as frequenting house. . . . The shutters of the front windows were seldom opened. Those in the rear were always closed" (539). Violently opening up channels of circulation between these three discrete pairs, the tale reflects some of the worst anxieties that accompanied urban encroachments on private space.

Second, Mme. L'Espanaye's decapitation has its parallel in Dupin's own absorption in the life of the mind, to the exclusion of material concerns. Until involving himself in this investigation, Dupin's description of the Prefect of police would apply equally well to himself: "In his wisdom is no *stamen*. It is all head and no body, like the pictures of the Goddess Laverna—or, at best, all head and shoulders, like a codfish" (568). Dupin's rejection of abstract, disembodied modes of analysis indicates an important development in Poe's conception of the intellectual aristocrat. Like Roderick Usher—cocooned in a realm of "excited and highly distempered ideality"—Dupin displays symptoms of "an excited, or perhaps . . . a diseased intelligence" in the early days of his acquaintance with the narrator ("Usher," 405; "Murders," 533). Something about this investigation, then, mends the split between Dupin's body and his mind. As Rosenheim argues, "it is the knowledge of his own embodiment that permits Dupin to solve the mystery of the L'Espanaye's deaths" (173). This is a deeply troubling knowledge, for the reader as well as for Dupin: "Insofar as 'stamen' refers to the male generative organ of a flower, it marks the (male) reader addressed by the text. . . . To have a male body seems inseparable from complicity in the orangutan's gendered violence" (Rosenheim, 174). Is Poe suggesting, then, that the reintegration of the masculine body is to be achieved through monstrous violence against women? By looking back at the emergence of the detective impulse in "The Man That Was Used Up," I would like to propose an alternative to this conclusion.

In "Used Up," the appearance of masculine bodily integrity is restored by the labor of an ill-treated black servant; by reassembling the General's dismembered body, Pompey provides the narrator with the closed text he has been trying so desperately to read. As a subversion of antebellum ideals of "national manhood," this solution to the mystery is humorously satisfying; but any reader misguided enough to have been hoping for a revelation about the essence of masculine integrity will be deeply disappointed by this tidy closure. By the same token, if "The Man That Was Used Up" and "The Man of the Crowd" have prepared us to see a crisis of sexual definition at the heart of Poe's detective fiction, we will remain skeptical about the air of supreme self-possession and masculine integrity that Dupin conveys at the end of "Murders." As Dupin reasons about the L'Espanaye's locked apartment, "there *must* be something wrong," some opening in this apparently impenetrable edifice.

In the clue that reveals the murderer's mode of egress, we see the convergence of the tale's two structuring metaphors: decapitation and the open window. As the police's investigation of the apartment has confirmed, the only possible means of egress is through the back windows—but these are nailed shut. Dupin's investigation, however, reveals that it is not the apartment itself, but the perception of the police, that has been "hermetically sealed" (558). Following his instinct that "these apparent 'impossibilities' are, in reality, not such," Dupin is led to the nail in one of the back windows:

> It had, I say, in every respect, the appearance of its fellow in the other window; but this fact was an absolute nullity (conclusive as it might seem to be) when compared with the consideration that here, at this point, terminated the clew. 'There *must* be something wrong,' I said, 'about the nail.' I touched it; and the head, with about a quarter of an inch of the shank, came off in my fingers. The rest of the shank was in the gimlet-hole, where it had been broken off. . . . I now replaced this head portion in the indentation whence I had taken it, and resemblance to a perfect nail was complete—the fissure was invisible. Pressing the spring, I gently raised the sash for a few inches; the head went up with it, remaining firm in its bed. I closed the window, and the semblance of the whole nail was again perfect. (553)

I have quoted at some length, because so much hangs on this tiny nail. It is the master clue that brings all the other clues together into a coherent narrative; it establishes a closed text by appearing to fix every divergent and unstable signifier in its place. Yet just as the nail gives the apartment the appearance of being sealed from within while in fact enabling its ventilation and penetration, Dupin's apparently airtight solution actually leaves the text open, by confounding the desire that has driven it. The homoerotic desire that initiates the detective impulse—the desire to apprehend an integral masculine subject—is redirected toward an irrational and unmotivated actor rather than a culpable human agent who might be brought to justice. In place of a criminal mastermind, we find simply a sailor who couldn't keep his beast in the closet.

The broken nail thus serves as a curious lynchpin for Poe's ratiocinative method. For all its thematic significance, it also serves to play a trick on the reader—teasing us with the promise of a tidy solution.[23] We are encouraged to unravel the mystery for ourselves, by reading between the lines, searching for hidden clues, filling in the gaps to create a coherent narrative and solve the crime. Like "The Man That Was Used Up" and "The Man of the Crowd," the tale trades in insinuation and innuendo, seducing us into the game of detection only to redirect our desire toward a broken object—a used-up man. But this image of dismemberment, this broken nail, is no joke. Dupin's discovery opens onto a new configuration of masculine bodily and intellectual potency that acknowledges the masculine subject's vulnerability as well as its propensity to inflict harm on others. If the open window represents a masculine subject that achieves potency by being opened, the broken nail suggests that this subject is irreparably fractured by the impulses of beastly violence that pass through it.

Leaving behind the security of purely abstracted intellectual life, Dupin enters a public sphere where his intellectual labor has a monetary rather than an intrinsic value. Despite his persistently condescending attitude toward the police, his transformation from the dilettante detective of the Rue Morgue to the investigator-for-hire in "The Mystery of Marie Roget" and "The Purloined Letter" demonstrates his interpellation by and service to the state legal apparatus. The pleasure Dupin takes in vicariously experiencing the orangutan's murder of Madame and Mademoiselle L'Espanaye proves that he has not remained uncontaminated by the perversions of this economy—but Poe is not finished with this character yet. In two subsequent tales, Dupin will continue to intervene in an economy of personhood that depends on the circulation of both texts and women's bodies. With Dupin, Poe mobilizes and sustains a narrative desire for a masculine subject that is defined not by wholeness, independence, purity, and integrity, but by fragmentation, contingency, desire, penetrability, and yes, violence. Dupin's life as a character, moreover, extends far beyond the three tales in which he first appeared. Siring a long line of literary detectives, Dupin is the very definition of an open subject—a man, it seems, who will never be used up.

NOTES

1. Taken from Bernard Ward's biography of Edward DeVere, the *Gentleman's* motto defines gentlemanliness as an intellectual quality, not a matter of family name or fortune: "By a gentleman, we mean not to draw a line that would be invidious between high and low, rank and subordination, riches and poverty. No. *The distinction is in the mind*" (italics in original).

2. In the order that they were published, Poe's major contributions to *Gentleman's* were "The Man That Was Used Up" (August 1839), "The Fall of the House of Usher" (September 1839), "William Wilson" (October 1839), "The Conversation of Eiros and Charmion" (December 1839), "Peter Pendulum (The Business Man)" (February 1840), "The Philosophy of Furniture" (May 1840), and "The Man of the Crowd" (December 1840).

3. Lee Edelman, *Homographesis: Essays in Gay Literary and Cultural Theory.* New York and London: Routledge, 1994, p. 12.

4. Dana Nelson, *National Manhood: Capitalist Citizenship and the Imagined Fraternity of White Men.* Durham and London: Duke University Press, 1998, p. x.

5. William Whipple's case for Richard Johnson (then vice president under Martin Van Buren) as the target of Poe's satire is probably still the strongest: "Poe's Political Satire," *University of Texas Studies in English* 25 (1956): 81–95. Robert Beuka suggests Winfield Scott and William Henry Harrison as other possible targets, but argues that *Gentleman's* readers could readily see that "in a larger sense Poe was satirizing a tendency toward self-aggrandizement in contemporary politics" (30). See also Daniel Hoffman, *Poe, Poe, Poe, Poe, Poe, Poe, Poe* (Garden City: Doubleday, 1972); and Richard A. Alekna, "'The Man That Was Used Up': Further Notes on Poe's Satirical Targets," *Poe Studies* 12 (Dec. 1979): 36.

6. Ortwin de Graef, "The Eye of the Text: Two Short Stories by Edgar Allan Poe." *Modern Language Notes* 104, no. 5 (Dec. 1989): 1113.

7. Roland Barthes, *S/Z*. 1970. Trans. Richard Miller. New York: Hill and Wang, 1974, p. 115

8. Compare "Ligeia," 311–312. The narrator's fetishization of the General's beautiful body parts also recalls the narrator of "Berenice," whose fetishization of his beloved's teeth takes a particularly grotesque turn.

9. As Mabbott notes, *Man-Fred* (as Poe spells it here) is the title of a popular minstrel burlesque of Byron's drama, first performed in 1834 ("Used Up," 390, note 19).

10. Eve Kosofsky Sedgwick, *Epistemology of the Closet*. Berkeley and Los Angeles: University of California Press, 1990, p. 23.

11. The object of queer reading, Valerie Rohy argues, is not the "truth value" of what queer readers see, but "the angle of vision itself" ("Ahistorical," *GLQ: A Journal of Lesbian and Gay Studies* 12, no. 1 (2006): 63). Drawing on recent theories of "queer time" in the work of Jonathan Goldberg, David Halperin, Terry Castle, Chris Nealon, and others, Rohy argues for the value of "ahistorical" reading, suggesting that the critical taboo against projection and identification unwittingly "upholds the illusion of a true, unidirectional history, whose effect of veracity and realism is in fact sustained by the very retroaction it condemns. Resistance to phobic definitions of homosexuality as anachronistic . . . might mean a turn away from the discipline of straight time, away from the notions of historical propriety that, like notions of sexual propriety, function as regulatory fictions" (70).

12. It was a common racist practice among slaveholders to name slaves after the heroes of antiquity and classical mythology. Harking back to the ancient Roman military hero, the name *Pompey* also provides an ironic counterpoint to the plebian "John A. B. C. Smith." It is also worth noting that Pompey is also the name of Psyche Zenobia's servant in "How to Write a Blackwood Article."

13. James V. Werner, *American Flaneur: The Cosmic Physiognomy of Edgar Allan Poe*. New York: Routledge, 2004, p. 32.

14. Walter Benjamin, *Charles Baudelaire: A Lyric Poet in the Era of High Capitalism*. Trans. Harry Zohn. London and New York: Verso, 1997, p. 33.

15. Gustavus Stadler, "Poe and Queer Studies." *Poe Studies: Dark Romanticism* 33. 1-2 (2000): 21.

16. John Bryant, "Poe's Ape of Unreason: Humor, Ritual, and Culture." *Nineteenth-Century Literature* 51.1 (June 1996): 32.

17. John Irwin, *The Mystery to a Solution: Poe, Borges, and the Analytic Detective Story*. Baltimore: Johns Hopkins University Press, 1994, pp. 1-2.

18. Shawn Rosenheim, "Detective Fiction, Psychoanalysis, and the Analytic Sublime." In Shawn Rosenheim and Stephen Rachman, eds., *The American Face of Edgar Allan Poe*. Baltimore: Johns Hopkins University Press, 1995, p. 163.

19. Despite his lack of guilt, paranoia, self-loathing, and homicidal tendencies, the narrator begins to resemble the husband/narrators in some of Poe's marriage tales, idolizing Dupin's mental abilities in much the same way as Ligeia and Morella's husbands prostrate themselves before their wives' prodigious talents. Like Morella's husband, who feels "a forbidden spirit enkindling within" under the influences of

Morella's "gigantic . . . powers of mind" (230), Dupin's narrator suffers the exquisite pains of intellectual arousal: "Above all," he confesses, "I felt my soul enkindled within me by the wild fervor, and the vivid freshness of his imagination" (532).

20.   Katherine Snyder, *Bachelors, Manhood and the Novel: 1850-1925*. Cambridge, U.K., and New York: Cambridge University Press, 1999, p. 21.

21.   Quoted in Bryce Traister, "The Wandering Bachelor: Irving, Masculinity, and Authorship." *American Literature* 74.1 (March 2002): 111.

22.   Drawing on Benedict Anderson's analysis, David Anthony shows how the emergence of tabloid journalism and scandal reporting during the early to mid-1800s provided space for a new type of violence-inflected, homosocial bonding among broader classes of urban men. In contrast to more staid newspapers such as the *Times*—which catered to "a landed citizenry [who] could supposedly debate political questions in a purely abstract, disembodied fashion"—upstart penny tabloids such as the New York *Herald* and *Sun* "provided a representational opportunity for a number of different voices, many of which were forcing vexed questions of class, gender, and 'self-possession' into public discourse in disruptive ways" ("The Helen Jewett Panic: Tabloids, Men, and the Sensational Public Sphere in Antebellum New York," *American Literature* 69, no. 3 (Sept. 1977): 491). Anthony shows how sensational reporting of the well-known prostitute Helen Jewett's murder, which dominated New York tabloids for several weeks in April 1836, brought readers into imaginative connections with one another over the site of her corpse. This is precisely what happens as Dupin and the narrator read the *Gazette des Tribunaux*'s account of the murders of Madame and Mademoiselle L'Espanaye. Poe based his next Dupin story, "The Mystery of Marie Roget," entirely on actual newspaper accounts of the murder of Mary Rogers in New York.

23.   In an 1846 letter to his friend Philip Cooke, Poe admits that his Dupin tales are not as "ingenious" as many readers have supposed: "Where is the ingenuity of unraveling a web which you yourself (the author) have woven for the express purpose of unraveling? The reader is made to confound the ingenuity of the suppositious Dupin with that of the writer of the story" (qtd. in Mabbott, 521).

FIVE

Gothic Displacements: Poe's South in *Politian*

Amy C. Branam

In his preface to *Tales of the Grotesque and Arabesque*, Poe writes: "I maintain that terror is not of Germany, but of the soul."[1] By refusing to acknowledge the Gothic as belonging to only one place, he legitimized the use of the Gothic by an American. Poe was adamant that the Gothic was the property of all humankind, and he had no qualms about appropriating this genre and its conventions for his own writing. Moreover, this declaration at once illustrates the Gothic's duality: as a locale and a universal condition. This duality implies that the genre operates in such a way that it can appear to discuss a specific time and place while it also engages the time and place of its audience. In recent Poe scholarship, Poe's articulation of universality through the particular is receiving increased attention. For instance, in *Poe's Children: Connections between Tales of Terror and Detection*, Tony Magistrale and Sidney Poger assert, "it seems impossible not to read Poe as somehow commenting upon his epoch, even when the writer appears most disengaged from American culture."[2] As this pronouncement suggests, Poe scholars are shifting from viewing Poe's works apart from their historical contexts to interrogations of how his works reflect content directly related to American historical moments.[3] This change in method is significant because it allows for apparently anomalous works, such as Poe's verse drama *Politian*, to realize more import than in past critical assessments. For instance, until the 1990s, scholars had focused almost exclusively on the play's literary merits and its potential literary and historical origins.[4] However, in 2002, Jeffrey H. Richards's article, "Poe, *Politian*, and the Drama of

Critique," finally engaged the play as a work of its time within the dramatic tradition rather than the literary tradition.[5] By discussing this work as a play for early nineteenth-century America, Richards opened the discussion for contextualizing this work in relation to the dramatic sphere. In 2007, in *"Politian's* Significance for Early American Drama," I also argued for the play's reading within a historical context; however, unlike Richards, I elaborated on how this work demonstrates a sincere engagement with its time as opposed to the burlesque of contemporary theatrical techniques and content posited by Richards.[6]

Even though American drama began to evolve into a distinctive national form, during the early 1800s, the older, European dramatic forms persisted, such as the sentimental drama, melodrama, and the Gothic drama.[7] In terms of the Gothic in particular, it facilitated "the exercise, release, and containment of personal and social anxieties."[8] By looking at Poe's drama within its theatrical context, as well as in conjunction with his sociohistorical position in American history, this article investigates Poe's Gothicism via his verse drama, *Politian.*[9] Not only does this play conform to many of the conventions of Gothic drama but it also engages sociopolitical issues common to the genre, including anxieties regarding power and identity.[10] Moreover, as the Gothic often displaces contemporary places to a distant locale and previous era, this argument also establishes how Poe's setting is superficially Renaissance Italy, yet it covertly addresses antebellum Virginia anxieties. Through isolating these concerns, the play can be understood more clearly in relation to Poe's philosophy of the Gothic, as well as within an American Gothic tradition.

In "'Gothic' and the Critical Idiom" Maurice Levy asserts: "The naturalization of ['gothic'] in a country with no medieval past and whose fiction owes more to Indian folklore than to European legends does not convince me."[11] The "country" to which he refers is America, and he objects to classifying any American writer as a Gothic writer because he believes that the term possesses "many specific connotations" that prohibit its applicability to American literature.[12] To apply this term to a nation that did not experience the first Gothic revival or the political turmoil under Georgian rule seems ludicrous to Levy.[13] However, he maintains that Poe is a Gothic writer in "Edgar Poe et la tradition 'gothique.'"[14] Levy avoids contradicting his argument in the "Critical Idiom" by asserting that Poe's Gothic aligns with traditional English and European Gothic conventions rather than the variation known as the American Gothic. He recognizes that Poe utilizes concrete Gothic imagery, such as the castle, underground labyrinths, and even the Inquisition. Although Poe is an American, Levy claims that Poe actually belongs in the European Gothic tradition due to Poe's decisions to situate most of his Gothic tales in England, Germany, or some other European clime.

In contrast to Levy's definition, European Gothic and American Gothic appear to be quite similar when the term is evoked to signify an understanding of the fear of living under a tyrant in an enlightened age. Since the Gothic's anxiety stems from the question of legitimacy, the nascent American government and the haunting by its English past parallel the European Gothic tradition.[15] Ultimately, the main ideological difference between European Gothic and American Gothic is negligible. Like English doubts regarding whether the country truly followed a path to realize sociopolitical improvement, American Gothic engaged the same notion. As Teresa Goddu notes, it often presented "a nightmarish vision of the American experiment gone awry."[16] According to David Reynolds, American Gothic "was . . . bent perversely on dismantling the complacencies of ideological investments in human perfectibility through tales of the perverse," and this approach "was a kind of political engagement rather than escapist storytelling."[17] In a sense, the American Gothic confronted the question of *what if*: what if the American experiment claimed casualties? In "Nineteenth-Century American Gothic," Allan Lloyd-Smith traces the evolution of these casualties from the settlers' decimation of the Native Americans through to the growing reliance on the slave system to support the American economy.[18] The apprehension regarding whether these acts could indeed be legitimized became increasingly exacerbated as the nation moved closer to civil war and the American government continued to persecute the Native Americans.

These oppressive tactics on the path to nation building align the American Gothic with the European in that both address issues of power and identity. However, America may claim an additional layer of anxiety: the additional urgency to avoid reinventing Old World tyranny highlighted in its nation-building rhetoric. The burgeoning country confronted many challenges to its utopia, including concerns regarding miscegenation, class relations, and the realization of democratic ideals (particularly for slaves and women), which contributed to a generalized fear that this new society would degenerate. These proofs against America's idealized conceptions constitute uniquely American anxieties. America's self-conscious identity formation as a nation in which all men "are endowed by their Creator with inherent and inalienable rights; that among these are life, liberty and the pursuit of happiness" was at stake.[19]

By the time Horace Walpole's *The Castle of Otranto* (1764) appeared in England, the controversy over the monarchy had already emerged.[20] As E. J. Clery and Robert Miles note, "from the seventeenth century onwards, British historians, legal commentators and political philosophers showed a deep interest in the historical role of Germanic tribes."[21] This scholarship resulted in the association of the Gothic with England's Saxon past. These historians believed that the Glorious Revolution of 1688 was not merely an uprising of the people but also a sanctioned event under the dictates of a pre-Norman Conquest constitution. Rather than claim that the ruler has a right to the throne through inheritance, the Saxon constitution bases the selection of a leader on the choice of the people.[22] This concept of government especially appealed to the populace under the reign of George III. "Before his illness," Backscheider asserts, "George III had first been in opposition to his own ministers, including the popular Pitt-Newcastle 'broad-bottom' coalition, and had then been the object of resolutions passed in Parliament condemning the increase in his exercise of power."[23] Eventually, the tyranny of George III's rule led to the American Revolution. The affinity of the American cause with this Gothic tenant was instrumental in the justification for the war against the crown. Because the British subjects in colonial America remained part of the political party system of Britain, they were just as involved in these debates as the subjects who remained in England. The Whigs tended to rely on the premise that the common man had inalienable rights that the monarch had no right upon which to infringe. In the wake of the American Revolution, the Whig party laid the foundation for American politics. In Demophilius's *The Genuine Principles of the Ancient Saxons, or English Constitution* (1776), an American colonist outlines the fundamental principles for the American constitution. He also distinguishes between pre-Norman versus post-Norman rule. The writer alleges: "The [pre-Norman is] founded upon the principles of liberty, and the [post-Norman] upon the principles of slavery."[24] As this treatise indicates, the Gothic's preoccupation with power relations is not only exclusive to an English cultural memory but also to colonial and postcolonial American memories.

SOUTHERN-NORTHERN TENSIONS DISGUISED AS ENGLISH-ITALIAN CONFLICTS

Set in sixteenth-century Rome, *Politian* begins with the appearance of two servants discussing the "untimely revels" of their master's son, Castiglione Di Broglio (249).[25] In addition to his inebriation, the audience learns that he has seduced his father's orphan ward, Lalage. In the first scene, three servants discuss the unhappy fate of Lalage. Then, the second scene cuts to Castiglione and his friend San Ozzo finishing a night of festivities; however, the focus remains on the plight of Lalage. Feeling guilty about his treatment of Lalage, Castiglione begins to regret how he seduced and abandoned her. Through his antics, San Ozzo convinces Castiglione to think no more of the affair—at least for the moment. Also, during this scene, the audience discovers that Castiglione's father, the Duke, has confined Lalage to a room in the castle. As the play progresses, an English Earl by the name of Politian arrives at the Duke's palazzo with his companion, Baldazzar. These men learn that Castiglione is preparing for his nuptials with his cousin, Alessandra. That very same evening Politian hears a woman singing a sorrowful, English song and discovers the forlorn Lalage at her window. He falls in love with her immediately and commits himself to her wholeheartedly *in spite of* her liaison with Castiglione. Lalage accepts Politian's pledge on the apparent condition that he kills Castiglione. Politian accepts these terms because of Castiglione's egregious injury against her. When the drama concludes, Lalage finds Politian in the Coliseum and relays to him that Castiglione is marrying Alessandra at that moment. The last action of the play is Lalage's farewell to Politian as he departs to confront Castiglione at the altar.[26]

Poe's *Politian* presents the quasi-medieval world of late fifteenth- to early sixteenth-century Rome, but, in actuality, it alludes to issues confronting the American South. These issues include the vilification of the Southern plantation owner who did not engage in the proper treatment of slaves, orphans, and women. Slavery and plantation life were linked inextricably. Imprisonment, chains, and torture—all elements of the Gothic—mirrored the ideas many persons held about how the slaves were abused in the American South. As Teresa Goddu notes in *Gothic America*, these abuses often were appropriated by American Gothic writers to be utilized as writing conventions.[27] Poe consciously exploited the tensions between the North and the South, knowing that his readers were often Northerners who hungered for stories that presented imagined horrors of plantation life. Even today, his exact position on slavery remains elusive. Though Poe did own a slave for a brief time, David Reynolds asserts that Poe "retained deep, if rather oblique and ambivalent connections to the most urgent and vexed question of his day."[28] Fiedler attributes this apathy to Poe's "aristocratic pretensions."[29] He believes that Poe lacked "the equivocations and soul-searching demanded of such liberal gothicists as the young Brockden Brown."[30] Goddu believes that he not only equivocates on the question but that he also uses "the conventions deployed by pro- and anti-slavery proponents alike to sell his own tales."[31] Poe's primary interest did not appear to be to sympathize with marginalized peoples, such as American Indians, slaves, and women. On the contrary, his lack of sympathy allowed for his use of these sensationalized scenes of oppression to further his literary career. This indifference further explains how Poe could treat such issues as feminism and racism with irreverent, albeit dark, humor in such tales as "Hop Frog" and "How to Write a Blackwood Article."[32]

The character of Lalage exhibits the affinity between the titillation of the Gothic and the sensationalism of slave depictions. The plight of the persecuted heroine parallels the experience of the slave. Because the plantation owner tried to paint himself as the caretaker of these allegedly childlike beings, the idea that a father would treat his "children" with such violence affected readers in much the same way as a guardian in the Gothic transgressing his duties. A slave master could beat his male slaves and rape the females, often producing mulattos, that is, the literal slave-child paradigm. From a Northern perspective, one imagined that, if the slave master could perpetrate these atrocities, very little could prohibit one of these men from pursuing his ward if he so desired. Poe adds an additional complication in the play in that Lalage is a fallen woman. The American South viewed infidelity as a grave matter. The preservation of the family line could not be risked by the female's proclivity to cuckold her husband. This outlook is promoted by the drama of this period. Traditionally, the heroine was to "embody sensibility, often in its purest, most idealistic form."[33] When she does signify these traits, she has a much greater chance of "bring[ing] out the latent benevolence of the protagonist."[34] Lalage has fulfilled this role before the play opens; however, her purity has suffered an irrecoverable blow at the play's commencement. Castiglione equates her beauty with her character when he initially defends her against San Ozzo's imprecations. Castiglione confesses: "If ever a woman fell / With an excuse for falling it was she! / If ever plighted vows most sacredly / Solemnly sworn perfidiously broken / Will damn a man, that damned villain am I! / Young, ardent, beautiful, and loving well / *And pure as beautiful*" (254, emphasis mine).

However, this beauty proves not to be pure but vulnerable. For this reason, Poe's play shows that his heroine cannot escape punishment entirely for her failure to protect her chastity. Depicting a mad character eventually will become one of Poe's hallmarks, although Lalage's madness is distinct from the many mad male narrators to follow. Many male Gothic writers created mad female characters. According to Backscheider this occurs "at points of action when heroines might have asserted themselves and attempted to assume control or might have submitted to some dishonorable action: the device, thus, serves to remove responsibility for immoral, 'unfeminine,' or effective action."[35] This maneuver allows the female character to fluctuate between a desire to repent and to seek revenge on the villain who reduced her to this abominable state. Because Lalage engages in premarital sex, she must die. Or does she? She references the "early grave untimely yawning" because this is how society expects a fallen woman to repent (263). Simultaneously, though, Poe depicts a woman who, on some level, cannot accept that she is solely accountable for her fall. These conflicting responses result in her competing desires for repentance, a gradual death by debilitating remorse, and the death of Castiglione. This internal strife leads to her descent into madness. Poe conveys the process of degeneration, which leads Lalage to conspire in the commission of unlawful actions. Moreover, he accomplishes a pseudo-pardon through the introduction of a hero who sympathizes with her. By taking this measure, he prevents his audience from distancing themselves from his main female character. In effect, through the paternalistic championship of her cause, Politian exculpates Lalage from any guilt because his status as a nobleman signals that her indignation is righteous. Politian's support and Lalage's madness eschew a demand from the audience to hold her accountable for her revenge impulse. Rather, these two conditions provide Lalage with a double absolution.

At the very beginning Lalage appears sane, although understandably distressed. She takes solace from reading about other women who have been betrayed by lovers and were "happy" enough to die. Upset from the recent death of her parents, the betrayal of her lover, and the impertinence of her servant, Lalage quickly deteriorates. Throughout the play, she is depicted as unstable. In the fourth scene, her fractured self is forecasted by the Monk, who deems her "words are madness" (264). According to Poe's stage direction for his final scene, Lalage has entered "wildly" (287). In his characterization of Lalage, Poe exploited shifting views of insanity. Sally Shuttleworth explains that, as the nineteenth century progressed, "madness is envisaged less as an inescapable physiological destiny, than as a partial state, to which anyone under stress is liable, and which endures only so long as passion overturns reason."[36] Since the public of the 1830s believed that any person could succumb to insanity, the audiences were less likely to distance themselves from Lalage just because she became frenzied after her seduction. Her reaction, when viewed within the context of the early nineteenth-century mentality that a fallen woman had destroyed her future prospects, would receive more audience sympathy than if the same situation would have occurred even ten years prior due to these new attitudes toward madness.

In addition to changing views on insanity, Poe's drama tapped into two significant cultural views regarding seduction: the emergence of reform movements and the Southern sense of chivalry. In New York in particular, the mission of a women's group called the Female Moral Reform Society was to ostracize "the most guilty of the two—the deliberate destroyer of female innocence."[37] Because many seduced women became prostitutes, these reform societies not only wanted to aid prostitutes but also deter the seductions. One of their most successful tactics was the public disclosure of the names of men who were known to have committed such egregious offenses. A couple of months before Poe began to compose his play this group began to circulate *The Advocate*, which printed these lists. Although these reform societies were composed predominantly of women, Rosenberg describes an incident in which an all-male group of female reformists suggested that, now that they had taken up the cause, the women could disband. In response, however, the women asserted that this "was decidedly a woman's not a man's issue."[38] Rather than kowtow to this paternalistic attitude, these women decided to insist on the opposite extreme: foregoing male assistance altogether. However, Poe's play retains this paternalism. Poe's Politian protects Lalage. Men, especially Southern gentlemen, often felt that they needed to stand up for women; many engaged in dueling to effect just this.[39] Rather than allow women to protect themselves or seek their own recompense through the courts, men continued to fight for women's honor. Like a deus ex machina, Politian appears at just the right moment to avenge Lalage.

Politian's intervention ensures the violent return of the repressed. Although society generally sanctioned repentance and death for fallen women, the American Gothic opened a space to expose the ferocity with which society clung to this "nostalgia." As Eric Savoy explains, this nostalgia is "a will to sustained cultural coherence."[40] In this case, that coherence relates to the idea that women should repent their falls. However, as Lalage's actions portend in the wake of her jilting, an alternative story contends with society's expectations. Whereas most fallen women might quietly disappear for propriety's sake, Lalage, like most Poe women, refuses to stay entombed. Her active empowerment may mark her as "wild," yet her aggressive return is both a hallmark of Poe's women and American Gothic. As one of Poe's tropes, this "return of what is unsuccessfully repressed" is the secret of aristocratic debauchery.[41]

If England possessed the medieval remnants of castles and Italy its palazzos, the American South paralleled these magnificent structures with its plantation houses. Indeed, many of these homes were fashioned after the Gothic and Palladian styles. In addition to architecture, the cultures' patriarchal value systems also coincided. The Southern gentleman, like the English and Italian aristocrat, was expected to live according to certain moral codes. One of these codes directed citizens on how to dispense with a dead relation's child. In these instances, the Southern gentleman did not hesitate to offer his home and raise this child with (and as) his own.[42] Priding themselves on self-education in the classics, Latin, and Greek, many Southern men looked to these civilizations as models for what to instill in their children. This included teaching females how to be respectable. For instance, in a letter to his niece, a Southern patriarch instructs: "Propriety is to a woman what the great Roman critic says action is to an Orator: it is the first, the second and the third requisite. A woman may be knowing, active, witty and amusing; but without propriety she cannot be amiable. Propriety is the center in which all the lines of duty and of agreeableness meet."[43] The word "propriety" included chastity, and the Southern culture placed the onus on women to protect this quality. However, there is one important exception. When guardians seduced their female wards, the seducer was held accountable for the woman's fall. According to Catherine Clinton, "Only if a man seduced a female 'under his protection' did the southern moral code shift the burden of guilt onto the male transgressor."[44] Part of the reason for this exception was the community's desire to ensure that all persons conformed to certain expectations. If a guardian who committed such an act was left unchecked, he was perceived to have degenerated into a tyrannical, terrorizing individual, which was quite similar to the earlier "feudal lords [who] saw themselves as the law."[45] In America, this tyrant was reincarnated as the evil plantation master. In "Slavery and the Gothic Horror of Poe's 'The Black Cat,'" Lesley Ginsberg argues for Poe's deliberate use of the Gothic to depict "the peculiar psychopolitics of the master/slave relationship."[46] Due to their similar legal statuses, Ginsberg asserts that the distinctions between slaves and women were negligible. In effect, both groups thrived or suffered according to the disposition and dispensations of the master. In essence, this totalitarian mentality denied the existence of natural rights of dependents. As the nineteenth century progressed, however, the South responded quite deftly to the apparently conflicting notions of authority and how this doctrine related to the issues of women's rights and slavery.

In *Politian,* Castiglione and his father embody American fears surrounding the sensationalistic image of the corrupted Southern plantation owner. Castiglione's trespass against Lalage marks him as a prime candidate for a Gothic villain. Although he contemplates his vile behavior, he ultimately chooses to stay the course. He stresses his treachery through declarations such as, "'tis but the headach - / The consequence of yestereve's debauch - / Give me these qualms of conscience" (255). Castiglione defines manliness as that which does not fall into bouts of reflective melancholy. Whenever he begins to consider remorse, his friend, San Ozzo, mocks Castiglione's worry over Lalage. He ridicules Castiglione's potential repentance, deriding him as a "cardinal" in the making (255). In the scene that parodies the donning of ashes for atonement, Castiglione conclusively decides to forsake Lalage altogether and to continue his debaucheries of "crack[ing] a bottle" and fraternizing with the buffo-singer, which are sanctioned by the aristocracy as young, masculine activities (257). The aristocratic characters consistently promote appearances above all else. For instance, his betrothed, Alessandra, instructs Castiglione on the importance of appearances for young, aristocratic men. She critiques him, noting that his "dress and equipage" are "over plain / For thy lofty rank and fashion" (258). Castiglione also mentions the importance of honor, clearly intending the word to mean avoiding an appearance of the debasement of his line rather than being virtuous or noble in his treatment of "lowly born" women, such as Lalage (255).

Although Castiglione commits the physical transgression, Castiglione's father, the Duke Di Broglio, possesses the power to suppress Lalage's story through her incarceration. Through this action, he supports his son's treacherous behavior. The audience learns in the very first scene that the Duke has not treated his ward properly. His servant, Benito, reports that the Duke "pardons his son, but is most wroth with her [Lalage] / And treats her with such marked severity / As humbles her to the dust" (249). The father originally had orchestrated an alliance between his son and Lalage, but now Lalage is a "plighted wife" (249). Her former "bosom friend," Alessandra, is to be married to Castiglione (250). We also learn that this transfer has taken nearly a year to accomplish. During this eleven-month period, the Duke has kept Lalage confined to her apartment, or, as Benito witnesses, behind "the lattice-work / Of her chamber-window" (250) and, as San Ozzo later expresses, "secluded from society" (254). The primary motive for the Duke's breach of promise is his perception that Lalage is destitute of wealth and titles. Moreover, she also lacks propriety in the word's sense of conforming to society's polite expectations regarding chastity and in the sense of without ownership, which by extension often implies protection. In contrast to Lalage, Alessandra, Castiglione's cousin, assures an honorable marriage, which will produce a legitimate heir for the house of Di Broglio.

THE GRANDEUR THAT WAS ROME

In addition to the Gothic images of the tyrannical master and guardian, preservation of a familial hierarchy, as well as suspicions of the Other (i.e., the North), are operative in this play. Unlike the North, the American South insisted on confining women to the domestic sphere. Whereas many Northern women began to enter the workforce as the North industrialized, Southern women instead became managers of "a complex household."[47] In addition to resisting progress in terms of women's roles, the South also experienced a decline in its prestige. According to Ann Douglas, "The South was on the defensive, was slowly but certainly being pushed from her position of pre-eminence. Now, Charleston could admit without qualms the superiority of London, and even more readily that of ancient Athens or Rome; but the superiority of New York was a dangerous supremacy, a condition in the making rather than an accomplished—or, possibly, an admitted—fact, and a condition to be fought."[48]

In the view of many Northerners, the plantation system was reminiscent of the maligned feudal pasts of England and Italy. The confrontation of the North's and South's respective ways of life could not be ignored, and many Southerners felt the impending loss of the region's prestige. For example, in a review of Lucian Minor's address advocating education in Virginia, Poe praised Minor for his forthright attempt to improve the waning lustre of Virginia. In the December 1835 issue of *The Southern Literary Messenger*, Poe writes:

> Virginia is indebted to Mr. Minor—indebted for the seasonable application of his remarks, and doubly indebted for the brilliant eloquence, and impressive energy with which he has enforced them. We sincerely wish—nay, we even confidently hope, that words so full of warning, and at the same time so pregnant with truth, may succeed in stirring up something akin to action in the legislative halls of the land. Indeed there is no time to squander in speculation. The most lukewarm friend of the State must perceive—if he perceives any thing—that the glory of

the Ancient Dominion is in a fainting—is in a dying condition. Her once great name is becoming, in the North, a bye-word for imbecility—all over the South, a type for "the things that have been." And tamely to ponder upon times gone by is not to meet the exigencies of times present or to come. Memory will not help us. The recollection of our former high estate will not benefit us. Let us act.[49]

This notice appeared the same year, 1835, in which Poe wrote *Politian*.

Based on these rivalries between the North and South, the stage is set for Poe to transpose these competing cultures discretely yet not too obscurely onto men of differing nationalities. Poe's substitution of an English Earl for an American hero results in a distinction of Southerners as different from Northerners, particularly in terms of class. From some vantage points, such as the Italian, this transfer is difficult to comprehend. Early nineteenth-century Italians envisioned an "American" as an aboriginal, or Native American; therefore, when Americans traveled to Italy, they were commonly assumed to be English.[50] However, Americans, especially those in the North, distinguished themselves from the English due to the wars and the English's emphasis on rank. For this reason, Poe's use of an English nobleman as a substitute for a Southern gentleman is quite appropriate for this displacement because it emulates the genteel tradition prized by the South's aristocracy and underscores even more the disparities between the two cultures.

The persistence of the South's hierarchical system assumed that the higher classes possessed a higher capacity for intelligence and sensibility. In the play, Poe uses the English to achieve a two-fold purpose: (1) to align his allegiance as a Southerner with the aristocratic class symbolized by his title character and (2) to create a hierarchy that ultimately privileges the English over the Italian aristocracy, thereby also intimating that the American South is above both Italian culture and the American North as well as its prejudices. The latter result appears to be contrary to Ann Douglas's aforementioned observation that the South already admitted inferiority to Rome, but the South's concession in terms of an inferiority complex was not based on the system of economy. The South did not seem to equate the Southern plantation structure with Italian feudalism; therefore, the South did not view itself as inferior to Rome for this reason. In order to understand why Poe and other Southerners apparently did not recognize this parallel, the prevalence of Jefferson's theory of agrarianism and the direct influence of the Scottish Enlightenment on this theory must be reviewed. Considering the sympathies between Lord Kames's theory of society and Jeffersonian agrarianism, an understanding of how the South could persist in its notions of superiority becomes apparent. Agrarianism emphasized the supremacy of tillers. Not only did this theory posit farming as the best way to live but it also represented the farmer as an inherently virtuous man. The link between farming and Godliness promoted a consensus that slavery may somehow be in tune with God's plan due to the perceived need for slaves in the tilling of the American South. This philosophy of "mutual benefits" (as Kames refers to it) through agriculture is encompassed by the American South's economic system. Poe's drama also emphasizes this blind spot. For example, in Lalage's description of the New World, she describes America as a place where breathing the air is "Happiness now, and . . . Freedom hereafter" (274). Although this freedom is denied to most of the population in the South, many Southerners refused to view slavery as anything but an unequivocal good.[51] Rather than view slavery as exploitative, Southerners could manipulate Kames's and Jefferson's ideas to rationalize this institution as peculiar, or different, and, therefore, better than the feudal system through its aggrandizement of all involved.

Italy also may have appealed to Poe because of its potential to symbolize an Other not altogether dissimilar from the American culture juxtaposed against it. Leonardo Buonomo argues that Italy attracted foreign visitors because it "functioned as a relatively accessible and not too disquieting Orient."[52] The dark-skinned people, the Catholic religion, the political system, the pastoral country, and the ruins of ancient Roman civilization provided points of contrast to America. As America industrialized, thereby gaining a reputation of wealth through capitalism, Italy, conversely, represented a land of an idyllic, rural past.[53] Also, the Catholic religion fascinated Americans, who were mostly Protestant, because of Catholicism's apparent affinity with paganism. Nowhere was this parallel more evident than Rome, a city where the statues and temples of Roman gods and goddesses commingled with religious statuary and churches. This juxtaposition gave rise to and supported notions that "at the bases of the Roman Catholic Church there is a simple disguise or adaptation of heathen customs."[54] Similar to the Orient, Italy represented a fascinating alternative to politics, religion, and life in general; however, it also functioned as a revenant civilization. Nineteenth-century Italy merely underscored the lack of greatness inherent in its present society as compared to the civilization of ancient Rome. In many periodicals of the early nineteenth century, articles argued that the fall of Rome could be attributed to the barbaric institution of feudalism, which neglected the rights of the individual. In order to avoid the same fall that Rome experienced, many Americans believed that America had to champion the dignity of the individual above all else. Americans could project their own fears concerning the limitations of American society on this former great society. This strategy was useful as a means to warn that, if America did not purge itself of the American South's same flaws as those of the Roman civilization, it too would crumble.

However, Poe's Italy did not function entirely as a substitute for the American South. It was also a point of contrast between the North's view of the South and the South's distinctions from Italy. Indeed, many of the American impressions of Italy were similar to the impressions Northerners held concerning the American South. Southerners, including Poe, could not have helped but notice the sympathies that their region shared with Rome. Both these regions experienced an awareness of their fading glory. Although the Italian High Renaissance of the late fifteenth century may have promised a great future for Italy, instead the works of Machiavelli, Ariosto, and Castiglione proved to be merely "the 'swan song' of late medieval Italian civilization."[55] This was even more apparent when travelers of the eighteenth and nineteenth centuries went to Rome in order to view its landscapes and its ruins rather than to appreciate the country's modernity.[56] Migration of the people from the rural to the urban areas of America also indicates the tendency to marginalize the non-industrialized South. Unlike its response to Italy, the North did not subscribe to nostalgic portrayals of the South as a land to be prized for its abilities to stave off "the irresistible march of technology."[57] Instead, the South's economic system was the bane of a country that hoped to throw off the plantation system and its association with slavery. The romantic potential of the Southern plantation was largely ignored by the North until it was clearly a remnant of a past that could not resurge, that is, after its destruction via the Civil War.

To underscore differences between Italy and the South, Poe evokes one of the High Renaissance figures, Castiglione, through the name of the main character in the play. As the author of *The Book of the Courtier*, Castiglione's ungentlemanly portrayal in *Politian* is ironic. Poe demonstrates how this great champion of courtly behavior does not necessarily privilege virtuous behavior. Castiglione lived in a nonindustrialized nation. However, an important contrast with the South is that Italy was steeped in Catholicism, which often stood for a debauched society.[58] In contrast to Poe's portrayal of the Italian Castiglione, the Southern gentleman resembled the impulses of Politian: the desire to impose moral standards, to ensure justice for those who have been wronged, and to abide by the chivalric code as a means to effect the first two impulses. The idea was that, if society conformed to these codes, it could reclaim a prelapsarian state of being. Since Italy held onto its old institutions of government, religion, and economy, its Edenic state appeared to be lost irrecoverably.

In Poe's play, the reference to Eden provides a foil to the corrupted state of Italy. In Gothic drama, the landscapes and their rendering in set design are part of the genre's popularity. The landscape paintings of Salvator Rosa were so popular, for example, that set designers endeavored to replicate these scenes onstage. Even Poe, who coined quite a few words, is credited with the word "Salvatorish." He employs the term in "Landor's Cottage" to describe the trees, implying that, like Salvator's, they are "lofty" and sublime.[59] Just as Radcliffe's heroines find solace in the contemplation of sublime nature, Poe's Lalage paints a vision of the New World as an Eden, as "the divine world," which reassures the persecuted heroine that there is a "spiritual power counteracting the forces of evil."[60] In contrast, "the Gothic world" is depicted "as a postlapsarian one that presents us with a powerful echo of the lost Eden, a physical and psychological wilderness that threatens virtually everyone and in which no one can be trusted to be what one appears or claims to be."[61] In Poe's play, Italy's postlapsarian status is underscored by the presence of "a spectral figure" in the *garden* of the palace (274). Similarly, Lalage's description of the New World leads the reader to draw the parallels between the promise of America as a paradise and its current, corrupted state. She waxes:

> A fairy land of flowers, and fruit, and sunshine,
> And crystal lakes, and over-arching forest,
> And mountains, around whose towering summits the winds
> Of Heaven untrammeled flow. (274)

Obviously, in the mid-1830s, the American North and its industrialized cities resembled this paradise much less than the expansive, natural beauty of the American South and its agrarian economy.

These doublings and redoublings in Poe's play are significant in that the use of Italy appears to obfuscate Poe's allegory. He at once tackles the issues of what it means to be a gentleman and who best embodies such qualities. In the process, a pressure arises for his audience to connect the metonymical Castiglione and Politian to the peoples each figure symbolizes. These correspondences are not simply to Italians and English, respectively. Rather, Politian, who appears as an Englishman, incarnates Southern ideals of the gentleman, including a defender of a lady's reputation. The English hero represents the South's idyllic view of its social codes, including its paternalistic, deferential culture. In contrast, the use of Italy as a stand-in for the North's perceptions of the South allows Poe to exploit tropes concerning tyranny. This approach also scratches at the South's anxieties regarding just how legitimate those Northern perceptions may be. In effect, the hero attempts to redeem the South's image through his noble-minded actions. However, he is haunted by "an imp" that he cannot shake (267). What is this imp that threatens to extinguish his life? Politian only identifies it as "that nature / Which from my forefathers I did inherit, / Which with my mother's milk I did imbibe" (268). Politian seeks an act of substance. As he confides to Baldazaar, "I am sick, sick, sick, even unto death, / Of the hollow and high-sounding vanities / Of the populous Earth!" (268). This hero may be a melancholic, yet his "imp" signifies a repression that he will not articulate to himself or others. The zeal with which he fights against the tyranny of the di Broglios may result in his expatiation as well as Castiglione's. However, Poe's play never directly reveals this oppressive secret.

In *Politian*, the repression is not merely the local situation between a libertine male and a seduced woman. Rather the repression is a generalized anxiety that the corrupted nature of the aristocracy might be revealed. The use of Gothic conventions displaces the Southern secret of the potential tyrannical effects of unlimited power of patriarchs over women, children, and slaves.[62] In addition to the sensationalism that the Gothic elicits from its readers, the Gothic also allows Poe to work through his own anxieties in terms of his marginalized status in relation to the Southern aristocracy. Poe's strained relationship with his foster father, John Allan, as well as his existence in the shadow of his grandfather, distinguished Revolutionary War Assistant Deputy Quartermaster "General" David Poe, simultaneously brought him close to the aristocratic circles of Southern gentlemen while also holding him at bay.[63] This frustration, as Ginsberg notes, continued to be exacerbated by Poe's continued close proximity to these aristocrats in his work as an editor for T. W. White at the *Southern Literary Messenger* and how they directed the views, particularly on slavery, while he worked for them.[64] Indeed, "Scenes from an Unpublished Drama" first appeared as a serial for this periodical in December 1835 and January 1836.[65] Interestingly, the scenes that condemn Castiglione through his crass epithets against Lalage are not included in the serial version of the text. On the contrary, the five scenes selected for the magazine appearance depict Castiglione's response to Lalage's condition as a genuine concern about the pivotal role he has played in her present distress. This decision indicates Poe's savvy regarding just how transparent the displacement of the setting could be and how it might potentially inflame his Southern audience's sensibilities. Rather than present a corrupted, mainly unrepentant, aristocratic rake, Poe tempers Castiglione's portrayal in the serial version for the *Messenger*'s primarily Southern audience.

THE GOTHIC AND THE SOCIOPOLITICAL AMBIVALENCE IN POE

In "Average Racism," Terence Whalen argues that Poe's position on slavery was neither "racism-positive" nor "racism-negative."[66] Instead, he constructs a meticulous case for Poe's occupation of a more moderate position. Similarly, *Politian* demonstrates that Poe's view on women's rights also appears to be average: neither feminist nor archaic. Whereas some Poe scholars have discovered a progressive, deconstructionist representation of women in his works, Poe's depictions reveal his greater interest in literary rather than socio-political ends.[67] Poe's potential interest in presenting a coherent, reliable message on either slavery or women's rights is elided in favor of titillating his audience in order to sell his works. His vacillation from the traditional European Gothic's focus on a woman transgressed and oppressed by a tyrant to the use of the transgressed and oppressed slave back to women again through parallels between slaves and women as dependents exemplifies Poe's genius as a Gothic writer. He reinvents the same sensationalist effect of the demented patriarch wielding his absolute tyranny over those in his care. *Politian* is just one of the many examples in Poe's oeuvre of this phenomenon to reveal the secrets that the characters work diligently to keep concealed in a closet, or for Poe, a tomb and locked chamber. Does this repetition indicate a proslavery and/or pro-feminist sympathy? This is indeterminate. However, what Poe does demonstrate without equivocation is that he is certainly Gothic-positive.

Politian's veiled references to the American South show Poe's use of a genre known for obscuring contemporary fears and issues of marginalized groups in England through displacing the concerns to a medieval past. Just like European Gothic, Poe's Gothic displaced his society's marginalized peoples and national anxieties in this same manner. Poe's sophisticated, multivalent removals of the American South to a foreign locale in the medieval era caused his own misplacement by his American public and many scholars, such as Levy, who did not trace these displacements fully but mistakenly categorized Poe as a European writer. On the contrary, as *Politian*'s displacements show, Poe's works prove that his allegiance exists more so with his craft than with presenting an unequivocally, pro-Southern idealization. However, even though Poe's personal stance may appear convoluted in his works, the fact that he utilizes contemporary controversies in this play establishes a strong connection between Poe and his American consciousness as well as reaffirms the theory that Poe's works should be read in conjunction with his historical moment.

NOTES

1. Edgar Allan Poe, Preface, vol. 1 of *Tales of the Grotesque and Arabesque* (Philadelphia: Lea & Blanchard, 1840), www.eapoe.org/works/misc/tgap.htm.

2. Tony Magistrale and Sidney Poger, *Poe's Children: Connections between Tales of Terror and Detection* (New York: Peter Lang, 1999), 98.

3. For example, Magistrale and Poger cite examples of this shift as that from F. O. Matthiessen's *American Renaissance* to David Leverenz's "Poe and Gentry Virginia" and Joan Dayan's "Amorous Bondage: Poe, Ladies, and Slaves" (98). Other recent examples of this trend in Poe scholarship include J. Gerald Kennedy, ed., *A Historical Guide to Edgar Allan Poe* (Oxford: Oxford University Press, 2001); J. Gerald Kennedy and Liliane Weissberg, ed., *Romancing the Shadow: Poe and Race* (Oxford: Oxford University Press, 2001); Meredith McGill, *American Literature and the Culture of Reprinting, 1834–1853* (Philadelphia: University of Pennsylvania Press, 2003), 141–217; Terence Whalen, *Edgar Allan Poe and the Masses* (Princeton: Princeton University Press, 1999).

4. For literary merit, see contemporary reviews: Dwight Thomas and David K. Jackson, comps., *The Poe Log: A Documentary Life of Edgar Allan Poe, 1809–1849* (New York: G. K. Hall & Co., 1987), 186, 188, 189; Beverly Tucker, "To Poe," in vol. 17 of *The Complete Works of Edgar Allan Poe*, ed. James A. Harrison (New York: Sproul, 1902), 22–23; David K. Jackson, "Prose Run Mad: An Early Criticism of Poe's *Politian*," in *Poe and His Time: The Artist in His Milieu*, ed. Benjamin Fisher (Baltimore: Edgar Allan Poe Society, 1990), 88–93. See also later scholars, such as N. Bryllion Fagin, *The Histrionic Mr. Poe* (Baltimore: The Johns Hopkins Press, 1949), 84; John Phelps Fruit, *Poe's Poetry*

(New York: AMS Press, 1969), 49; Daniel Hoffman, *Poe, Poe, Poe, Poe, Poe, Poe, Poe* (Baton Rouge: Louisiana State Univ. Press, 1998), 37. For literary sources, see Karl Arndt, "Poe's *Politian* and Goethe's Mignon," *Modern Language Notes* 49 (1934): 101–4; William Bryan Gates, "Poe's *Politian* Again," *Modern Language Notes* 49 (1934): 561; Thomas O. Mabbott, "Another Source of Poe's Play, 'Politian,'" *Notes and Queries* 194 (1949): 279; Palmer Holt, "Poe and H. N. Coleridge's Greek Classic Poets 'Pinakidia,' 'Politian,' and 'Morella' Source," *American Literature* 34 (1962): 8–30. For articles that link the play to the historical incident referred to as the Kentucky Beauchamp-Sharp tragedy, see William Goldhurst, "The New Revenge Tragedy: Comparative Treatments of the Beauchamp Case," *Southern Literary Journal* 22 (1989): 117–27; William Kimball, "Poe's *Politian* and the Beauchamp-Sharp Tragedy," *Poe Studies* 4 (1971): 24–27.

5. Jeffrey H. Richards, "Poe, *Politian*, and the Drama of Critique," *The Edgar Allan Poe Review* 3, no. 2 (2002): 3–27.

6. Amy C. Branam, "*Politian's* Significance for Early American Drama," *The Edgar Allan Poe Review* 8, no. 1 (2007): 32–46.

7. In early American drama, American innovations included the integration of Native American characters, such as in John Augustus Stone's *Metamora; or the last of the Wampanoags*, and also patriotic productions, such as William Dunlap's *The Glory of Columbia; her Yeomanry.*

8. Paula Backscheider, *Spectacular Politics: Theatrical Power and Mass Culture in Early Modern England* (Baltimore: The Johns Hopkins University Press, 1993), 168.

9. In terms of viewing the play as Gothic, many scholars have discussed the work's Gothicism in relation to Byron's influence on Poe. See Fagin, *The Histrionic Mr. Poe*, 85–86; Katrina Bachinger, *The Multi-Man Genre* (Salzburg: Institut für Anglistik und Amerikanistik, 1987); Kenneth Silverman, *Edgar A. Poe: Mournful and Never-ending Remembrance* (New York: Harper Perennial, 1992), 93; Roy P. Basler, "Byronism in Poe's 'To One in Paradise,'" *American Literature* 9 (1937): 236.

10. For further discussion on the Gothic conventions in the play, see Branam, 35–39.

11. Maurice Levy, "Gothic' and the Critical Idiom," in *Gothick Origins and Innovation*, ed. Allan Lloyd Smith and Victor Sage (Atlanta: Rodopi, 1994), 1–15.

12. Levy, 14.

13. Levy, 4.

14. Maurice Levy, "Edgar Poe et la tradition 'gothique,'" *Caliban* 5 (1968): 35–51.

15. Robert Miles, "The Gothic and Ideology," in *Approaches to Teaching Gothic Fiction*, ed. Diane Long Hoeveler and Tamara Heller (New York: MLA, 2003), 62.

16. Teresa Goddu, "Historicizing the American Gothic: Charles Brockden Brown's *Wieland*," in *Approaches to Teaching Gothic Fiction* (see note 15), 186.

17. David S. Reynolds, *Beneath the American Renaissance: The Subversive Imagination in the Age of Emerson and Melville* (Cambridge, MA: Harvard University Press, 1988), 175.

18. Allan Lloyd-Smith, "Nineteenth-Century American Gothic," in *A Companion to the Gothic*, ed. David Punter (Oxford: Blackwell Publishers, 2000): 110.

19. Thomas Jefferson, "A Declaration by the Representatives of the United States of America, in General Congress Assembled," in *The Norton Anthology of American Literature*, shorter 6th ed., ed. Nina Baym (New York: W. W. Norton and Company, 2003), 337.

20. For a discussion of Walpole's political affiliations, see Markman Ellis, *The History of Gothic Fiction* (Edinburgh: Edinburgh University Press, 2000), 37–43.

21. E. J. Clery and Robert Miles, ed., *Gothic Documents: A Sourcebook 1700–1820* (Manchester: Manchester University Press, 2000), 48.

22. Clery and Miles, 48.

23. Backscheider, 160.

24. Demophilius, *The Genuine Principles of the Ancient Saxons, or English Constitution*, 1776, in *Gothic Documents: A Sourcebook 1700–1820* (see note 21), 225.

25.   Edgar Allan Poe, *Politian*, in vol. 1 of *The Collected Works of Edgar Allan Poe*, ed. T. O. Mabbot (Cambridge, MA: Belknap Press, 1969), 247–98. All subsequent quotations are taken from this edition and are given in parentheses in the text.

26.   Many scholars presume that the play would have ended with the death of Castiglione at the hand of Politian. For example, see John H. Ingram, 'Poe's "Politian,"' *The Southern Magazine*, 17 (1875): 588–94.

27.   Teresa A. Goddu, *Gothic America: Narrative, History, and Nation* (New York, Columbia University Press, 1997), 93.

28.   Reynolds, 181.

29.   Leslie Fiedler, *Love and Death in the American Novel*, 2nd ed. (New York: Stein and Day, 1966), 397.

30.   Fiedler, 397.

31.   Goddu, 93.

32.   For further discussion, see Lloyd-Smith, 113–14.

33.   Backscheider, 195.

34.   Backscheider, 198.

35.   Backscheider, 204.

36.   Sally Shuttleworth, *Charlotte Bronte and Victorian Psychology* (New York: Cambridge University Press, 1996), 35.

37.   Carroll Smith Rosenberg, "Beauty, the Beast and the Militant Woman: A Case Study in Sex Roles and Social Stress in Jacksonian America," *American Quarterly* 23 (1971): 572.

38.   Rosenberg, 579.

39.   The prevalence of duels led to aggressive legislation against the practice in the early nineteenth century. See Andrew J. King, "Constructing Gender: Sexual Slander in Nineteenth-Century America," *Law and History Review* 13 (1995): 63–110.

40.   Eric Savoy, "A Theory of American Gothic," in *American Gothic: New Interventions in a National Narrative*, ed. Robert K. Martin and Eric Savoy (Iowa City: University of Iowa Press, 1998), 3–19.

41.   Savoy, 4. In this article, Savoy defines one of American Gothic's characteristics as "the imperative to repetition, the return of what is unsuccessfully repressed, and, moreover, that this return is realized in a syntax, a grammar, a tropic field."

42.   Catherine Clinton, *The Plantation Mistress: Woman's World in the Old South* (New York: Pantheon Books, 1982), 39.

43.   Campbell qtd. in Clinton, 102.

44.   Clinton, 112.

45.   Backscheider, 164.

46.   Lesley Ginsberg, "Slavery and the Gothic Horror of Poe's 'The Black Cat,'" in *American Gothic: New Interventions in a National Narrative* (see note 40), 99–128.

47.   Ann Douglas, *The Feminization of American Culture* (New York: Alfred A. Knopf, 1977), 49.

48.   Douglas, 151.

49.   Edgar Allan Poe, "Critical Notices," *Southern Literary Messenger* 2 (1835): 41–68.

50.   Leonardo Buonomo, *Backward Glances* (Madison: Fairleigh Dickinson University Press, 1996), 18–19.

51.   For instance, in Terence Whalen, "Average Racism: Poe, Slavery, and the Wages of Literary Nationalism," in *Romancing the Shadow*, ed. J. Gerald Kennedy and Liliane Weissberg (Oxford: Oxford University Press, 2001), 9, he discusses Beverly Tucker's stance on slavery as a strong belief in its moral benefit to all parties involved.

52.   Buonomo, 15.

53.   Buonomo, 21.

54.   Buonomo, 23.

55.   Theodore J. Cachey, "Italy and the Invention of America," *The New Centennial Review* 2(2002): 17–31.

56.   Cachey, 19.

57.   Buonomo, 16.

58. Poe once commented that he did not respect any religion, although he did not mind the Jesuits because they "smoked, drank, and played cards like gentlemen, and never said a word about religion." See Silverman, 341.

59. Edgar Allan Poe, "Landor's Cottage," in vol. 3 of *The Collected Works of Edgar Allan Poe*, ed. T. O. Mabbot (Cambridge, MA: Belknap Press, 1969), 1332.

60. Marshall Brown, "Philosophy and the Gothic Novel," in *Approaches to Teaching Gothic Fiction* (see note 15), 46-57.

61. Stephen C. Behrendt, "Teaching the Gothic through the Visual Arts," in *Approaches to Teaching Gothic Fiction* (see note 15), 66–72.

62. Ginsberg also notes that one of the South's most common depictions in the face of abolition "was the domestic fiction of the happy slaveholding family" (105). Unfortunately, this façade is undercut not only by the instances of abuses against slaves but also by Thomas E. Buckley's report which uncovered that the highest number of divorces filed in antebellum Virginia cited domestic violence as the impetus (107).

63. See Leland S. Person, "Poe and Nineteenth-Century Gender Constructions," in *A Historical Guide to Edgar Allan Poe*, ed. J. Gerald Kennedy (Oxford: Oxford University Press, 2001), 130; David Levernz, "Poe and Gentry Virginia," in *The American Face of Edgar Allan Poe*, ed. Shawn Rosenheim and Stephen Rachman (Baltimore: The Johns Hopkins University Press, 1995), 210–36. Poe's grandfather actually only held the rank of major, but was given the courtesy title "General" because he donated much money in support of the Revolutionary cause.

64. Ginsberg, 120–22.

65. There are three different published versions of this play: the 1835–1836 serialization in the *Southern Literary Messenger*; T. O. Mabbott's 1923 authoritative edition of Poe's manuscript version included in his *The Collected Works of Edgar Allan Poe*, and the 1845 version printed in *The Raven and Other Poems*.

66. Whalen, 35.

67. See Cynthia S. Jordan, "Poe's Re-Vision: The Recovery of the Second Story," *American Literature* 59 (1987): 1–19; Joan Dayan, "Poe's Women: A Feminist Poe?" *Poe Studies: Dark Romanticism* 26 (1993): 1–12; Marita Nadal, "'The Death of a Beautiful Woman Is, Unquestionably, the Most Poetical Topic in the World': Poetic and Parodic Treatment of Women in Poe's Tales," in *Gender, I-Deology: Essays on Theory, Fiction and Film*, ed. Chantal Cornut-Gentille D'Arcy, García Landa, and José Angel (Netherlands: Rodopi, 1996), 151–63.

SIX

Poe in the Ragged Mountains: Environmental History and Romantic Aesthetics

Daniel J. Philippon

A later work, written at the same time as some of his best-known tales of horror and ratiocination—such as "The Tell-Tale Heart," "The Gold-Bug," "The Black Cat," "The Premature Burial," and "The Purloined Letter"—"A Tale of the Ragged Mountains" (1844) has never been considered one of Edgar Allan Poe's more successful stories. As Doris V. Falk has noted, the plot seems to be "deliberately obscure, full of multifarious Romantic-Gothic elements which never quite cohere," and as a result, the very intricacy of the tale has probably "discouraged criticism, to say nothing of readers."[1] At the same time, however, Poe is said to have identified "A Tale of the Ragged Mountains" as one of his favorite compositions,[2] and it is the only work in which he refers specifically to his experience in Charlottesville, where he attended the new University of Virginia during most of 1826.[3] Despite its weaknesses, "A Tale of the Ragged Mountains" raises two important questions that deserve consideration: first, did Poe base his tale on the actual landscape of the Ragged Mountains, and second, how might his having done so affect our reading of the tale?

William Carlos Williams claimed that Poe was "intimately shaped by his locality and time" and that the local was Poe's "constant focus of attention."[4] "It is the New World," Williams wrote in *In the American Grain* (1925), "or to leave that for the better term, it is a new locality that is in Poe assertive; it is America, the first great burst through to expression of a reawakened genius of place" (216). Yet Williams also suggested that

Poe's work grew out of the local conditions "not of trees and mountains, but of the 'soul'" (227). Although most of Poe's tales do indeed explore the inner landscape of his characters at the expense of the natural world, "A Tale of the Ragged Mountains" is an important exception to this rule. Close attention to the environmental and cultural history of the Ragged Mountains demonstrates not only that Poe most likely did base his tale on this familiar landscape, but also that the discrepancy between the actual Ragged Mountains and the fanciful landscape his protagonist envisions is crucial to a complete understanding of the story.

"A Tale of the Ragged Mountains" opens with the narrator's description of Augustus Bedloe, one of Poe's typical protagonists—a thin, corpse-like young man, pale and melancholy, who suffers from neuralgia. For this condition, he has long been treated by Doctor Templeton, an elderly physician trained in mesmerism. As a result, says the narrator, "a very distinct and strongly marked rapport, or magnetic relation" had grown up between the patient and his doctor.[5] A sensitive and excitable character, with a vigorous imagination and a heavy morphine habit, Bedloe would each day "set forth alone, or attended only by a dog, upon a long ramble among the chain of wild and dreary hills that lie westward and southward of Charlottesville, and are there dignified by the title of the Ragged Mountains" (942).[6] One evening, when Bedloe returns home late from one of his daily jaunts in "rather more than ordinary spirits," Templeton and the narrator are treated to a most extraordinary tale.

After several hours of walking in a drug-induced swoon through the "dreary desolation" of the mountains, Bedloe says, he was surprised to hear the beating of a drum, "a thing unknown" in these hills. Soon thereafter he encountered "a dusky visaged and half-naked man" rushing past him, followed closely by a hyena. When Bedloe paused a moment to collect himself, he then discovered that the tree beneath which he rested was a palm. Astonished by these strange events, he found himself entering into a dream like state in which he was overlooking—and then entering—an arabesque city with "long winding alleys" that "absolutely swarmed with inhabitants" (945). As he became caught up in the tumult and excitement of the crowd, "by some inconceivable impulse" he joined a British-led party battling the city's inhabitants, but was quickly killed in combat, shot in the right temple by a poisoned arrow "made to imitate the body of a creeping serpent" (947). Following his death, Bedloe says, he experienced a violent shock "as if of electricity"; he seemed to rise above his corpse; and he departed the city. Upon returning to the location where he first encountered the hyena, Bedloe was then awakened by another sudden shock, and he bent his steps "eagerly homewards" (948).[7]

At the conclusion of Bedloe's tale, a visibly shaken Doctor Templeton announces that "the soul of man today is upon the verge of some stupendous psychal discoveries," and proceeds to inform Bedloe that "at the very period in which you fancied these things among the hills, I was engaged in detailing them on paper" (949). According to Templeton, Bedloe's vision perfectly matched a memoir he had been writing of his own experiences as a twenty-year-old British officer in Benares, India, serving under the administration of Warren Hastings. "The riots, the combats, the massacre, were the actual events of the insurrection of Cheyte Sing, which took place in 1780," Templeton says, "when Hastings was put in imminent peril of his life" (949). Moreover, says Templeton, Bedloe's experience not only paralleled the shooting death of a fellow British officer named Oldeb, but Bedloe's "miraculous similarity" in appearance to Oldeb was what first attracted the doctor to his patient many years ago.

At this, Poe's narrator closes the story by reprinting the newspaper obituary of Bedloe, who died one week after the events narrated. According to the death notice, Bedloe had contracted a slight cold and fever on his expedition to the Ragged Mountains, and to relieve the swelling in his head, Doctor Templeton bled Bedloe with leeches applied to the temples. Unfortunately, Templeton unknowingly applied a poisonous leech—the "poisonous sangsue of Charlottesville"—to Bedloe's right temple, thus causing his untimely death. As the newspaper account reveals, the "poisonous sangsue of Charlottesville may always be distinguished from the medicinal leech by its blackness, and especially by its writhing or vermicular motions, which very nearly resemble those of a snake" (950). Just as Oldeb was killed by a snakelike, poisoned arrow to his right temple, therefore, Bedloe died in a similar fashion from a snakelike, poisoned leech applied to his right temple by Templeton. Finally, to cement the connection between the two men, the narrator notes that Bedloe's name was misspelled in the obituary as "Bedlo"—a fact "stranger than any fiction," he declares, "for Bedlo, without the e, what is it but Oldeb conversed?" (950).

To make sense of this swirling mass of incidents and coincidence, most commentators have understandably turned their attention to the tale's most prominent themes: mesmerism, metempsychosis, and animal magnetism. In an influential 1947 article on "Poe and Mesmerism," Sidney E. Lind distinguished between the mesmerism (hypnosis) and metempsychosis (the transmigration of souls) in the tale, arguing that "A Tale of the Ragged Mountains" was "intended by Poe to be a study in hypnosis, with the theme of metempsychosis subordinated to one character, Dr. Templeton."[8] In 1969, however, Doris V. Falk argued, contra Lind, that Poe meant the story to be a study not in mesmerism but in "animal magnetism—that electromagnetic force capable of maintaining the nervous organization, complete with physical sensations, even after death, making time and space unreal and relative."[9]

These and other critics have avoided much discussion of the landscape of Poe's tale in part because it seems so irrelevant to the plot.[10] James Southall Wilson, a professor of English at the University of Virginia and the first editor of the *Virginia Quarterly Review*, for instance, claimed that "A Tale of the Ragged Mountains" had "no local color."[11] Likewise, Frances Winwar wrote that although Poe "drew on the nature he observed . . . the story was as far removed from normal experience as an opium dream could make it."[12] And Daniel Hoffman has even suggested that "for those Poe stories in which the characters are still alive, it may be inessential, indeed distracting, to establish a recognizable place as the locus of the action."[13] Taken in by the circuitous windings of Poe's plot, critics such as these fail to recognize the degree to which Poe not only grounded his tale in the Virginia landscape, but also used the realities of that landscape to both justify and spoof the Romantic visions Bedloe claims to experience.

Although the extent of Poe's familiarity with the Ragged Mountains cannot be determined with certainty, documentary evidence suggests that the region sometimes served as a refuge for students, possibly including Poe, during the early years of the University of Virginia. The most detailed record of this practice appears in a letter of Thomas Goode Tucker, one of Poe's classmates, to Douglass Sherley, a student at the University in the late nineteenth century. Sherley incorporated the substance of the letter into one of his columns, called "Old Oddity Papers," published in the *University of Virginia Magazine* in April 1880. According to Sherley, in May 1826, when Poe was enrolled at the University, a number of students fled to the Ragged Mountains to escape the local sheriff, who was seeking to bring them before the Albemarle County grand jury on charges of gambling. "With Edgar Allan Poe for a leader," Sherley recounts, "they, to use the college expression, indiscriminately 'bolted' . . . off to the 'Ragged Mountains' over an unfrequented by-path, but one well known to Poe, and over which he had often travelled."[14] Although the minutes of the Faculty and other University records confirm the main features of this story, "Tucker's statement that Poe was the ringleader of the band is unconfirmed and probably fictitious," Floyd Stovall suggests.[15] Likewise, John S. Patton, librarian of the University of Virginia in 1908, characterized Poe's leadership of the fleeing collegians as "a graceful fiction."[16]

With the exception of his own participation, Poe himself confirmed the basic facts of Tucker's account in a letter written to his foster father, John Allan, on May 25, 1826:

> Soon after you left here the Grand Jury met and put the students in a terrible fright—so much so that the lectures were unattended—and those whose names were upon the Sheriffs list—travelled off into the woods & mountains—taking their beds & provisions along with them—there were about 50 on the list—so you may suppose the College was very well thinned—this was the first day of the fright-the second day, "A proclamation" was issued by the faculty forbidding "any student under pain of a major punishment to leave his dormitory

between the hours of 8 & 10 AM—(at which time the Sheriffs would be about) or in any way to resist the lawful authority of the Sheriffs"— This order was very little attended to—the fear of the Faculty could not counterbalance that of the Grand Jury—most of the "indicted" ran off a second time into the woods and upon an examination the next morning by the Faculty—Some were reprimanded—some suspended—and one expelled. (*Letters* I: 4)[17]

Because Poe was not among the "indicted," if he went with the students who fled to the Ragged Mountains, Stovall concludes, "it was evidently not as ringleader and apparently not from fear of the sheriff; it might have been for fear he would be called as a witness, or it might have been only for the fun of it or because he was better acquainted with the area than other students."[18]

Even if Poe did not participate in this particular trip, it seems more than likely he at some time traveled to the mountains—or at the very least was acquainted with their characteristics. Poe's best biographer, Arthur Hobson Quinn, claims that the description of the scenery in this tale "probably was based on memories too deeply impressed on a young imaginative mind to be forgotten,"[19] and the many accounts of student excursions to the mountains of Virginia during the nineteenth century suggest that Quinn is probably correct. Antebellum novelist William Alexander Caruthers, for instance, described his 1818 expedition to the Natural Bridge with three friends from Washington College in "Climbing the Natural Bridge" (1838); Henry Ruffner recounted his many visits to House Mountain, west of Lexington, in his autobiographical novel *Judith Bensaddi* (1839); and Henry Clay Pate's *American Vade Mecum; or, The Companion of Youth, and Guide to College* (1852) includes a representative account of a trip to the Peaks of Otter, near Bedford. Just as Poe seems to have derived his description of the streams of the imaginary island of Tsalal in *The Narrative of Arthur Gordon Pym* (1838) from his knowledge of the mineral springs of Virginia, so too did he probably base his description of the "chain of wild and dreary hills" in "A Tale of the Ragged Mountains" on his knowledge of the local landscape.[20]

Poe's likely familiarity with the Ragged Mountains is further indicated by a close reading of the early portion of the tale, in which Poe alludes to the historic inhabitation of this region by American Indians. According to the narrator, Bedloe departed for the hills "upon a dim, warm, misty day, towards the close of November, and during the strange interregnum of the seasons which in America is termed the Indian Summer" (942). Bedloe himself also refers to the distinctiveness of the season when he notes that "the thick and peculiar mist, or smoke, which distinguishes the Indian summer, and which . . . hung heavily over all the objects, served, no doubt to deepen the vague impressions which these objects created" (943). One of the earliest references to the term "Indian Summer" was made by J. Hector St. John de Crevecoeur in a 1778 essay on "A Snow-

Storm as It Affects the American Farmer," in which Crevecoeur simply described the period as "a short interval of smoke and mildness," but a later, further detailed reference to the term is more revealing—and may even have influenced Poe's own usage. In his *1824 Notes, on the Settlement and Indian Wars, of the Western Parts of Virginia and Pennsylvania*, the historian Joseph Doddridge claimed that the "smokey time" known as Indian Summer was so called "because it afforded the Indians another opportunity of visiting the settlements with their destructive warfare" (266). A popular text in mid-nineteenth-century Virginia, Doddridge's *Notes* were appended to Samuel Kercheval's widely read *History of the Valley of Virginia* (1833), a book with which Poe may well have been familiar. Placed in the context of Doddridge's definition, then, Poe's choice of seasons can be seen not only to foreshadow the events that take place in the "Indian" city of Benares, but also to link these events to the American Indian history of central Virginia.

Although no battles similar to the insurrection of Cheyte Sing occurred between Indians and settlers in Albemarle County (in which Charlottesville is located), warfare was common between rival tribes before the arrival of Europeans. The earliest reference to the Indians of this region appears on John Smith's 1612 map of Virginia, in which Smith indicates that a group of Indians called the Monacans lived in this area and that their chief village was named Monasukapanough. Amoroleck, a Manahoac Indian from the Rappahannock River region, described the Monacans as peaceful in August 1608, according to Smith's *General Historie* (1624): "The Monacans he sayd were their neighbors and friends, and did dwell as they in the hilly Countries by small rivers, living upon rootes and fruits, but chiefly by hunting."[21] But in the text accompanying his 1612 map, Smith offered a more bellicose description of the tribe, in his discussion of the tidewater Powhatans in relation to the Monacans: "They seldome make warre for lands or goods, but for women and children, and principally for revenge. They have many enemies, namely all their westernely Countries beyond the mountaines, and the heads of the rivers."[22]

Another important source from which Poe may have learned of the Indian inhabitants of this region was *Notes on the State of Virginia* (1785), written by Thomas Jefferson, founder of the University of Virginia. In Query XI of his *Notes*, Jefferson explained how he examined a Monacan burial mound north of the Ragged Mountain region, "on the low grounds of the Rivanna [River], about two miles above its principal fork, and opposite to some hills, on which had been an Indian town [Monasukapanough]."[23] The mound, Jefferson says, "was of a spheroidical form, of about 40 feet in diameter at the base, and had been of about twelve feet altitude, though now reduced by the plow to seven and a half, having been under cultivation about a dozen years."[24] After making a number of excavations, Jefferson observed that the mound held about one thousand bodies arranged in several layers, with each layer being covered with dirt and stones. Given that he discovered no holes "as if made with bullets, arrows, or other weapons" in any of the bones, Jefferson also conjectured that this was probably not the grave marker of a great battle, nor was it "the common sepulchre of a town."[25] Whatever the occasion for the mound, Jefferson concluded, the bones "are of considerable notoriety among the Indians": "for a party passing, about thirty years ago, through the part of the country where this barrow is, went through the woods directly to it, without any instructions or enquiry, and having staid about it some time, with expressions which were construed to be those of sorrow, they returned to the high road, which they had left about half a dozen miles to pay this visit, and pursued their journey."[26] Although no burial mounds of this size exist farther south, twelve sites—including two rock shelters—are located in the Ragged Mountain region, along the north and south forks of the Hardware River.[27]

According to Albemarle County historian John Hammond Moore, local legend also has it that another party of Indians appeared in the county sometime around 1840, seeking permission to perform memorial services at a burial mound near the Ragged Mountains. When their request was granted, the Indians "conducted a series of dances watched with considerable interest by many citizens," and then, like the Indians observed by Jefferson, went away without incident.[28] Poe, in Philadelphia at the time, in all likelihood remained unaware of this particular event (if indeed it did occur), but he nevertheless must have learned something about the situation of the American Indians by the mid-1840s, because he was clearly growing sympathetic to their cause. Two years after "A Tale of the Ragged Mountains" appeared, Poe argued in *Graham's Magazine* (Dec. 1846) that the term "Appalachia" was preferable to "America" as a name for the United States because "in employing this word we do honor to the Aborigines, whom, hitherto, we have at all points unmercifully despoiled, assassinated and dishonored."[29]

In addition to his allusions to the American Indian inhabitants of the region in his tale, Poe also relied on popular stereotypes of the poor whites who lived in the Ragged Mountains to strengthen the credibility of Bedloe's visionary experiences. Although Bedloe emphasizes that he may have been "the first adventurer—the very first and sole adventurer who had ever penetrated . . . [the mountains'] recesses," he also claims to have remembered "strange stories told about these Ragged Hills, and of the uncouth and fierce races of men who tenanted their groves and caverns" (943).

Despite the limited information that exists about the mountain people of this region during the mid-nineteenth century, a few pieces of evidence suggest that Poe's characterization of their unfavorable reputation was in keeping with the popular beliefs of his time. In a April 15, 1875 letter to John Henry Ingram, Poe's English biographer, George Long, one of the first professors at the university, wrote that the Ragged Mountains were "inhabited by a considerable number of very ignorant, brutal whites. This hilly region is very picturesque and the geology very interesting. I often rode out to see it, but I kept clear of the barbarous inhabitants one of whom I had unintentionally offended by a harmless joke. In those days a Virginian was a dangerous man to joke with, for he could not comprehend a joke and could only take it as an insult."[30]

A similar account appears in a fictional sequel to "A Tale of the Ragged Mountains" written by Emory Widener, a student at the University, for the *University of Virginia Magazine* in 1909. In Widener's updated "Tale," the narrator describes an expedition he and two other students took to the Ragged Mountains one morning in May, in tribute to "poor Eddie Poe."

> The little hills seemed only a short distance away when we started, but it was high noon ere we reached their summit. And such mountains! Only a nest of hills, inhabited by a strange, rude people, who have lived in the shadow of Mr. Jefferson's institution since its founding without ever being able to write a word that is spoken there. As we climbed the mountain, one of these fellows was standing in his yard. He motioned us towards him. "Any booze?" he queried, and when we denied him, he went into his cabin, sad. Such is the life of the inhabitants of Ragged Mountains.[31]

The economic circumstances of these people is further illustrated by a comment in the Rev. Edgar Woods's 1909 history of Albemarle County, in which Woods writes that "in early times the Mountains . . . were called Ragged, from their disordered appearance, and not from the garments of their inhabitants, as has sometimes been suggested."[32]

Unfortunately, the most detailed discussion of the residents of this region does not appear until more than sixty-eight years after Poe's story first appeared, when the University of Virginia Civic Club in 1912 published *An Investigation of Conditions in the Ragged Mountains of Virginia.* Assuming that the situation of the inhabitants of this region would most likely have improved, and not declined, over time, this twenty-six-page booklet—heavily marred though it is by class bias—may nevertheless offer some indication of the conditions in which the inhabitants of the Ragged Mountains must have been living in the mid-nineteenth century. "The larger part of the Ragged Mountain people," the club found, "are reasonably prosperous, of good intelligence and moral fiber, and possess at least a rudimentary education."[33] A small portion of the inhabitants, however, were discovered to be living "in a practically separate community—which is vastly more backward, in greater poverty and moral darkness than its neighbors."[34] Situated within a narrow strip of land eight miles long and from two to four miles wide, and located a little more than two miles southwest of Charlottesville, this community was said to be composed of people "not only very poor, but also tainted with various forms of physical and moral degeneracy which make them not only useless citizens but bad neighbors."[35] It is their moral laxity, according to the Civic Club, that "has in times past cast an unmerited reproach upon all the inhabitants of the Ragged Mountains."[36]

Given the continuity that seems to have existed throughout the years in the perception of these people by outsiders, Poe's local audience in the nineteenth century probably would have recognized a similarity between Bedloe's fear of the "uncouth and fierce races of men" who lived in the Ragged Mountains and the "deep sense of animosity" he felt toward "the swarming rabble of the alleys" in Benares (946), just as they might have associated the Indian summer of the tale's setting with the idea of warfare. Nevertheless, in the same way Poe's sympathy with the American Indian today helps us find irony in his use of the Indian summer as a foreshadowing device, Poe's local audience would no doubt also have recognized a difference between the dwellings of this poorest class of Ragged Mountain residents and the Oriental city envisioned by Bedloe. According to the Civic Club, the homes of "this community of backward and, in part, aberrant individuals" are "of the wretchedest type":

> The cabins are pitifully small, the families occupying them pitifully large; and often the pigs and chickens live in the same room with seven or eight people. Some of the cabins are so tumbled down and open to the weather that it is amazing that human beings can dwell in them, particularly in the winter. The premises about the cabins are in equally as bad condition; stables, pigsties and privies are placed without regard for drainage into the wells and springs; the stables and other outbuildings are often merely shelters, sometimes built of the thick branches of trees; and the fences, porches, and yards are ill kept and unkempt to a degree that is astonishing. Horses and cows are rarely owned by these people, but nearly every family has one or more pigs and a collection of chickens; there are few agricultural implements, and these are of the poorest type, and in bad repair.[37]

The contrast between this description and Bedloe's view of Benares could not be more striking. Looking down on the Indian city from above, Bedloe notes:

> The houses were wildly picturesque. On every hand was a wilderness of balconies, of verandahs, of minarets, of shrines, and fantastically carved oriels. Bazaars abounded; and in these were displayed rich wares in infinite variety and profusion—silks, muslins, the most dazzling cutlery, the most magnificent jewels and palanquins, litters with stately dames close veiled, elephants gorgeously caparisoned, idols grotesquely hewn, drums, banners and gongs, spears, silver and gilded mace. And amid the crowd, and the clamor, and the general intricacy and confusion—amid the million of black and yellow men, turbaned and robed, and of flowing beard, there roamed a countless multitude of

holy filleted bulls, while vast legions of the filthy but sacred ape clambered, chattering and shrieking, about the cornices of the mosques, or clung to the minarets and oriels. (945)

Noting that Poe's references to "strange stories" and "fierce races" are reminiscent of similar devices used by Washington Irving in "Rip Van Winkle" (1819), Stuart Levine suggests that Poe "may have selected the mountains of Virginia for much the same reason that Irving chose the Catskills: because he thought he could 'get away' with more than he could in more prosaic places."[38] Moreover, Levine argues, the hint of folklore present in the tale suggests that Poe, "like Hawthorne and other contemporaries, was worried by the problem of creating romance in a matter-of-fact new country."[39] While Levine is correct in suggesting that Poe was following the practices of other Romantic authors in his use of folkloric elements in "A Tale of the Ragged Mountains," unlike them, Poe was also interested in satirizing Romantic aesthetics. Indeed, if Poe's only intent was to romanticize the mountainous Virginia landscape, he could have developed the roles of the Indian and the mountaineer much further than he did. Instead, by turning to India to provide the substance of his tale—by choosing to transform "A Tale of the Ragged Mountains" into "A Tale of Benares"—Poe was able to poke fun at the very Romantic practices he seemed to be embracing. As Mukhtar Ali Isani points out, "Poe's choice of an Oriental element for his tale appears to have been influenced by the contemporary vogue for Orientalism in America. Only in this case, Poe was not writing an Oriental tale, though he may for a while give this impression. . . . Poe's Orientalism is a lure, the claims to authenticity skillfully diverting the reader from the more mundane truth that the story is a tale of Charlottesville, with a psychological explanation of the exotic cover."[40] In other words, as Edward Said has written, Poe's Orientalism "has less to do with the Orient than it does with 'our' world."[41]

Poe further suggests that Bedloe's Romantic vision is literally "out of place" in the Virginia mountains by borrowing elements of his Orientalized landscape from other sources. Of the many studies that trace the sources of this tale, the most convincing are those that discuss the similarities between "A Tale of the Ragged Mountains" and Thomas Babington Macaulay's famous essay on Warren Hastings, which first appeared in the *Edinburgh Review* in October 1841. Like Poe, Macaulay writes of Benares as a "labyrinth of lofty alleys, rich with shrines, and minarets, and balconies, and carved oriels, to which the sacred apes clung by hundreds"; he describes India as filled with "the black faces, the long beards, the yellow streaks of sect; the turbans and the flowing robes; the spears and the silver maces; the elephants with their canopies of state"; and he refers to "the jungle where the lonely courier shakes his bunch of iron rings to scare away the hyaenas" (Mabbott III: 937–38).

The extent of Poe's borrowings from Macaulay to orientalize his Virginia setting also suggests the degree to which we should interpret the rest of his tale as a spoof on popular Romanticism in America. Poe not only plays on the contemporary taste for exotic destinations, but he also makes fun of those Romantic writers who suggest that every landscape is a knowable entity with which one can communicate. Between the delight Bedloe expresses in the "pleasant fog" of Indian summer and the oppression he feels from his "thousand vague fancies" about the mountains and their inhabitants, Bedloe also experiences another emotion—a drug-induced Romantic reverie. As his walk progressed, Bedloe recounts, "the morphine had its customary effect—that of enduing all the external world with an intensity of interest. In the quivering of a leaf—in the hue of a blade of grass—in the shape of a trefoil—in the humming of a bee—in the gleaming of a dewdrop—in the breathing of the wind—in the faint odors that came from the forest—there came a whole universe of suggestion—a gay and motley train of rhapsodical and immethodical thought" (943).

Such rhapsodies do not bring about transcendence for Bedloe, of course, but rather the heightening of terror, a state of fearful agitation, and, ultimately, complete delusion. Our attempts to "commune" with nature in the Romantic fashion, Poe seems to suggest, are doomed to utter failure. Nature, despite our deepest desires, will always remain a foreign country.

Poe's expose of Romantic aesthetics in "A Tale of the Ragged Mountains" culminates in the device by which the narrator announces the death of Bedloe: his contact with "one of the venomous vermicular sangsues which are now and then found in the neighboring ponds" (950). As Thomas Ollive Mabbott points out in his introduction to the tale in the *Collected Works of Edgar Allan Poe*, "Neither in fact, nor in fable (before Poe's), can a poisonous sangsue (or leech) be found" (936). In addition, according to W. Otto Friesen, Professor of Biology at the University of Virginia, of the ten or so pond leeches found in and around the Charlottesville area, not only is none poisonous, but many are not even bloodsuckers. As Mabbott also notes, although Poe may have found the French term for the leech (sangsue) in either Cuvier's *Le Regne Animal* (1817) or Victor Hugo's *Notre-Dame de Paris* (1832), he may also have chosen to pun on the name of Samuel Leitch, Jr., a Charlottesville merchant who billed John Allan for a debt of $68.46, incurred by "Edgar A. Powe," while at the University (952–23).[42] Whatever the source of his leech, Poe's intention is clear: Romantics who surrender themselves completely to nature—who allow their imaginations to overwhelm their perceptions—can expect to meet with a deadly fate. Inattention to the actualities of the landscape, in short, can have tragic consequences.[43]

Although the mesmerism, metempsychosis, and animal magnetism of "A Tale of the Ragged Mountains" all provide a convenient explanation for Bedloe's Romantic vision, these aspects of the tale fail to address the full significance of his experience. Restoring the centrality of the landscape to Poe's tale helps us better to understand Bedloe's vision as an expression of both the ease with which we can find the supernatural in the natural and the consequences of our looking for more in a landscape than it actually contains. According to Reinhard H. Friederich, "In a number of ways 'A Tale of the Ragged Mountains' is typical of what irritates the reader in much of Poe's fiction: there are both oblique and obvious repetitions, excitement and exhaustion, exotic prospects which turn out to be commonplace. For a while life seems to invent exciting alternatives to a normally drab existence, but after a short while such semblances collapse in death."[44] Yet this is precisely the point of Poe's tale: "exotic prospects" often exceed the ability of the "commonplace" to sustain them, and "exciting alternatives" are usually nothing but "semblances" of daily life. To succeed, therefore, any search for a "whole universe of suggestion" must be held in check by the realities of the landscape in which it occurs.

NOTES

1. Doris V. Falk, "Poe and the Power of Animal Magnetism." *PMLA* 84 (1969): 542.

2. John Carl Miller, *Poe's Helen Remembers* (Charlottesville: University Press of Virginia, 1979), 419.

3. Although the narrator dates the events of "A Tale of the Ragged Mountains" as occurring during the fall of 1827, Poe attended the university from February to December of 1826.

4. William Carlos Williams, *In the American Grain* (New York: New Directions, 1956), 216; 218.

5. *Collected Works of Edgar Allan Poe*, ed. Thomas Ollive Mabbott, 3 vols. (Cambridge: Harvard University Press, 1969–1978) III: 941. Subsequent references to this volume will be made parenthetically in the text by page number.

6. Modern geological survey maps confine the Ragged Mountains to a few square miles, which include four main peaks: Round Top (919 ft.), Bear Den Mountain (1,248 ft.), Newcomb Mountain (1,262 ft.), and Woodson Mountain (1,297 ft.). Earlier maps of Albemarle County are more generous, however, and the first county history shows the term "Ragged Mountains" to be rather flexible, sometimes designating mountains in the northwest part of the county in addition to those "heaped up for some miles" to the southwest. (See Rev. Edgar Woods, *History of Albemarle County in* Virginia. [Charlottesville: Michie Company, 1901], 15.)

7. Portions of Bedloe's vision resemble Thomas De Quincey's dreams in *Confessions of an English Opium-Eater* (1822), which Poe had read by 1835, especially De Quincey's imagery of mountains and valleys, solitude and crowds, and the terror of the East (Poe, Letters I: 58). For more on Poe and opium, see Hayter and Milligan.

8. Sidney E. Lind, "Poe and Mesmerism," *PMLA* 62 (1947): 1085.

9. Falk, 540.

10. An important exception to the general disregard for the landscape of Poe's tales is Ljungquist, although his discussion of "A Tale of the Ragged Mountains" is all too brief (*The Grand and the Fair: Poe's Landscape Aesthetics and Pictorial Techniques* [Potomac, MD: Scripta Humanistica, 1984], 127–29).

11. James Southall Wilson, "Poe and the University of Virginia," *Corks and Curls* (University of Virginia) 42 (1929): 216.

12. Frances Winwar, *The Haunted Palace: A Life of Edgar Allan Poe* (New York: Harpers, 1959), 242.

13. Daniel Hoffman, *Poe Poe Poe Poe Poe Poe Poe* (Garden City, New York: Doubleday, 1972), 206.

14. [Douglass Sherley,] "Old Oddity Papers," *University of Virginia Magazine* 19 (1879–1880): 432.

15. *Edgar Poe the Poet* (Charlottesville, VA: University Press of Virginia, 1969), 6–7.

16. John S. Patton, "Poe at the University," *New York Times Book Review* (Dec. 5, 1908): 726.

17. Only twenty-five students' names were on the "Proclamation," according to Stovall, and Poe's name was not among them (p. 9).

18. Stovall, p. 10.

19. Arthur Hobson Quinn, *Edgar Allan Poe* (New York: Appleton, 1941), 114.

20. For a comparison of Pym and the mineral springs, see L. Moffitt Cecil, "Poe's Tsalal and the Virginia Springs," *Nineteenth-Century Fiction* 19 (1965): 398–402.

21. John Smith, *The Complete Works of Captain John Smith*, ed. Philip L. Barbour (Chapel Hill: University of North Carolina Press, 1986), vol. 2, 176.

22. Smith, vol. 1, 165.

23. Thomas Jefferson, *Notes on the State of Virginia* (1785), ed. William Peden (Chapel Hill: University of North Carolina Press, 1955), 98.

24. Jefferson, 98.

25. Jefferson, 99.

26. Jefferson, 100.

27. Charlton Gilmore Holland, Jr., "Albemarle Before 1700," *Magazine of Albemarle County History* 9 (1940): 8.

28. John Hammond Moore, *Albemarle: Jefferson's County, 1727–1976* (Charlottesville: University Press of Virginia, 1976), 5–6. These beliefs are consistent with the long-standing negative perception of Appalachian mountain dwellers by outside observers. For the history of the idea of Appalachia, see Allen Batteau, *The Invention of Appalachia* (Tucson: University of Arizona Press, 1990), and Henry D. Shapiro, *Appalachia on Our Mind: The Southern Mountains and Mountaineers in the American Consciousness, 1870–1920* (Chapel Hill: University of North Carolina Press, 1978).

29. Poe, *The Brevities: Pinakidia, Marginalia, Fifty Suggestions, and Other Works*, ed. Burton R. Pollin (New York: Gordian Press, 1985), vol. 2 of *Collected Writings of Edgar Allan Poe*. 4 vols. (1981–1986), 310.

30. Patton, 166.

31. Emory Widener, "A Tale of the Ragged Mountains," *University of Virginia Magazine* 52 (1908–1909): 217.

32. Woods, 20.

33. University of Virginia Civic Club, *An Investigation of Conditions in the Ragged Mountains of Virginia* (Charlottesville: University of Virginia Civic Club, 1912), 25.

34. Op. cit., 25.

35. Op. cit., 16.

36. Op. cit., 25.

37. Op. cit., 20.

38. Stuart Levine, *Edgar Poe: Seer and Craftsman* (Deland, FL: Everett/Edwards, 1972), 138–39.

39. Levine, 139.

40. Mukhtar Ali Isani, "Some Sources for Poe's 'Tale of the Ragged Mountains,'" *Poe Studies* 5, no. 2 (1972): 38.

41.   Edward Said, *Orientalism* (New York: Pantheon, 1978), 12. For more on Orientalism and Romanticism in America, see Dorsey Rodney Kleitz, "Orientalism and the American Romantic Imagination: The Middle East in the Works of Irving, Poe, Emerson, and Melville," Diss. University of New Hampshire, 1988.

42.   Several critics have noticed this similarity, the most recent being Isani. Poe probably read the essay in the first two volumes of the (unauthorized) Philadelphia edition of Macaulay's *Critical and Miscellaneous Essays* (1841), which he reviewed for *Graham's Magazine* in June (Mabbott III: 937).

43.   Bedloe's reliance upon morphine to induce his hyperesthesia, or intensity of sense perception, heightens the discrepancy between real and imagined landscapes in the tale. See also De Quincey's contrast between the "Pleasures" and "Pains" of opium.

44.   Reinhard H. Friederich, "Necessary Inadequacies: Poe's 'Tale of the Ragged Mountains' and Borges' South," *Journal of Narrative Technique* 12 (1982): 155–56.

SEVEN

"King Pest" and the *Tales of the Folio Club*

Benjamin F. Fisher

"King Pest" has never spurred the lively critical controversies that several of Poe's other works have invited. In fact, this tale has been frequently omitted from selective anthologies, just as it has attracted little notice from Poe specialists. Long ago, expanding leads from G. E. Woodberry, Ruth Leigh Hudson assessed Poe's debts in "King Pest" to Disraeli's popular novel *Vivian Grey*, arguing that Poe targeted for comic purposes Disraeli's handling of the grotesque in that book, and also targeted conceptions of farther ranging literary uses of the grotesque. More influential, perhaps, has been William Whipple's treatment of "King Pest" as a satire upon political issues related to Andrew Jackson's presidency, a viewpoint that is essentially repeated lately in a study by Duncan Faherty and by G. R. Thompson in his recent Norton Critical Edition of Poe's writings.[1] I wish to propose another possibility inherent in "King Pest": that it may have played an important role in Poe's experimentation with *Tales of the Folio Club*. Specifically, I believe that Poe may have thought of using this tale as the concluding piece in the Folio Club book, as I will elaborate below. I will also indicate why "King Pest" should not be relegated to "minor" status in the Poe canon.

I

Before moving to my own central focus, I address several other relevant ideas about "King Pest" offered by influential Poe scholars. Seldom have I found occasion to take issue with opinions concerning Poe registered by that late doyen among Poe scholars, Thomas Ollive Mabbott. Nevertheless, to my way of thinking, in his headnote to "King Pest" in *Collected Works of Edgar Allan Poe* he seems to be off center when he dismisses this tale as "one of the least valuable of Poe's stories," citing for support Robert Louis Stevenson's deploring of that tale when in 1875 he was reviewing J. H. Ingram's edition of Poe's works and, because of Ingram's arrangement of the tales, thought that "King Pest" was one of Poe's later stories. When Mabbott in 1928 speculated about likely authors for individual stories in *Tales of the Folio Club*, he ruled out "King Pest" as part of the project, commenting, without elaboration, that the tale had not been written sufficiently early, that is, in 1833, which year, he suggests in the headnote to the tale in *Collected Works*, was the date for Poe's composing the prologue to what was then an eleven-tale collection.[2]

Other critiques by James Southall Wilson, Claude Richard, Alexander Hammond, and Louis Renza have prompted my own speculations about the possible role of this early tale in the Folio Club scheme.[3] Of course, I know that precision and the Folio Club tales are not typically or necessarily intimates. To take the most relevant example that bears on my topic, I mention Alexander Hammond's study of the role "Lionizing" may have played in the Folio Club.[4] He thinks that that tale was intended as the final piece in one version of the collection. My intent here is not to refute Hammond, but to suggest that "King Pest" might repay consideration of its possible role as the concluding tale in either the same or another version of the project, whatever other implications may be inherent. Hammond commented briefly in his 1972 "Reconstruction" about the role of "King Pest" in the Folio Club, and though my approach and Hammond's are by no means identical, they may with equal validity serve as windows onto aspects of the Folio Club.

"King Pest" was not specifically mentioned as a Folio Club tale by Poe nor in any other response to his projected book as it apparently existed in 1833, when the project was first mentioned, on through the remainder of Poe's lifetime. After its publication in the *Southern Literary Messenger* for September 1835, the tale was republished with revisions in *Tales of the Grotesque and Arabesque* (1839), and in the *Broadway Journal*, October 18, 1845. The version that appeared in the posthumous edition of Poe's writings, assembled by Griswold, reveals a few more revisions, which, Mabbott states, were Poe's own (*CW* 2: 239). Wilson located "King Pest" among the original eleven Folio Club tales ready in 1833, which hypothesis differs from what Mabbott presents in *Collected Works*, as does Hammond's in his 1972 study. Woodberry and Hudson's more detailed linking of Poe's story with *Vivian Grey* has continued as a reasonable idea among Poe scholars, although my own sense is that in "King Pest" Poe may well have targeted more than just Disraeli's novel. For comparison's sake, we might remember that ties between "A Tale of Jerusalem" and Horace Smith's once popular novel, *Zillah: A Tale of the Holy City* (1828)—in which the running headers read "A Tale of Jerusalem," which provided Poe a ready title for his tale, as well as an undeniable clue to the book he was using up—reveal a far more limited range for satire than what may reside in "King Pest."

First, to Poe's hinting a larger range. Although Irving and Scott have understandably been cited as models for the "Stout Gentleman," presumed Folio Club author of "King Pest," additional possibilities may exist.[5] That the tale opens in an inn where two initially unnamed men drink may well point to episodes in Sir Walter Scott's fiction, for example, in *The Bride of Lammermoor* (1819), which Poe admired, but such a scene may as readily recall popular fiction by Harrison Ainsworth, Edward Bulwer-Lytton, and G. P. R. James. For example, Ainsworth's best-seller, *Rookwood* (1834), opens in a tomb where two initially unidentified men, supplied with liquor, converse about topics that expand to inform the rest of the novel. The supernaturalism that enlivens theme and scene in *Rookwood* may understandably be transformed in "King Pest" to create the hallucinatory sensations that often accompany very nonsupernatural drunkenness, thereby imparting a satiric element to Poe's tale, which is nonexistent, or certainly muted, in Ainsworth's novel.

Furthermore, as Wilson commented (220), some Folio Club members may actually have told more than one tale. If we allow such latitude, we must concede that each tale may at some stage have been part of Poe's experimenting with the Folio Club. Perhaps we might take a leaf from another among Poe's earlier academic champions, Arthur Hobson Quinn, who included "King Pest" among those tales he termed "Arabesques," in which, he emphasized, "occur some of the very greatest short stories in the literature of the world. They are the products, either of Poe's inspired imagination or of his fertile fancy, and while irony appears in a few cases, like 'King Pest,' he never loses, in the Arabesques, respect for his material. That material is selected with care on account of its strangeness."[6] Quinn's admiration dovetails with Hudson's outlook on Poe's intent, mentioned above. Moreover, Poe's careful revisions in "King Pest" attest his high regard for the tale.

Another aspect of Poe's intent in "King Pest" now comes to the fore. If the six grotesque personages encountered by Legs and Tarpaulin may not be supernatural beings at all, but, rather, live actors, as revealed toward the close, Poe may have aimed a satiric shaft at the renowned "explained supernaturalism" of Mrs. Radcliffe and her heirs. Such fictions kept readers titillated, often through several long volumes, with

expectations that an otherworldly agency would have caused the villain-
ies, to learn in the end, however, that some very earthly being or beings
had perpetrated the troubles and mysteries. British and American authors, whose propensities may be exemplified by Irving's "Rip Van Winkle," Paulding's "Cobus Yerks," Hawthorne's "Young Goodman
Brown," and Poe's own "The Murders in the Rue Morgue," were adept in
fashioning that for much of their spans seemed to be based upon supernatural causes for terrors, only to have those about to meet ghastly fates
awaken from a dream—or to reveal that a drunkard's muddled perceptions had evoked such apparent otherworldliness.

Poe's contemporaries who produced Southwest Humor yarns, for example, George Washington Harris, Henry Clay Lewis ("Madison Ten-
sas"), or T. B. Thorpe, were never behindhand at creating fantastic situations that emanated from apparently occult sources, ultimately to reveal
that the protagonist had a nightmare, with or without help from alcohol,
and Poe seems to align with them in this respect.[7] Early on, he learned
well and practiced cleverly how to establish alcoholic and other dream-
like atmospheres that double subtly as seemingly supernatural causes for
fears and horrors. He soon realized that he could employ similar repetitive speech patterns, confused minds that occur among the intoxicated,
and mood swings in drunkards and gluttons, to create the weird and
terrifying as emanations from minds distorted, but distorted from mental, not swallowed or inhaled intoxicants. "The Fall of the House of Usher," "William Wilson," "The Masque of the Red Death," "The Raven" and
"Ulalume" are prime examples of this technique.

Understandably, many present-day readers, who know little about
alcohol or drug use in Poe's day, may plausibly tend toward interpreting
drug-induced states as motivating his narrators, or toward thinking that
Poe's own abuses of alcohol or drugs were transformed into his fiction,
but revisions in the tales often demonstrate how he eliminated alcoholic
and drug-related causes for what he called "terror of the soul."[8] In other
words, Poe came to realize that the mind itself contained sufficient potential for horrors, consequently negating the need for any outside help. In
"The Fall of the House of Usher," for instance, the narrator likens his
emotional tortures to those of an opium addict, but he gives no reason for
readers to believe that in the immediate circumstances he is indulging an
addiction; and the admitted opium influence in the opening of "The Oval
Portrait" was removed after that tale first appeared. Or, in "The System
of Dr. Tarr and Professor Fether," albeit alcohol and, perhaps, some of the
food, may intensify mindsets and uproarious displays among the in-
mates of the madhouse, their mental problems had become well en-
trenched before such drinking and eating.

Written later than the tales for the Folio Club project, such works
display a modified purpose on the part of their author, who had learned
that the human mind needs no stimulation from externals to perceive

horrors; hallucinatory states or manic-depression may substitute for those resulting from drugs or alcohol. Poe's awareness of drug uses, as they were employed for medical purposes, may have derived not nearly so much from any habit of his own, as from familiarity with De Quincey's *Confessions of an English Opium Eater* and the many spinoffs, serious and comic, from that renowned work which adroitly mingles fact with fiction. He may also have derived knowledge of warped psychology from reading medical literature current in his times.[9] The jury remains out as regards Poe's own uses of alcohol, though he may have derived his literary uses of alcohol and alcoholism from literary sources extending from the ancient classics to publications in his own day which mingled comic and serious elements.

II

Regarding "King Pest" more particularly, we might also mull the likelihood that Poe may have had in mind some farther reaching aspects of Gothicism and Romanticism overall. First, the paradigmatic haunted castle, usually found in rural territories in earlier Gothic tradition, is transformed here into equally grim, "haunted," urban environs and architecture, from the "Jolly Tar" alehouse that figures in Legs and Tarpaulin's first adventure, on to the desolate plague-ridden slum where they confront the council of grotesque personages assembled in the "gigantic and ghastly-looking building," an undertaker's establishment located amidst a veritable cesspool of decay and poisonous air. Below stairs is a well-stocked wine cellar, comparable with Montresor's in that superb later liquorish tale, "The Cask of Amontillado": alcohol and death are to be found in both. In combination with the mirth that hovers just beneath the surfaces in "King Pest," we might discern Poe's experimenting with the grotesque (the intersection of horror with humor), as Hudson's approach to the tale posits. If "King Pest" figured as part of some version of the Folio Club experiments, then the urban Gothic would operate as a neat foil to its converse in a tale like "Metzengerstein," which is set in the countryside of Hungary. In landscape, characterization and overall aura of doomedness, "Metzengerstein" for the Folio Club members would have represented an unmistakable traditional "German" variety of the Gothic.[10]

Second, in centering on the pair of sailors in loathsome urban squalor, which foregrounds architectural ruins associated with physical and spiritual decay emanating from the ravages of the plague, could Poe in a spirit of lampoon have inverted the Romantic penchant for ruins and rural environs as well as that for "medievalism"? Might he have had in mind popular works like Scott's *Ivanhoe* and *The Monastery*, or G. P. R. James's *The Castle of Ehrenstein*, to which he applied deflating methods similar to those in an earlier satire on the Gothic fad, E. S. Barrett's *The Heroine* (1813), a lampoon of "medieval" Gothic that Poe may have reviewed and that was popular this side of the Atlantic during his work for the *Southern Literary Messenger*?[11] Reading "King Pest," one might suppose that here is Tintern Abbey gone to the inferno.

Finally, we might also read the tale as a satire upon the drastically over-sensationalizing chapbooks and penny dreadfuls that literary Gothicism had spawned some years before Poe commenced writing fiction, and that would continue to enjoy great currency well through the Victorian age. For comparison's sake, I cite a convenient reprinting of just one of the many chapbooks that catered to readers' desires for cheap thrills, the anonymously authored *The Bloody Hand; or, the Fatal Cup. A Tale of Horror! In the Course of which is described the TERRIBLE DUNGEONS and CELLS in the PRISONS OF BUONAPARTE* (c. 1800).[12] The title alone enticingly forecasts the sufferings and tortures to be discovered in the narrative. Unlike the genuine bleakness and sufferings highlighted in this brief work, "King Pest" shifts between possibilities of gruesome punishments to be inflicted upon the intruding sailors to spirited comedy which culminates in the amusing flight of the sailors with the females. Legs and Tarpaulin are for some time threatened by little other than words, whereas characters in the chapbooks were often subjected to genuinely stark frights and tortures, details of which are unsparing. In *The Bloody Hand* the narrator ultimately escapes his tormentors, but not before several of his teeth had been knocked out in an attempt to force a drug promoting hallucinations down his throat. Resisting his captor, he ultimately spit some of the deranging substance into his enemy's eye, which brought on rapid death for that persecutor. Poe's alacrity to mock what he perceived as excesses in any literary mode gives what I submit about "King Pest" a decided credibility as a critique of the grotesque and of the extravagances that were often found in Gothic works.

III

Focusing again on "King Pest" and its role in the Folio Club, we may comprehend that certain features readily place it, during at least one stage in the evolution of Poe's abortive book, as a potentially concluding tale, that which would mime the prologue narrator's rage over having had *his* tale voted the worst yet one more time, and his consequent running away with the manuscripts, hoping that publication and circulation among a wider readership would vindicate his own abilities and reveal the overblown fictions and critical notions of the others in the Club. As Poe wrote to Harrison Hall, a Philadelphia publisher whom he was trying to interest in publishing his book, "the author of the tale adjudged the worst demurs from the final judgment, seizes the seventeen MSS. upon the table, and, rushing from the house, determines to appeal, by printing the whole, from the decision of the Club, to that of the public."[13]

At this point it may be appropriate to pause over Poe's precise title and epigraph to "King Pest," as it appeared in the *Southern Literary Messenger* for September 1835, since they point the way toward what follows in the text.

> King Pest the First. A Tale Containing An Allegory — By___.
> The Gods do bear and will allow in kings
> The things which they abhor in rascal routes.
> *Buckhurst's Tragedy of Ferrex and Porres.*

These lines direct our attention to allegory and to the concept of "rascal routes" (uproars caused by rioting lowlifes), so we might plausibly see affinities between "King Pest" and "Lionizing," the tale Hammond reasonably places as a contender for the final piece in the Folio Club book. "Routes," as it appears in the lines from Thomas Norton and Thomas Sackville's (Lord Buckhurst's) play, *Gorboduc* (1561) used by Poe as the motto for "King Pest," is *old* spelling, which might be far more quickly apprehended as what the tale seems to bear out as Poe's design, were the word spelled "routs." In other words, instead of going off track if one construes "routes," as "traveled ways," we should interpret this word by means of its other spelling, "rout," that is, "a state of wild confusion or disorderly retreat," or "a precipitous flight," as that word is commonly defined (Webster). This word in the latter sense would have borne the same meaning during the medieval time frame in Poe's tale, and so it perfectly conveys Legs and Tarpaulin's fleeing with the captive females.

Considering that Poe also used the subtitle of *Gorboduc* (1561) as if it were the title, and since Ferrex and Porrex are Gorboduc's sons, who quarrel, after which Porrex is murdered by his mother, who wants Ferrex to inherit the throne, we may detect signs of Poe's deliberate slantwise intentions. Ambiguities of this nature continue within the tale proper, evinced early on in the opening, where we learn that "Free and Easy" is the name of the sailors' ship, for which a major port of call is "Sluys" (slys). There is, to be sure, a free and easy slyness coursing throughout the tale, and "Allegory" in the title may hint of slyness and the freedom and ease in placing "King Pest" as the concluding tale in the Folio Club book or in shifting it to some other position. Such characteristics coalesce artistically with information furnished by the narrator in the prologue to *Tales of the Folio Club* and with the precipitous exit of Legs and Hugh with their "ladies."

Poe's wordplay is evident elsewhere, in names like "Legs," "Tarpaulin," as well as in all the Pest family names. Then, too, "Allegory" in the title may alert us to take more than cursory notice of characters who represent, or, in this case, who misrepresent, or satirize, some one or another quality that inheres in their names, just as the names in the Folio Club prologue hint the nature of their bearers and the nature of the tales they read to each other and critique.[14] Whether the group into whose company the two sailors stumble may in part represent hits at persons close to Andrew Jackson and his cohorts, they certainly bear striking resemblances as well to the odd-featured members in the Folio Club. To exemplify the correspondences, let us consider, for example, King Pest the First, as he styles himself, "who appeared to be the president of the table."

> His stature was gaunt and tall. . . . His face was yellower than the yellowest saffron—but no feature of his visage, excepting one alone, was sufficiently marked to merit a particular description. This one consisted in a forehead so unusually and hideously lofty, as to have the appearance of a bonnet or crown of flesh superadded upon the natural head. His mouth was puckered and dimpled into a singular expression of ghastly affability, and his eyes, as indeed the eyes of all at table, were glazed over with the fumes of intoxication. (*CW* 2: 245)

Compare now this vignette from the Folio Club prologue: "The members, generally, were most remarkable men. There was, first of all, Mr. Snap, the President, who is a very lank man with a hawk nose, and was formerly in the service of the Down-East Review" (*CW* 2: 205).

Like the Folio Club members, the "King Pest" group amidst funereal surroundings—where, perhaps, they should not be—are respectively marked out by a single distinctive, and, in this tale, repulsive feature, although all share close connections with death, to whose royal eminence they demand that the sailors defer. The character sketches quoted above may in fact demonstrate that Poe actually had the Folio Club President in mind when he designed the character of King Pest as presiding official among the revelers. In fact, since the narrator in the Folio Club prologue pronounces the club members "quite as ill-looking as they are stupid" (*CW* 2: 203), should we doubt that the bizarre family in "King Pest" bear kinship with them?

Like the Folio Clubbers, too, this group evince considerable pretentiousness and pomposity. From the repeated responses of Legs and Tarpaulin, that King Pest is actually Tim Hurlygurly (thus, as his name betokens, a pretender, as actors are by virtue of their profession, or an organ-grinder, that is, a second-rate musician), we might discern an appearance-reality syndrome operating here as it would have among the Folio Club members: in regard to their physiognomies, their literary work, and their critical abilities. All these phenomena fall under a rubric of plague and death in "King Pest" that only enriches the cream of the jest in the tale, and that is compounded by death's signaling an ending. The entire tale hints at conclusiveness, terminus—"death," of itself and of the Folio Club foolishness.

The Folio Club purpose of amusing and instructing seems to resonate in King Pest's response to Legs's questioning the group's presence in such surroundings:

> [W]e are here this night, prepared by deep research and accurate investigation, to examine, analyze, and thoroughly determine the indefinable spirit—the incomprehensible qualities and nare of those inestimable treasures of the palate, the wines, ales, and liqueurs of this goodly Metropolis: by so doing to advance not more our own designs than the true welfare of that unearthly sovereign whose reign is over us all—whose dominion is unlimited—and whose name is 'Death.' (*CW* 2: 250)

So, like the Folio Club members, the personages in "King Pest" have stated principles, which, Renza points out, emphasize the literary qualities in these characters and their circumstances in the undertaker's establishment.[15] Combined with the quoted passage just above, these elements might as readily serve as a paradigm of the absurdity surrounding the enterprise as the narrator sets it forth in the prologue:

> The Folio Club is, I am sorry to say, a mere Junto of *Dunderheadism*. I think too the members are quite as ill looking as they are stupid. I also believe it their settled intention to abolish Literature, subvert the Press, and overturn the Government of Nouns and Pronouns. These are my private opinions which I now take the liberty of making public. (*CW* 2: 203)

Finally, as the much-belabored Folio Clubber whose tales were repeatedly voted worst would in high dudgeon have finally darted away with the manuscripts, the sailors instigate a rout (such as would no doubt have ensued within the Folio Club, too, as the members realized that the evidence of their folly was vanishing), wherein they nab their prizes, and no unimportant prizes either.

Significantly, in context, the abducted females are, as Renza designates them, "muse figures of poetic speech."[16] The serio-comic episodes in which they figure, in tandem with the rapid exit of the quartet in the conclusion, surely signal that "King Pest" was at some point intended to be the closing tale in Poe's collection. Arch Duchess Ana-Pest's name being the concluding phrase in the tale makes it impossible for us to conclude our reading of "King Pest" by ignoring that an important literary purpose had been insinuated into the tale, with comic intent, to be sure, whatever other implications may also reside there. From the privacy and security dear to the six deathly figures, the sailors will take literary value into the public domain. After the abduction of the literary spirit, Ana-Pest, what is left for those who remain but triumph of the plague, metaphor for their high-flown but empty aspirations and pretensions, as well as for the plaguing result of the sailor's intrusions, but death (literal and metaphoric)?

We might interpret this movement toward death as analogous to that in several of Poe's tales that are usually considered far more serious productions than "King Pest": "Berenice," "Morella," and "The Fall of the House of Usher." In all, the departure or death of a feminine presence, represented by Berenice, Morella, and Madeline, signals eventual death for the survivor protagonist because if these tales embody symbolic implications regarding the essential integration of male-female qualities to maintain a balanced self, then loss of one-half of that makeup will not permit the one who survives to continue a normal existence. Just as credibly, but from a different perspective, we must remember that Queen Pest and Arch Duchess Ana-Pest are actresses, and that stage players in Poe's era were often regarded with suspicion concerning their sexual morality. Thus Legs and Tarpaulin could be running away with death if in fact the females were sexually promiscuous, therefore easy prey for sexually transmitted diseases, which were indeed "pests" or plagues to those with such afflictions.

Additional undercurrents of suggestion reinforce the role of "King Pest" as the conclusion to *Tales of the Folio Club*. Like "Shadow—A Parable," "King Pest" centers on a group whose concerns mingle alcohol and death in zesty wordplay.[17] Poe evidently recognized how he had seized upon a good method in creating these early tales because he was to recycle it, sometimes with, sometimes without, alcoholic trappings, in works like "Ligeia," *The Narrative of Arthur Gordon Pym*, "William Wilson," "Usher," "Eleonora," "The Angel of the Odd," "Tarr and Fether," "Cask," and "Hop-Frog," to name some obvious choices. Moreover, "The Masque of the Red Death" and "The System of Dr. Tarr and Professor Fether" may be read in part, at least, as material recycled from preceding tales.[18]

Correspondences to "King Pest" are noteworthy in "Masque": in both we find attempts by unrealistic characters to create an illusory fantasy "world" where no plague, that is, displeasing reality, can intrude. The plague does enter, however, because nobody can elude death, which makes its presence felt in both works. Reading each tale, readers swiftly come to anticipate the onset of circumstances adverse to the fantasies of those who have (vainly) secreted themselves from what they fear. "Masque" might be considered a refinement of the high jinks and somewhat coarse sexual humor in "King Pest": the later tale proceeds in slow motion toward Prospero's confrontation with his antagonist, followed by a stillness (in multiple implications) related to death. The slow movement of Prospero's pursuit of the Red Death bears out the inexorability of time, the passage of which is symbolized in the function of the giant ebony clock; its striking the hours suddenly halts the music and movement of the revelers participating in a masked ball, their movements resuming only slowly or tentatively once the striking has ceased. The entire setting in "Masque" is far less immediately horrifying than that in the earlier tale. Similar in kind, different in degree, "King Pest" and "Masque" bear close resemblances in terms of actors/pretenders and deception. Both tales remind us of the nature of nightmarish dreams: they commence in the mundane, shift into the fantastic, and conclude at their respective climactic moments. So, too, the *Tales of the Folio Club* would have concluded in an exciting episode.

Equally significant, we repeatedly find in "King Pest" the word "appearance" itself, or what involves appearance, from the description of the tap-room in the "Jolly Tar," to the architectural exteriors and interiors elsewhere, on through vignettes of the characters, commencing with the introduction of Legs and recurring as other characters appear. When Legs and Tarpaulin balefully eye the "No Chalk" ("No Credit") sign over the doorway of the Jolly Tar tavern, as the tale opens, that phrase sets the mood for events that follow. Moreover, although the sailors cannot read, they sense what the phrase means: pay or leave. The "certain twist in the formation of the letters" is a subtlety that bonds "twist" as it may imply confusion or deception to a context of literacy and literariness, thus paving the way for what ensues. When we learn that "No Chalk" is written *with* chalk the blurring of appearance versus reality cannot be ignored.

Not only do these techniques suggest a tactic resembling that in those character introductions more tersely presented in the Folio Club prologue, as well as a presumable failure among the club members to read or comprehend clearly, they also impart a stylization to the bizarre characters who enliven "King Pest" while their situation is conducive to a dream aura that enhances the overall prose movement in the tale. The insistent repetitions and alliterations may constitute a perfect means of expression for a drunkard's vision and speech, but they may also constitute a prose poem with hypnotic impact. The "Then there was" phrase that begins each character delineation in the Folio Club prologue (and which is repeated in sections of "Lionizing") is omitted in "King Pest" in favor of a rotating visual movement that comes to rest briefly on each character as he or she is introduced. This particular prose poem has a decided staccato movement and an insistent note in the sound effects throughout, witness the repetition of "'A sentence!—a sentence!—a righteous and just sentence!'" cried by all the Pest group after the King pronounces the fate of the sailors if they do not yield to his will. Or Tarpaulin's coughing: "Ugh! ugh! ugh!" (which may seem like an anticipation of Fortunato's coughing in "The Cask of Amontillado"), continuing with "'I was saying . . . I was saying . . .'" And the final repeated shouts of "Treason" to express the outrage of the group when Tarpaulin identifies King Pest as Tim Hurlygurly (*CW* 2: 252–53). These repetitions approximate the speech of a drunkard, kindred, perhaps, to those in "Silence—A Fable," or in the opening in "Loss of Breath" (in its several versions). These verbal structures also recall those repetitive effects in the prologue to the Folio Club and similar rhetorical outbursts in "Lionizing,"[19] whereas some of Poe's other prose poems, such as "Masque," are less strident in tone.

A variation on this technique occurs in "The Assignation." The opening paragraph is less raucous in sound than the examples I have just assessed because in this tale the visual appeal is more prominent, as if to shift emphasis toward the unreliable narrator as visionary. Akin to the incoherent speech that characterizes drunkards, the torrent of words, which are so structured as to resemble a kaleidoscopic series of pictures, attests to the narrator's unreliable perceptions about what he "sees," or thinks he sees. His imperfect ocular ability dovetails well with his emotional bewilderment. Such vision-sound connections—which are hypnotic both to characters within the work where such techniques occur, as well as to readers, who by dint of their reading respond to the sound-sense combination—also enhance Poe's art in "Metzengerstein," "Silence—A Fable," "Shadow—A Parable," "The Assignation," "Eleonora," "The Cask of Amontillado," "The Raven," "Ulalume," "Eldorado," or "Annabel Lee," as well as many sections in *The Narrative of Arthur Gordon Pym* (and probably many more works by Poe, which are too numerous to list here).

Appearance, we know, too, may symbolize in part what lies beneath, but externals are not always reliable gauges of the precise nature of such interiority. Shrouds, palls, and winding sheets in "King Pest" remind us of death, but likewise of the concealments of those they enclose from penetrating gaze. Elsewhere Poe uses words like "shroud" and "ghost" such that readers are kept on a intellectual tightrope, as it were, of deciding is this or is it not "Gothic" rhetoric? Is Poe creating mere Gothic atmosphere to titillate readers eager for lurid thrills, or is he employing sophisticated language strategies? The House of Usher, we may recall, is "enshrouded," but what precisely does that mean? We do not read far into "The Raven" before encountering embers from a dying fire throwing their "ghosts" upon the floor, but "ghost" in context is nineteenth-century slang for the shadow created by a dying fire, instead of the term for a supernatural visitant. Other phrasing in "King Pest," for example, "in the opinion of," "seemed to possess a monopoly of some particular portion of physiognomy," combines with the aura of drunkenness to emphasize that what is seen or supposed may be no accurate barometer to truth. Individual words, for example, "nare" (in context of alcohol) and "Junto" too closely echo the prologue to the Folio Club tales to go unnoticed in connection with the role of "King Pest" in that project.

That the President is an actor (and I assume that once this aspect of his being is discovered we must conceive of the others in the strange group as actors, too), clinches, for me, the Folio Club context of "King Pest." After all, we might well designate the members of that bogus literary group as actors, role-players, just as the characters in "King Pest" are. We do not encounter Poe's typical first-person narrator, but we do discover that time, place, and characters deceive us, just as the Folio Clubbers would like to remain, by means of their monthly, select gatherings, an elite society, thoroughly unaffected by any harsh realities in the literary world, thus wholly deceiving themselves into believing that their own literary endeavors and status are august. In the Folio Club and "King Pest" we confront uncertainties and instabilities from the "No Chalk" in the tavern to the characters themselves being actors, who seem to be unaware that they are role-playing. In sum, too many elements in this tale conspire to leave us unaware or uninformed about its serving as *a* conclusion to *Tales of the Folio Club*, whether or not it would have been *the* conclusion as Poe contemplated his design.

IV

Divorced from the Folio Club framework, thereby becoming something of a puzzler as other Folio Club tales have been, "King Pest" might well strike readers as a piece of mere repulsiveness from Poe's pen, serving little purpose other than as a tale published with deliberate intent to horrify readers, much as several others of his early tales elicited puzzled reactions among readers or as that later tale, "The Facts in the Case of M. Valdemar," was received when it appeared in England.[20] Like "The Assignation," however, which has sometimes been dismissed as having little or no important substance, or like so many others among Poe's tales and poems that have at one time or another been willfully dismissed as Poe the madman's, the drunkard's, the incompetent bungler's maunderings, for example, "Silence—A Fable" or "The Raven," "King Pest" merits a revisitation to ensure that it is recognized as an important work in the Poe canon. In terms of characterization, prose-poetry techniques, themes (literary, political, sexual), and undercurrents that manifest subtle literary art, this tale should not be dismissed as sleazy froth unsuitable for serious reading or extended analytic approach. The tale ranks with other works by Poe in which the comic and the serious function with equal importance, and in which their teamwork, so to speak, demonstrates Poe's unquestionable creative artistry at its best.

NOTES

1. I dedicate this critique to the memory of Richard P. Benton, whose publications and repeated wise, generous counsel shaped many of my thoughts concerning the Folio Club. I also acknowledge gratitude to Professor Scott Peeples for initially providing me a forum for ideas which I have expanded here; and to Professors Louis Renza and Dennis W. Eddings for courtesy and alacrity with suggestions that have stimulated my thinking and improved this study. For early commentary on "King Pest" see

George E. Woodberry, "Notes," *The Works of Edgar Allan Poe*, ed. Edmund Clarence Stedman and George E. Woodberry (Chicago: Stone and Kimball, 1894–1895), 4: 295; and his *The Life of Edgar Allan Poe* (Boston: Houghton Mifflin, 1909), 1: 130; Ruth Leigh Hudson, "Poe and Disraeli," *AL* 8 (1937): 402–16; William Whipple, "Poe's Political Satire," *UTSE* 35 (1956): 81–95. Interestingly, Ernest Marchand does not mention "King Pest" in "Poe as Social Critic," *AL* 6 (1934): 28–43. See also Duncan Faherty, "'A Certain Unity of Design': Edgar Allan Poe's *Tales of the Grotesque and Arabesque* and the Terrors of Jacksonian Democracy," *Edgar Allan Poe Review* 6, no. 2 (2005): 4–21; G. R. Thompson, ed., *The Selected Writings of Edgar Allan Poe* (New York: W. W. Norton, 2004): 148–59.

2. Thomas Ollive Mabbott, ed., with the Assistance of Eleanor D. Kewer and Maureen C. Mabbott, *Collected Works of Edgar Allan Poe* (Cambridge, MA: Belknap Press of Harvard University Press, 1978), 2: 238. I cite (parenthetically) and quote from this text. See also Robert Louis Stevenson, "*The Works of Edgar Allan Poe*, Edited by John H. Ingram," *Academy* 2 (January 1875): 1–2; and Mabbott, "On Poe's 'Tales of the Folio Club,'" *Sewanee Review* 36 (1928): 171–76, where, Mabbott states, his assignments of tales to individual Folio Club members are mainly speculative.

3. Wilson, "The Devil Was In It," *American Mercury* 24 (1931): 214–20; Richard, "Les Contes du Folio club et le vocation humoristique d'Edgar Allan Poe" (Paris: Minard, 1969), transl. by Mark L Mitchell as "The Tales of the Folio Club and the Vocation of Edgar Allan Poe as Humorist," *UMSE* n.s. 8 (1990): 185–99, especially 187–91; Hammond, "A Reconstruction of Poe's 1833 *Tales of the Folio Club*: Preliminary Notes," *PoeS* 5 (1972): 25–32; "Further Notes on Poe's Folio Club Tales," *PoeS* 8 (1975): 38–42; Renza, "Poe's King: Playing It Close to the Pest," *Edgar Allan Poe Review* 2 (2001): 3–18.

4. Hammond, "Poe's '*Lionizing*' and the Design of *Tales of the Folio Club*," *ESQ* 18 (1972): 154–65. Worth mentioning, too, are my own remarks on potential how's, why's and wherefore's connected with the Folio Club, expressed in *The Very Spirit of Cordiality: The Literary Uses of Alcohol and Alcoholism in the Tales of Edgar Allan Poe* (Baltimore: Enoch Pratt Free Library et al., 1978), especially 3–5, 9–11. Here I first speculated on some of the matters I consider and expand in my text. Surprisingly, G. R. Thompson in *Poe's Fiction: Romantic Irony in the Gothic Tales* (Madison: University of Wisconsin Press, 1973): 6, 42, 221n31, 224n22, does little more than mention "King Pest" in lists of Poe's comic tales.

5. Hammond, "A Reconstruction," 31. See also Mabbott (1928), 176; *CW* 2: 201 and note; and my *The Very Spirit of Cordiality*: 2, 10–11, 14n4.

6. Arthur Hobson Quinn, *American Fiction: A Historical and Critical Survey* (New York: D. Appleton-Century, 1936), 80–81.

7. I address such combinations in "Devils and Devilishness in Comic Yarns of the Old Southwest," *ESQ* 36 (1990): 39–60; and "George Washington Harris and Supernaturalism," *Sut Lovingood's Nat'ral Born Yarnspinner: Essays on George Washington Harris*, ed. James E. Caron and M. Thomas Inge (Tuscaloosa: University of Alabama Press, 1996), 176–89. See also the high praise awarded by Constance Rourke: "Yet *King Pest*, with its background of the plague and the night, is one of the most brilliant pure burlesques in the language, transmuting terror into gross comedy, as it had often been transmuted in the western tall tales" (*American Humor: A Study of the National Character* [New York: Harcourt Brace, 1931], 145–49). That Poe continued to draw upon techniques more commonly associated with frontier humorists is reinforced in Harry M. Bayne, "Poe's 'Never Bet the Devil Your Head' and Southwest Humor," *ARLR* 3 (1989): 278–79.

8. "Preface" to *Tales of the Grotesque and Arabesque* (1840 [1839]), quoted in *CW* 2: 475.

9. David W. Butler, "Usher's Hypochondriasis: Mental Alienation and Romantic Idealism in Poe's Gothic Tales," *AL* 48 (1970): 1–12; David E. E. Sloane, "Gothic Romanticism and Rational Empiricism in Poe's 'Berenice,'" *ATQ* 19 (1972): 19–25; George R. Uba, "Malady and Motive: Medical History and 'The Fall of the House of Usher,'"

SAQ 85 (1986): 10–22. See also, for extensive commentary on Poe's medical knowledge, Carroll D. Laverty, "Science and Pseudo Science in the Works of Edgar Allan Poe," unpublished Ph.D. Dissertation, Duke University, 1951.

10. I argue thus in "Poe and the Gothic Tradition," *The Cambridge Companion to Poe*, ed. Kevin J. Hayes (Cambridge: Cambridge University Press, 2002). 80–81.

11. *The Heroine*, which Thomas W. White much admired, appeared in an edition published in Richmond in 1835 by P. D. Barnard, T. W. White's son-in-law. The review in the *Southern Literary Messenger* for December 1835 may or may not be by Poe, according to Mabbott in a letter to me, June 9, 1966. See J. Lasley Dameron, "Thomas Ollive Mabbott on the Canon of Poe's Reviews," *PoeS* 5 (1972): 56–57; and *Collected Writings of Edgar Allan Poe*, ed. Burton R. Pollin (New York: Gordian Press, 1997), 5: 75. Nonetheless, Poe would have been aware of the book, and his own treatments of Gothicism often parallel the humor found there.

12. Franz J. Potter has edited *The Bloody Hand* (Camarillo, CA: Zittaw Press, 2004). See also Michael Anglo, *Penny Dreadfuls and Other Victorian Horrors* (London: Jupiter Books, 1977); the introduction to *The Penny Dreadful*, ed. Peter Haining (London: Victor Gollancz, 1975); Louis James, *Fiction for the Working Man: 1830–1850* (London: Oxford University Press, 1963), especially chapters 3 and 5.

13. *The Letters of Edgar Allan Poe*, ed. John Ward Ostrom, rev ed. (New York: Gordian Press, 1966): 103–4.

14. Mabbott's note on allegory (*CW* 255), in which the various Pest family members are categorized as figurative characters, is challenged by Renza (2, 11), who warns that Mabbott bypasses the importance of Legs and Tarpaulin, that no single allegorical meaning may attach to this tale, and that Poe was allegorizing allegory to prove this point. My view is not so anti-allegorical as Renza's; I think that Poe originally employed the term as much to its placement within Folio Club contexts, and that, in his own spirit of perversity, perhaps, he permitted it to stand just to tease readers—to be a pest.

15. Renza, 13–14.

16. Renza, 13-14.

17. In *CW* 2: 202 Mabbott claims it would have been the eleventh tale, though in 1928 he had placed "Lionizing" as eleventh, and, paradoxically, in *CW* 2: 207 he places "Silence—A Fable" there.

18. Burton R. Pollin, "Poe's 'Shadow' as a Source of his 'The Masque of the Red Death,'" *SSF* 6 (1969): 104–7; and my "Poe's 'Tarr and Fether': Hoaxing in the Blackwood Mode," *The Naiad Voice: Essays on Poe's Satiric Hoaxing*, ed. Dennis W. Eddings (Port Washington, NY: Associated Faculty Press, 1983),136–47.

19. "Lionizing" features a similar group dynamic, but without any discernible alcoholic aura. Repetitions in phrases and in mouthing individual synonyms at various points do, of course, resemble those in "Shadow" and "King Pest."

20. A comparable notion of horrifics was aroused in England concerning "The Facts in the Case of M. Valdemar," reprinted as a pamphlet with a different title, which many readers construed as unmitigated horrifics, not hoax (*CW* 3: 1230–31).

EIGHT

Understanding "Why the Little Frenchman Wears His Hand in a Sling"

Kevin J. Hayes

"Why the Little Frenchman Wears His Hand in a Sling," Edgar Allan Poe's playful dialect tale, amused many contemporary readers, including the popular British novelist, William Harrison Ainsworth. Having taken over the editorship of *Bentley's Miscellany* from Charles Dickens, Ainsworth read this story in *Tales of the Grotesque and Arabesque* and decided to reprint it, along with "The Duc de l'Omelette," "The Fall of the House of Usher," and "The Visionary." The London setting of "Little Frenchman" and its humorous use of Irish brogue to spoof the gentry made the tale especially appropriate for British readers. Although Ainsworth selected four Poe stories for *Bentley's*, "Little Frenchman" was the first he reprinted. Ainsworth did make one key change: he retitled the tale. In the July 1840 issue of *Bentley's*, Poe's story appeared as "The Irish Gentleman and the Little Frenchman."[1]

Ainsworth's enjoyment of the tale verifies the positive British reception of Poe's humorous tale. Contemporary American readers also appreciated it. When William T. Porter, editor of the weekly sporting paper *Spirit of the Times*, came across the July 1840 issue of *Bentley's*, he liked the story well enough to reprint it in his paper.[2] This formerly neglected reprint of Poe's story affirms its positive reception among contemporary American readers. Neither reprint helped Poe's personal reputation, however. *Bentley's* had reprinted the tale anonymously, and the *Spirit of the Times* followed suit.

Despite the contemporary response, modern readers have largely failed to appreciate "Little Frenchman." It is "one of Poe's poorest" tales according to one, "almost the slightest story that Poe ever wrote" according to another, and "at best witty hack work" according to a third.[3] The story is not without modern enthusiasts. Jack Kaufhold, for one, characterized "Little Frenchman" as a "Chaplinesque comedy."[4] Recently, a Pennsylvania teacher had great fun sharing the text with her students. She assigned it in a literary survey course without identifying its date or its author. The story differs so much from Poe's best-known tales, she argued, that "Little Frenchman" could be used as a pedagogical tool to challenge the preconceptions about Poe that students bring to class.[5] Perhaps "Little Frenchman" is not so different from Poe's other tales as it may seem. Its simplicity is deceptive. This tale embodies many of the same complex issues common to Poe's most respected works. By taking it seriously instead of maligning the story, its artistry becomes apparent.

Like some of Poe's other tales and sketches of the late 1830s and early 1840s—"The Philosophy of Furniture," "The Man of the Crowd," "Murders in the Rue Morgue"—"Little Frenchman" takes the idea of urban spectatorship as a central theme. Kaufhold's association between this story and the cinema of Charlie Chaplin suggests not only the importance of visual culture to "Little Frenchman" but also the importance of the modern city to the tale. Cinematic comparisons work well to explicate Poe's work: much of what he did in words prefigures what filmmakers would do in images in the following century.

"Little Frenchman" develops ideas Poe had been contemplating for years. The story is set in London, specifically in Russell Square, Bloomsbury, where Poe lived as a child with his foster parents, John and Frances Allan. Furthermore, it develops an idea he had suggested in "Metzengerstein" (1832), which predates "Little Frenchman" by eight years. In that story, the inhabitants of the Castle Berlifitzing look with jealousy into the windows of the Chateau Metzengerstein. Some readers have seen the proximity of these two castles as an absurdity that verifies the story's supposedly satirical nature.[6] Alternatively, this detail adds another layer of interpretation to "Metzengerstein," for Poe draws an analogy between the feudal castle and the modern apartment building. "Metzengerstein," too, can be interpreted as a clash between neighboring city dwellers. This minor detail, however, may have seemed to Poe insufficient to develop in "Metzengerstein" further. Poe may subsequently have turned the theme into the central motif of "Little Frenchman."

The title Ainsworth assigned Poe's tale, "The Irish Gentleman and the Little Frenchman," gives readers an idea of the story's characters, the two men who are rivals for a widow named Mrs. Treacle. But Ainsworth ignored the purposefulness of Poe's original title, which explicitly conveys the story's aetiological nature. In other words, Poe's title suggests that the purpose of the story is to explain the cause or causes of one particular phenomenon, namely, why the Frenchman happens to be wearing his hand in a sling. Expressed in the present tense, Poe's title also suggests that the wearing of the sling and the telling of the tale are simultaneous events. The tale is being told after the little Frenchman has received his injury yet before it has healed.

William T. Porter's enjoyment of "Little Frenchman" should come as no surprise. The *Spirit of the Times* published much of the best literary humor of Poe's day and greatly encouraged the humorists of the Old Southwest. Poe's use of dialect in "Little Frenchman" closely resembles the dialect used by his contemporaries further south, who often structured their stories as frame tales. Typically, a frame tale begins in the voice of an outside narrator whose words establish the situation and introduce an inside narrator to relate the main story. As the inside narrator takes over, the outside one shifts from teller to listener and thus serves as a surrogate for the reader. In the end, the outside narrator finishes the story; his final words create the closing narrative frame. Among the humorists of the Old Southwest, the frame tale was particularly amenable because it allowed them to begin their stories in a voice not dissimilar to their own, that of an urbane Southern gentleman, and then indulge their fascination for folk speech by giving the story over to some loose-limbed, slack-jawed rustic, who narrates the main story in dialect.

Throughout his career, Poe continually experimented with different literary forms and genres, always seeking either to invent new genres or, at least, to expand the possibilities of preexisting ones. With "A Descent into the Maelström," for instance, he experimented with the frame tale by leaving off the closing frame. "Little Frenchman" is even more experimental. It is an implicit frame tale, one that has been completely stripped of its outside narrative. Told by Sir Patrick O'Grandison, a rough-hewn Irishman from Connaught who unexpectedly had become a baron six weeks earlier and who has since come to London to acquire "iddication and the graces" (183), the story begins in a thick brogue, which is maintained through its completion. Sir Patrick's remarks imply that he is telling the story orally to a houseguest who sits within his apartment and who can see the sling-wearing Frenchman through a window across the way.

Beginning his story by describing himself, Sir Patrick notices that his description elicits an expression of disagreement from his guest and tells him to "be plased to stop curling your nose."[7] Besides indicating the guest's presence within his apartment, Sir Patrick's comment reveals his own characteristic behavior. He sees someone make a gesture and quickly assumes that he understands what that gesture means. Excluding an opening frame, Poe forces readers to make up their own minds about this dialect narrative. Whereas the frame tale positions the outside narrator as a surrogate for the reader, Poe's story works the opposite way. The reader must stand in for the outside narrator. Structuring the story as he does, Poe lends a sense of immediacy to it, placing us in the room with Sir Patrick.

Although stripping his tale of its narrative frame, Poe does make extensive use of another framing device, the window frame. Next door to Sir Patrick lives the widow Mrs. Treacle, and the Frenchman lives across the way. From his apartment, Sir Patrick can look out his window to see Mrs. Treacle, and she, of course, can look out hers to see him. From his window, the Frenchman can see across the way into the apartments of both Mrs. Treacle and Sir Patrick. According to Sir Patrick, the Frenchman spends the whole day at his window "a oggling and a goggling" (184). To know how his neighbor spends each day, Sir Patrick obviously spends his days staring from his own window. The sight of the sling-wearing Frenchman prompts Sir Patrick to explain why the Frenchman appears as he does.

Poe would make use of the window as a framing device again in "The Man of the Crowd," a tale he published in 1840, soon after "Little Frenchman" appeared as part of *Tales of the Grotesque and Arabesque*. Like the earlier story, "The Man of the Crowd" is also set in London. It begins with the narrator looking onto a busy London street through a coffeehouse window, which mediates what he sees.[8] The crowded street in "The Man of the Crowd" and the proximity of the neighboring apartments in "Little Frenchman" emphasize how the modern city effectively reduced everyone's personal space.

"The Man of the Crowd" is the classic tale of the flaneur, the spectator who strolled the city streets and arcades making observations and attempting to discern the meaning of what he observed.[9] By definition the flaneur takes the urban public space as both the place and subject of his activities. Though the act of walking is typically associated with the flaneur, "The Philosophy of Furniture" offers a paradoxical variant, the stationary flaneur.[10] The narrator of "The Philosophy of Furniture" remains within a private interior space but restricts his gaze to that space. Sir Patrick's gaze in "Little Frenchman" represents a more intrusive form of urban spectatorship. From the interior of his own apartment, he gazes into the private spaces of others' apartments. He is a voyeur, not a flaneur. As of 1840, the term voyeur had yet to enter English usage, so a synonym must suffice. Sir Patrick is a Peeping Tom.

"The Man of the Crowd" has been compared to Alfred Hitchcock's *Rear Window* (1954).[11] "Little Frenchman" may make for a better comparison. After all, Sir Patrick's behavior is much the same as that of L. B. "Jeff" Jefferies, the character Jimmy Stewart plays in *Rear Window*. Stationed in their apartments, both Jeff and Sir Patrick look through their own windows into their neighbors' apartments and assume that they know what the others are thinking. Furthermore, both make their guests complicit in their intrusive gaze. Through his manipulation of point of view and other cinematic techniques, Hitchcock makes the audience complicit in Jeff's voyeurism. Much the same can be said about Poe. Through his clever manipulation of narrative techniques, he makes his readers complicit in the acts of a Peeping Tom.

The similarity between the situations of "Little Frenchman" and *Rear Window* allows further generalizations regarding the relationship between Poe's story and the cinema. The Frenchman's window frame anticipates the motion picture frame, and the sight of him in his window is not dissimilar to an opening shot in a motion picture. Since this image triggers Sir Patrick's narrative, the story itself works like a voiceover narration. The events Sir Patrick narrates resemble a long flashback sequence.

Reading "Little Frenchman" in terms of its relationship to the frame tale, the window frame, and the motion picture frame offers three different ways of understanding how the story is mediated. Seeing it as a frame tale stripped of its outside narrative emphasizes its immediacy. As a crucial motif in the story, the window suggests that physical circumstances mediate Sir Patrick's perception. Seeing the story as a kind of voiceover narration emphasizes that the tale of the Frenchman is being mediated by Sir Patrick. Poe complicates matters further by making Sir Patrick an unreliable narrator, which is obvious from the first paragraph.[12] The dichotomy between what Sir Patrick says and how he says it reveals that his perception of reality cannot be trusted. For example, he calls himself the leader of London's haut ton or, in his words, "the laider of the hot tun in the houl city o' London," but his colloquial dialect reveals that he is certainly not a member of London's high society (183). The story about the injured Frenchman is being mediated by a narrator who bends the truth to cast himself in the best possible light.

Perhaps the events Sir Patrick describes never occurred. Think about it. He is entertaining a houseguest. Together they look across the way and see a man with his arm in a sling. Sir Patrick invents a humorous episode, which he tells for his guest's amusement. (Another comparison here might be to the film, *The Usual Suspects* (1995)—frame tale, unreliable "narrator" spinning a wild tale, gazing at objects in the police detective's office that give him launching points for storytelling. That film's "Keyser Söze" might, in turn, be compared to Hitchcock's MacGuffin, the element that we think is the central goal of the hero's quest but is really secondary.) Though plausible, this particular interpretation does little to advance our understanding of the tale. In the name of critical appreciation, we must assume that some kind of encounter between Sir Patrick and the Frenchman did occur and that now Sir Patrick is telling a tale based on his personal experience regardless of how much his prismatic ego has refracted the truth.

The unreliability of Sir Patrick's narration encourages readers to scrutinize his perception and make sense of how he interprets what he sees. With this character, Poe takes the opportunity to explore one of his favorite topics, the relationship between surface appearance and the truth beneath the surface. Physiognomy, phrenology, autography, apparel, home decor: all are exterior indicators of personality, and Poe used each, separately or in combination, as crucial building blocks to construct his stories. To what extent, Poe wondered, do exterior signs represent personality?

Using Sir Patrick's visiting card as the story's opening motif, Poe makes the theme of representation explicit. After all, the visiting card is a device deliberately intended to represent the person it identifies. Sir Patrick begins to describe himself to his guest by describing his card. The information it contains verifies his social status: "It's on my wisiting cards sure enough (and it's them that's all o' pink satin paper) that inny gintleman that plases may behould the intheristhing words, 'Sir Pathrick O'Grandison, Barronit, 39 Southampton Row, Russel Square, Parrish o' Bloomsbury.'" After mentioning the pinkish hue of his visiting cards, he attempts a clever play on words, telling his guest, "And shud ye be wantin to diskiver who is the pink of purliteness quite . . . why it's jist mesilf" (183).

Having Sir Patrick use the word "pink" to describe both the color of his visiting cards and the essence of his personality, Poe reinforces the connection between the visiting card and the person it identifies. Sir Patrick's fascination with the color and quality of the paper on which his cards are printed anticipates Patrick Bateman's fascination with his handsomely printed business cards in *American Psycho* (2000). In both instances, the elegant appearance of the card bears little resemblance to the person it identifies. In Sir Patrick's case, the falseness of the impression is revealed as soon as Sir Patrick opens his mouth. The spoken word exposes what the printed word masks.

Characterizing the impression he strikes in public, Sir Patrick describes how his personal presence affects women: "But it's the iligant big figgur that I have, for the reason o' which all the ladies fall in love wid me. Isn't my own swate self now that'll missure sure the six fut, and the three inches more nor that in me stockings, and that am excadingly will proportioned all over to match?" (183–84). Asserting that he is well proportioned all over, Sir Patrick engages in a little sexual boasting. His bawdy humor is not without serious implications. This bit of vulgarity reveals how widely accepted was the idea that a person's appearance in public accurately indicated what was hidden from public view.

Besides his rough-hewn diction and coarse humor, Sir Patrick's opening words supply other details about him. His name, O'Grandison, recalls the title character of Samuel Richardson's *History of Sir Charles Grandison* (1753). Since the book's publication in the mid-eighteenth century, Richardson's title character had become a masculine ideal among English and American readers. Only in the most ironic sense can Poe's O'Grandison be considered a masculine ideal. Poe uses the character to spoof the whole notion of a masculine ideal.

Sir Patrick's speech is liberally peppered with proverbial comparisons, which impugn the character even further. Describing his new lifestyle as a baron, for example, Sir Patrick explains that for the past six weeks he has been living "like a houly imperor" (183). Unlike other contemporary American authors—Herman Melville comes to mind—Poe generally avoided incorporating traditional sayings in his work. His obsession with originality often prevented him from using proverbs in earnest. Calling "the whole race of what are termed maxims and popular proverbs," Poe identified "nine-tenths" of them as "the quintessence of folly."[13] When he did use proverbs, he usually put them in the mouths of characters he intends to ridicule. Think of all the clever sayings Peter Proffit spouts in "The Business Man" (and General John A. B. C. Smith in "The Man That Was Used Up").[14] Sir Patrick's use of proverbial comparisons in the early parts of "Little Frenchman" offers an indication that he, too, will become an object of the author's ridicule during the story.

Sir Patrick's opening words also provide an initial impression of the Frenchman, whom he calls "the three fut and a bit that there is, inny how, of the little oul furrener Frinchman" (184). Poking fun at the Frenchman's diminutive stature, Sir Patrick implicitly denigrates his sexual prowess. Poe's use of a little Frenchman is typical of the times. In American culture, the little Frenchman had already become an object of humorous derision. A tall tale entitled "A Prodigious Nose," which appeared in the May 1835 issue of the *Southern Literary Messenger*, for example, makes a little Frenchman the victim of a large-nosed man with whom he must share a room. Poe reviewed this issue of the *Messenger* for the Baltimore press and said that it was "upon the whole the best yet issued."[15] In "The Character of a Native Georgian," Augustus Baldwin Longstreet includes "a gay, smerky little Frenchman."[16] The author who most strongly influenced Poe in this regard was George P. Morris. A story of his entitled "The Little Frenchman" was reprinted in the *Southern Literary Messenger* in 1838 as part of a biographical sketch of the author.[17] Morris's little Frenchman was a recurring character. His most famous tale was "The Little Frenchman and His Water Lots," which initially appeared in the *New-York Mirror* in 1836 and was reprinted in a collection of his stories.[18] In North and South American culture, the little Frenchman would continue to be a stock humorous character. Consider the role Arduíno Colassanti plays in the Brazilian film, *How Tasty Was My Little Frenchman*.

Before finishing his introduction to the story, Sir Patrick mentions the pretty widow Mrs. Treacle or, as he says, the "purty widdy Misthress Tracle." Calling Mrs. Treacle his "most particuller frind and acquaintance," Sir Patrick reaffirms his unreliability as a narrator. She is certainly no friend of his and can scarcely be called an acquaintance. He knows her almost solely from seeing her at her window. According to him, Mrs. Treacle fell in love with him at first sight. Looking through her window toward his, she saw him and then, in order to get a better look, quickly lifted her window and raised a gold spyglass to her eye. Sir Patrick considers himself so adept at reading people's gestures that he can instantly tell what her eyes are saying: "Och! the tip o' the mornin to ye, Sir Pathrick o'Grandison, Barronitt, mavoureen; and it's a nate gintleman that ye are, sure enough, and it's meself and me fortin jist that'll be at yur sarvice, dear, inny time o' day at al at all for the asking" (184).

Sir Patrick's depiction of Mrs. Treacle provides a good indication of how his mind works. As he sees people, he knows what they are thinking from their appearance, particularly from their gestures. Their thoughts seem so real to him that he can convert their physical gestures directly into words. Both the narrator of "The Man of the Crowd" and the narrator of "The Philosophy of Furniture" possess similar abilities to understand personality by reading external signs. One understands people by their apparel, physiognomy, and mannerisms. The other understands people by their home decor. Sir Patrick thinks that he can understand people by their appearance and physical gestures. Of course he cannot, but much of the tale's humor stems from the incongruity between reality and Sir Patrick's perception and articulation of reality. Sir Patrick is an ironic precursor to Auguste Dupin, for whom all men have "windows in their bosoms."

The next day, while considering whether he should send a love letter to Mrs. Treacle, he receives a visit from the little Frenchman. Though Sir Patrick has difficulty understanding the Frenchman's words "excipting and saving that he said 'pully wou, woolly wou,'" he does get the message that the Frenchman "was mad for the love o' my widdy Misthress Tracle" (185). Furthermore, the Frenchman leads him to understand that the widow had a penchant for him—"a puncheon," Sir Patrick calls it. Upon learning this information, Sir Patrick becomes angry, but, refusing to show his anger, he feigns friendship. As he tells his guest, "I made light o' the matter and kipt dark, and got quite sociable wid the little chap" (186). The cleverness of Sir Patrick's expression reveals the artifice underlying his story. Furthermore, his words reveal an inconsistency in his thinking. While he acknowledges his own ability to make light while keeping dark, he does not recognize this ability in others. He can mask his true feelings from them, but they cannot mask their true feelings from him.

To keep an eye on the Frenchman, Sir Patrick must accompany him to Mrs. Treacle's apartment. Suddenly, Sir Patrick is forced from the safety of his own private space and into the dangerous space of the widow's apartment, where he can no longer control what will happen. Once inside, the Frenchman takes a seat to her right. Not to be outdone, Sir Patrick sits to her left. As they converse, Sir Patrick imagines he has the upper hand in the matter of her affection because he has "divarted her leddyship complately and intirely, by rason of the illigant conversation that I kipt up wid her all about the swate bogs of Connaught" (187). He becomes so confident of her affection that he makes an effort to hold her hand. For safety's sake, she puts her hands behind her back to avoid both his grasp and the Frenchman's.

The rest of the story is predictable. The Frenchman reaches behind her with his left hand, Sir Patrick with his right, and they squeeze one another's hands, each thinking the other has hold of the widow. As they argue over her, she rises from the sofa. Only then do they realize they have hold of one another. Mrs. Treacle's footmen soon roust the two suitors from her apartment. Sir Patrick ends his tale as follows:

> Ye may jist say, though for its God's truth that afore I lift hould of the flipper of the spalpeen, (which was not till afther her leddyship's fut-men had kicked us both down the stairs,) I gived it such a nate little broth of a squaze, as made it all up into raspberry jam.
> "Wouly-wou" says he "pully-wou" says he "Cot tam!"
> And that's jist the thruth of the rason why he wears his lift hand in a sling. (191)

Sir Patrick's closing sentence brings the tale to the present and reminds his guest what had initiated the story in the first place, the sight of the Frenchman in his window.

As Sir Patrick stands at his window looking toward the Frenchman and the Frenchman stands at his window looking back, they create mirror images of one another. The Frenchman's physical injury is matched by Sir Patrick's psychical injury. As he tells the story to his guest, Sir Patrick replicates the behavior he evinced while in conversation with the Frenchman. He makes light of the encounter with Mrs. Treacle but keeps dark the hurt he feels from her rejection. Restored to the safety of his own apartment, he once more can see the Frenchman and Mrs. Treacle from a distance, both framed by their windows. He can now reestablish control over what he sees.

The action of "Why the Little Frenchman Wears His Hand in a Sling" anticipates the action of "The Man of the Crowd." The Frenchman's behavior forces Sir Patrick to leave his apartment window to enter the perilous world of Mrs. Treacle's parlor; the sight of a mysterious old man jars the narrator of "The Man of the Crowd" from his complacency and compels him to leave his comfortable coffeehouse window seat to enter the mean streets of London to follow the old man in an attempt to read his personality. Poe gives Sir Patrick an option he withholds from the narrator of "The Man of the Crowd." Poe almost wears the narrator out by making him wander the London streets for a day and a half, but he never lets him return to the comfort of his coffeehouse window. After forcing Sir Patrick from his apartment and showing him the difficulties and uncertainties that lurk beyond its bounds, Poe lets him return to his apartment window. Home from his adventure at Mrs. Treacle's, he can now recapture his previous fantasies. He looks in one direction to see the woman he loves and who, he imagines, loves him. He looks in another direction to see his wounded rival and imagines himself a triumphant lover. The fantasy is complete. It will remain so—providing Sir Patrick O'Grandison no longer ventures outside. Perceiving the world from his apartment, he has imprisoned himself within his own window lattices.

NOTES

1. [Edgar Allan Poe,] "The Irish Gentleman and the Little Frenchman," *Bentley's Miscellany* 8 (1840): 45–48.

2. [Edgar Allan Poe,] "The Irish Gentleman and the Little Frenchman," *Spirit of the Times* 10 (1 August 1840): 254–55.

3. Arthur Hobson Quinn, *Edgar Allan Poe: A Critical Biography* (1941; reprinted, Baltimore: Johns Hopkins University Press, 1998), 289; Thomas Ollive Mabbott, ed., *Collected Works of Edgar Allan Poe*, 3 vols. (Cambridge, MA: Belknap Press of Harvard University Press, 1969–1978), 2: 462; J. Gerald Kennedy, "The Limits of Reason: Poe's Deluded Detectives," *American Literature* 47 (1975): 186.

4. Jack Kaufhold, "The Humor of Edgar Allan Poe," *Virginia Cavalcade* 29 (1980): 143.

5. Beverly Peterson, "Inviting Students to Challenge the American Literature Syllabus," *Teaching English in the Two-Year College* 28 (2001): 379.

6. Stuart Levine and Susan Levine, eds., *The Short Fiction of Edgar Allan Poe: An Annotated Edition* (1976; reprinted, Urbana: University of Illinois Press, 1990), 295.

7. Edgar Allan Poe, "Why the Little Frenchman Wears His Hand in a Sling," in *Tales of the Grotesque and Arabesque*, vol. 2 (Philadelphia: Lea and Blanchard, 1840), 183. Subsequent references to this story come from this edition and will be cited parenthetically.

8. Kevin J. Hayes, "Visual Culture and the Word in Edgar Allan Poe's 'The Man of the Crowd,'" *Nineteenth-Century Literature* 56 (2002): 450–51.

9. Kevin J. Hayes, "Early-Nineteenth-Century American Literature," in *American Literary Scholarship: An Annual, 1998*, ed. David Nordloh (Durham: Duke University Press, 2000), 221–22.

10. Kevin J. Hayes, "The Flaneur in the Parlor: Poe's 'Philosophy of Furniture,'" *Prospects* 27 (2002): 103.

11. Dana Brand, "Rear-View Mirror: Hitchcock, Poe, and the Flaneur in America," in *Hitchcock's America*, edited by Jonathan Freedman and Richard Millington (New York: Oxford University Press, 1999), 123–34; Dennis R. Perry, *Hitchcock and Poe: The Legacy of Delight and Terror* (Lanham, MD: Scarecrow Press, 2003), 146–56.

12. Daniel Royot, "Poe's Humor," in *The Cambridge Companion to Edgar Allan Poe*, edited by Kevin J. Hayes (2002; reprinted, Shanghai: Shanghai Foreign Language Education Press, 2004), 61.

13. Poe, *Essays and Reviews*, 679.

14. J. A. Leo Lemay, "Poe's 'The Business Man': Its Context and Satire of Franklin's *Autobiography*," *Poe Studies* 15 (1982): 33.

15. Democritus, Jr., *pseud.*, "A Prodigious Nose," *Southern Literary Messenger* 1 (1835): 468; David K. Jackson, "Four of Poe's Critiques in the Baltimore Newspapers," *Modern Language Notes* 50 (1935): 254.

16. Augustus Baldwin Longstreet, *Georgia Scenes, Characters, Incidents, &c. in the First Half Century of the Republic* (Augusta: S. R. Sentinel, 1835), 41.

17. "Biographical Sketch of George P. Morris," *Southern Literary Messenger* 4 (1838): 663–71.

18. George P. Morris, *The Little Frenchman and His Water Lots with Other Sketches of the Times* (Philadelphia: Lea & Blanchard, 1839).

NINE

"Eyes Which Behold": Poe's "Domain of Arnheim" and the Science of Vision

Laura Saltz

In Poe's "Domain of Arnheim," Ellison, the tale's only character, advances a theory of landscape gardening in which he justifies the need to modify "supreme" nature.[1] Though each of nature's components is perfect in itself, the arrangement or "composition" of these parts "will always be susceptible of improvement" (3: 1273). According to Ellison, the landscape's composition appears flawed because God originally designed the world for immortal man. Ellison believes that there probably exists a species of quasi-immortal, angel-like beings possessed of a "death-refined appreciation of the beautiful" to whom the earth's surface yet appears perfect (3: 1274). To human eyes, however, even "the most enchanting of natural landscapes" will always contain "a defect or an excess" (3: 1272). Correcting these defects and accommodating "the mortal or human *point of view*" are paramount in Ellison's art of landscape design (3: 1274). The height of his art will be reached when he has adapted nature's physical loveliness for "the eyes which were to behold it on earth" (3: 1272), a phrase the unnamed narrator of "Arnheim" dramatically repeats for emphasis: "In its adaptation to the eyes which were to behold it on earth."

The story's contrast between the perspectives of "the eyes which were to behold [the landscape] on earth" and of "a class of beings, human once, but now invisible to humanity" who gaze at the earth "from some point distant from [its] surface" might strike twenty-first-century readers as odd, to say the least (3: 1274). But it is crucial to Poe's depiction of Ellison's art. As the narrator of "Arnheim" explains, Ellison is a poet "in the widest and noblest sense" (3: 1271), a view that recalls Poe's own statements in "The Poetic Principle," where he notes that "the composition of the Landscape Garden" offers a "peculiarly . . . wide field" in which "the Poetic Sentiment . . . may develope [sic] itself."[2] Although Poe does not explain why landscape gardening is a "peculiar" medium for the expression of the poetic sentiment, the reason is implicit in his view that poetic sentiment is manifested in the ethereal and immaterial.

In "The Poetic Principle," Poe suggests that the highest aim of the poetic sentiment is to elevate the soul by revealing to it the supernal loveliness of eternity. As Poe explains in "The Philosophy of Composition," beauty is "not a quality, as is supposed, but an effect" (*ER* 16). It is therefore felt rather than perceived through the eyes and ears. Supernal beauty—precisely because it *is* supernal—is best apprehended in the transcendence of the physical senses rather than directly through them; thus, the human pursuit of beauty is "ecstatic" (*ER* 77). Because music and poetry have immaterial, nonrepresentational means for creating the effect of beauty, Poe points to them as especially important modes of conveying the poetic sentiment. "The Poetry of Words," Poe explains, can thus be defined as "*The Rhythmical Creation of Beauty*," which enables the hearer/reader to divine supernal beauty "*through* the poem, or *through* the music" in "brief and indeterminate glimpses" (*ER* 77, 78, Poe's italics). That a poem's rhythm can generate "glimpses" of the supernal, that rhythm produces an effect in and for the reader, suggests that Poe views poetry as a kind of contemplative medium.[3] By inducing a hypnagogic state in the reader, a poem might free "the soul" from the spatial and temporal restrictions of the body and put it in direct contact with the supernal. In Poe's tales, the organs of sense are usually overridden before a "glimpse" of the eternal can be attained. In "Mesmeric Revelation," Mr. Vankirk is granted a glimpse of the divine forces of the universe while he is in a mesmeric trance, explaining that "it is to the absence of idiosyncratic organs [such as the eyes] that we must attribute the nearly unlimited perception of the ultimate life" (1038). "Mesmeric Revelation" is typical in that it represents what Poe calls in "The Poetic Principle" the "ecstatic prescience of the glories beyond the grave" (*ER* 77).[4]

Ellison's emphatic interest in "the eyes which behold" the landscape on earth seems to challenge Poe's metaphysical notion of the poetic sentiment. By highlighting the perspective of a human observer, Ellison suggests that supernal beauty might somehow be glimpsed not by transcending the senses but through their normal operation. When he insists on the need to accommodate "the mortal or human *point of view*," Ellison apparently rejects the disembodied perspective advocated in "The Poetic Principle" and exemplified in stories such as "Mesmeric Revelation" (3: 1274). Ellison, in fact, makes the "peculiar" choice of landscape gardening over and against music or poetry because his interests are "tinged" with "what is termed materialism." According to the narrator,

Ellison wants only to create "purely *physical* loveliness" (3: 1271). Yet despite Ellison's materialism, which manifests itself both in his choice of the land as his medium of artistic expression and his concern for the vision of mortal humans, he manages to create in his garden an "intermedium" between human art and "the Almighty design" (1276). His garden forms a bridge between human and divine creation, as well as between human perception—"the eyes which behold"—and supernal beauty. In creating this "intermedium," Ellison fulfills "not only his own destiny as a poet, but . . . the august purposes for which the Deity had implanted the poetic sentiment in man" (3: 1272).

My essay addresses the apparent paradox of Ellison's materialist approach to the production of poetic sentiment. In "The Domain of Arnheim," Poe imagines a garden that creates the effect of transcendence by manipulating rather than suppressing "the eyes which were to behold it on earth." Poe was able to conceive and represent Ellison's garden in a way such that it would appeal optically to the hypothetical "visiter" [*sic*] who travels through it in the final pages of the tale because of his long-standing interest in the science of human vision (3: 1278). In particular, Poe had a working knowledge of Scottish physicist Sir David Brewster's *Letters on Natural Magic* (1831), in which Brewster describes dozens of optical illusions. He debunks these illusions, which were formerly attributed to the supernatural, by explaining how reflection, refraction, and the physiology of the eye work together to produce otherworldly effects. As a number of scholars have demonstrated, Poe often turned to *Natural Magic* for inspiration in the representation of uncanny phenomena. I believe that *Natural Magic* is not simply a source of optical tricks that Poe imports into "Arnheim." Poe also shares with Brewster an understanding of how the eyes work: why a glance can be more effective than a direct view, how the eyes perceive depth, and how the physical eye and the mind's eye are related. Through his scientific understanding of vision, Poe simulates in "Arnheim" a set of optical effects that parallel the out-of-body states in which the poetic sentiment, in Poe's view, is best apprehended.

Much critical discussion of "The Domain of Arnheim" has focused on Poe's use and abuse of the aesthetic discourse of the picturesque. I want to look briefly at this discussion in order to suggest how some of the notions that underpin the picturesque converge with the science of vision as Poe deploys it in "Arnheim." In the first part of the tale (which is a slightly revised version of Poe's "The Landscape Garden" of 1842), Ellison expounds on the aesthetic principles of landscape gardening, developing his own ideas and quoting and refuting "a writer" (3: 1274) on the subject. Jeffrey A. Hess has demonstrated that the "writer" with whom Ellison disagrees is Andrew Jackson Downing, whose *Treatise on Landscape Gardening* appeared in 1841 and was reviewed that year in the *Unit-*

ed States Democratic Review.[5] Catherine Rainwater develops this idea by placing Downing's work and Poe's response to it within the context of discussions of the picturesque in Europe and the United States.[6]

The picturesque emerged in reaction to Edmund Burke's *Inquiry into the Origin of Our Ideas of the Sublime and Beautiful* when writers such as Uvedale Price and Richard Payne Knight proposed a third category, neither sublime nor beautiful but picturesque. Where Burke sought to understand the emotional or moral responses provoked by sublime and beautiful scenes, Price and Knight emphasized the formal attributes—textural roughness and compositional complexity, for example—of the picturesque. Yet, as Rainwater notes, discussions of the picturesque by Archibald Alison, William Howitt, and William Gilpin reinvested the aesthetic category with a moral dimension. In their view, the ability to identify picturesque "compositions" in the land and therefore to recognize God's design becomes a moral good. Rainwater argues that Ellison's aim to restore "order and design" to the land, to create a supernal realm on earth, closely parallels the "Alisonian notion that human creativity improves nature by rearranging it, and thereby, making God's design perceptible to the mortal mind" (36). Because the garden itself is "far more grotesque and bizarre than these 'picturesque' conventions [of roughness, ruggedness, and complex or difficult harmony] allow" (36), Rainwater makes the case that Poe engages the picturesque in "Arnheim" in order to parody it.[7]

However much the tale might parody the advocates of the moral benefits of the picturesque, Ellison himself does not invest his domain or the art of landscape gardening generally with any moral dimension, though his interlocutor, the unidentified writer, does. The writer suggests that "mixture of pure art in a garden scene adds to it a great beauty. This is partly pleasing to the eye, by the show of order and design, and partly moral" (3: 1275). When Ellison responds, he avoids any mention of moral value, noting simply that "a mixture of pure art in a garden scene adds to it a great beauty" (3: 1276). Ellison continues that a poet might "so imbue his designs at once with extent and novelty of beauty, as to convey the sentiment of spiritual interference" (3: 1276), but this "spiritual interference" is curiously devoid of moral content. It simply lends "a charm" to the garden "far surpassing that which a sense of merely human interest could bestow" (3: 1276). Likewise, Poe's discussions of supernal beauty carefully distinguish the spiritual and moral. Poe makes clear in "The Poetic Principle" that true beauty is spiritual and that while beauty—the province of the poetic sentiment—is informed by taste, morality is tied to duty. Taste is so far distinguished from the moral sense that it can only approach morality in aesthetic terms as yet another source of beauty.[8] In striving to create a beautiful garden, Ellison directs his efforts at the eye rather than at the moral sense of the beholder.

If Ellison's domain embodies neither the moral nor the formal proper-ties (roughness, etc.) of a picturesque landscape, it does participate in the tendency of the picturesque to address "the eyes which behold it" by isolating the visual aspects of a scene in order to produce effects devoid of moral content.[9] "Arnheim" does not so much parody the picturesque as enact one of its basic objectives: the exercise of the sensation of sight. In one of the classic studies of the picturesque, Christopher Hussey explains that "the romantic movement was an awakening of sensation, and among the other sensations, that of sight required exercising. Thus the pictu-resque interregnum between classic and romantic art was necessary in order to enable the imagination to form the habit of feeling through the eyes."[10] In Hussey's view, the picturesque stimulates the imagination by appealing to the eyes rather than to intellect or reason. By emphasizing the rough or tactile features of the surfaces contained within a scene, the picturesque encourages the morally neutral "habit of feeling through the eyes." Martin Price concurs, writing that the picturesque is marked by "the dissociation of visual, pictorial, or generally aesthetic elements from other values in contemplating a scene."[11]

Although the formal aspects of the scenery in "The Domain of Arn-heim" differ from those of the picturesque, Poe's text cultivates in readers the "habit of feeling through the eyes." This interest in the *sensation* of sight is consistent with Poe's predilection for producing sensationalist gothic texts. It is also shared by the scientific community, which in the early decades of the nineteenth century increasingly turned its attention to the behavior of the eye in the production of sight. Before looking specifically at how the science of human vision engages "the habit of feeling through the eyes," I want to explore how the garden appeals to "the eyes which behold it."

Ellison's garden is described in the final pages of the tale, which Poe added when he expanded "The Landscape Garden" and published it as "The Domain of Arnheim" in 1847.[12] Ellison set out to create a landscape marked by "*strangeness*" (3: 1276) and the result is dark, claustrophobic, and disorienting—in a word, uncanny rather than picturesque. But there is no necessary or implied contradiction between the garden's strange effects and its beauty. As Poe was fond of remarking, "there is no exqui-site beauty which has not some strangeness in its proportion" (*ER* 140).[13] Much of the garden's strangeness is attributable to the sequence in which it is viewed. Ellison intended his domain to be approached by boat. As the narrator takes the hypothetical "visiter"—the reader—on this boat journey, he links the features of the landscape inextricably to the reader's situated point of view by describing only what the visitor/reader can see at each stage of the voyage. The garden's "arrangement of . . . parts" unfolds during the journey in a spatial and temporal sequence designed to disorient the reader, for the river follows a maze-like course (3: 1272). As the boat moves forward, space begins to contract horizontally and expand vertically, and the bottom drops out of the scene: "at every instant the vessel seemed imprisoned within an enchanted circle, having insuperable and impenetrable walls of foliage, a roof of ultra-marine satin, and *no* floor" (3: 1279). The visitor/reader is surrounded and engulfed by the landscape. Unlike the angelic beings who might view Ellison's domain all at once from "some point distant from the earth's surface" (3: 1274), the voyager only apprehends the features of the garden in fragments as they are revealed to the eye over time.

In presenting the elements of the landscape sequentially to the visitor/reader, "Arnheim" begins to enact "the dissociation of the visual" that Price identifies with the picturesque. As Joan Dayan argues, individual objects in the landscape present themselves directly to the reader as the narrator's voice recedes and the passive voice takes over the narrative.[14] Lacking the mediating presence of the narrator, the reader relies increasingly on optical cues in the landscape itself. As if moving through the virtual space of a computer-simulated environment, the voyager experiences the domain of Arnheim as a disembodied eye. For instance, as the boat continues to move forward, "the eye trace[s] upward the myriad-tinted slope," and "the crystal water well[s] up against the clean granite" walls of steep river banks "with a sharpness of outline that delighted while it bewildered the eye." "The eye" is indeed bewildered. As chasms of space appear and disappear, the reader becomes disoriented by a stream that takes "a thousand turns, so that at no moment could its gleaming surface be seen for a greater distance than a furlong." Thus, "the eye" is deprived of ordinary perceptual markers of recession and depth (3: 1279–80). Encountering blockages on all sides, "the eye" is made to feel its way almost blindly through the domain of Arnheim. By manipulating point of view so radically, "The Domain of Arnheim" draws attention to the workings of "the eye" and to the uncanny effects of claustrophobia and disorientation produced by the eye's limitations.[15]

The attention to the sensate eye, which Hussey and Price associate with the picturesque tradition and Poe exploits in "The Domain of Arnheim," coincides with emerging scientific explanations of vision. In *Techniques of the Observer*, art historian Jonathan Crary notes the convergence of aesthetic and scientific discourses of vision in a new visual paradigm that emerged in the 1820s.[16] Since the Renaissance, visual phenomena had been understood in terms of geometry and classical space. By contrast, the new paradigm, which Crary labels "subjective vision," understood vision as an effect of the body's physiology and its subjective response to stimuli. For example, in the 1830s, Johannes Müller showed that the application of electricity to the optic nerve produces the experience of light, as does a concussion or blow, certain chemicals (such as narcotics or digitalis) when they are absorbed into the bloodstream, and illnesses that stimulate the blood.[17] As a result of such experiments, scientists began to hold that visual phenomena had no independent existence apart from the physiological processes that produced them. With this shift to physiological optics, the eye became increasingly isolated as an object of study. Just as the picturesque divorced the visual from the rational and moral, so too did the science of vision dislodge sight from its place in a unified sensorium. The senses were no longer treated as accessory to the rational mind but as individual physiological organs. This "separation of the senses" (Crary's phrase) from each other and from rational knowledge was crucial to the invention of a number of visual technologies, including David Brewster's stereoscope, which creates the sensations of depth or relief through purely optical cues.[18]

The focus in "Arnheim" on the optical progress of "the eye" through space is deeply bound up with the physiological model of vision that came into ascendancy in Poe's day. This model held a powerful appeal for a number of American writers, including Fuller, Emerson, and Thoreau.[19] In "The Domain of Arnheim," the eye of the visitor (as well as the reader) is given primacy by becoming isolated and disembodied.[20] In what follows, I will examine the correspondence between "Arnheim" and the writings of one of the important contributors to the science of vision, David Brewster. Renowned for his work in polarized light and optics, Brewster studied the anatomy and behavior of the eyes: the response of the retina to various stimuli, binocular vision, and such phenomena as blind spots and afterimages. This work led him to invent the kaleidoscope in 1815 and the lenticular stereoscope over the course of the 1840s. He was a prolific writer whose research appeared in such prestigious publications as the *Edinburgh Journal of Science* (which he edited) and the *Philosophical Transactions of the Royal Society of London*. He also exerted a profound influence on Poe.

Over the course of his career, Poe repeatedly turned to Brewster's *Letters on Natural Magic* (1831) as a source.[21] Written as a series of letters to Sir Walter Scott, *Natural Magic* promises to enlist science, in the name of democracy and the diffusion of knowledge, to explain the illusions and tricks perpetrated by representatives of state and religious authority (kings, sorcerers, and priests) that had historically been used to awe subjects and keep their minds enslaved. Because the eyes are "the principal seat of the supernatural," Brewster focuses on "those illusions which have their origin in the eye" (*NM* 21). He explains how mirrors and lenses can be used to reflect and refract light, producing specific effects that range from the uncanny to the entertaining. Poe was clearly intrigued by the mysterious optical (and aural) phenomena Brewster describes, and borrowed nearly two dozen of them for his fiction. These include the mysterious appearance of the word "DISCOVERY" on the ship's sail in "MS Found in a Bottle," William Wilson's death-duel with his mirror image (Brewster explains how to orchestrate this illusion in letter IV), the specter images of ships in *The Narrative of Arthur Gordon Pym*, and the mysterious handwriting in "A Tale of the Ragged Mountains." What's more, "Maelzel's Chess-Player" is based entirely on Brewster's letter on automata.[22] In "Arnheim," Poe's debt to Brewster takes a different form than in these other stories. He does not borrow specific images (such as a man's duel with his own reflection) from *Natural Magic* so much as he appropriates Brewster's way of thinking about vision. The distinction is analogous to the one Poe makes with regard to beauty, which he asserts is "not a quality . . . but an effect" (*ER* 16). "Arnheim" owes something to the qualities of the illusions discussed in *Natural Magic*, but more importantly, the tale reproduces their effects by attending to the idiosyncrasies of human vision.

The first of these visual idiosyncrasies is oblique or indirect vision. In *Natural Magic*, Brewster notes that in ordinary vision, objects viewed directly are seen distinctly. However, in some exceptional cases, objects are seen more clearly when we look away from them: "The eye has the power of seeing objects with perfect distinctness, only when it is directed straight upon them; that is, all objects seen indirectly are seen indistinctly; but it is a curious circumstance, that when we wish to obtain a sight of a very faint star, such as one of the satellites of Saturn, we can see it most distinctly *by looking away from it*, and when the eye is turned full upon it, it immediately disappears" (*NM* 24-25, Brewster's italics). Indirect vision, explains Brewster, is usually inferior to direct vision because it exercises parts of the eye that are less capable of registering fine resolutions or of exerting prolonged attention. Nevertheless, certain small or luminous objects such as faint stars come into focus when the eye looks away from them because the parts of the eye used in oblique vision are more sensitive than those used in direct vision: the "inability of the eye to preserve a sustained vision of objects seen obliquely is curiously compensated by the greater ability of those parts of the eye that have this defect" (*NM* 24). Brewster's choice of faint stars is not incidental. In other discussions of oblique vision, he credits "several astronomers" with discovering this example of the efficacy of oblique vision, and even names Sir John Herschel and Sir James South as similarly recommending this "rather singular method" of viewing faint stars, "viz. *to direct the eye to another part of the field*."[23] By looking away, the viewer is able to see stars otherwise obliterated by brighter stars in their vicinity.

This kind of sidelong glance or glimpse, as David Ketterer has brilliantly shown, is one of Poe's favorite tropes.[24] In Ketterer's analysis, the half-closed eye allows the imagination to escape the conditions of the external universe and "eradicate the barriers erected by time, space, and self" (28). To be sure, an over-reliance on the data of senses leads to certain kind of blindness, as when, in "The Murders in the Rue Morgue," Dupin accuses Vidocq of "impair[ing] his vision by holding the object too close. He might see, perhaps, one or two points with unusual clearness, but in so doing he, necessarily, lost sight of the matter as a whole. Thus there is such a thing as being too profound. Truth is not always in a well"

(1: 545). In contrast, Dupin looks to his intuition as often as he looks at the world around him when solving a crime. Yet even here, where Dupin seems to recommend a kind of shutting down or blurring of the senses so that the whole is not sacrificed to the details, he justifies this approach by referring back, in Ketterer's words, to the physical "laws of space and self"—to astronomy and optics:

> The modes and sources of this kind of error are well typified in the contemplation of heavenly bodies. To look at a star by glances—to view it in a side-long way, by turning toward it the exterior portions of the *retina* (more susceptible of feeble impressions of light than the interior), is to behold the star distinctly—is to have the best appreciation of its luster—a luster which grows dim must in proportion as we turn our vision *fully* upon it. A greater number of rays actually fall upon the eye in the latter case, but, in the former, there is more refined capacity for comprehension. (1: 545)[25]

Dupin advocates not an escape from the senses but a proper understanding of their functions. Through such comprehension, the human sense of sight can be employed strategically to give a more correct and complete view of the universe.

In "Arnheim," white pebbles are substituted for stars as the objects of oblique vision. Nevertheless, the gesture of looking away from them is the same as the one described in "Rue Morgue" and *Natural Magic*, and it too is underpinned by a knowledge of the workings of the human eye. When an "unexpected turn of the vessel [brings] it suddenly, as if dropped from heaven, into a circular basin," the narrator instructs the reader on the exercise of oblique vision: "This basin was of great depth, but so transparent was the water that the bottom, which seemed to consist of a thick mass of small round alabaster pebbles, was distinctly visible by glimpses—that is to say, whenever the eye could permit itself *not* to see, far down in the inverted heaven, the duplicate blooming of the hills" (3: 1280). In this passage, the faint stars of Brewster's example have been brought to earth and transformed into alabaster pebbles, a process echoed in the "flowers de luce" of the tale's epigraph, which "hung upon their azure leaves . . . / Like twinkling stars" (3: 1267). To see the pebbles, the eye must "permit itself *not* to see" the "inverted heaven" and the "duplicate blooming of the hills" reflected on the water's surface. Only "by glimpses" does the eye avert the distorting power of the water—its ability to reflect, invert, and duplicate. Yet this passage is not about the dangers of illusion. It is about the eye's ability to see multiple or superimposed images and about the pleasure of these juxtapositions. By exerting a conscious effort to look forward or askance, the beholder determines which objects will be perceived.

Poe prescribes oblique vision here because the water both reflects and refracts light. The clear water of the basin performs a double visual function, acting as a surface on which "the inverted heaven" and "the duplicate blooming of the hills" are mirrored, and as a transparent medium through which the pebbles on the bottom of the basin might be viewed. Letter IV of *Natural Magic*, the one most frequently consulted by Poe, contains ample discussion of the use of mirrors and lenses in magic lanterns, phantasmagorias, and other apparatuses to produce optical illusions through the reflection and refraction of light. By the time Poe wrote "Arnheim" in 1847, however, visual culture had provided another more popular technology that embodied the properties of mirror and glass: the daguerreotype. The mirrored surface of the daguerreotype makes the image elusive and ambiguous. As Alan Trachtenberg notes, if a daguerreotype is not held at precisely the correct angle, the beholder's optical focus shifts from the permanent photographic image beneath the glass to the viewer's own reflection on the daguerreotype's surface.[26] Like the transparent water of the basin, the daguerreotype permits image and reflection either to alternate or to be superimposed. Divining the image beneath the reflection requires a sidelong glimpse similar to the one necessary to see the pebbles at the bottom of the basin. The daguerreotype's specific physical properties produce strange flitting images that elicit reactions ranging from perceptual confusion to enchantment—as do the properties of the basin.

Early discussions of daguerreotypes frequently distinguished them from other kinds of images (such as drawings, lithographs, and engravings) by the distinct outlines and minute details of their images, which seemed to constitute a "perfect fidelity" to the objects they pictured. Samuel F. B. Morse, the first American to see a daguerreotype, told his readers that "the exquisite minuteness of the delineation cannot be conceived. No painting or engraving ever approached it."[27] In Poe's own review of the new medium, he stresses the homology between daguerreotype and mirror: "if we imagine the distinctness with which an object is reflected in a positively perfect mirror, we may come as near the reality [of the daguerreotype] as by any other means.[28] Unlike paintings, the daguerreotype image shares with mirror images the appearance of infinite accuracy: "If we examine a work of ordinary art by means of a powerful microscope, all traces of resemblance to nature will disappear—but the closest scrutiny of the photogenic drawing discloses only . . . a more perfect identity of aspect with the thing represented" (38). These qualities of sharp delineation and accuracy characterize the water in "Arnheim" and its "pendant," "Landor's Cottage" (1849). The waters of Arnheim "duplicate" the landscape that surrounds them, reproducing it exactly, and the water's edge is remarkable for "a sharpness of outline that delighted while it bewildered the eye" (3: 1280, 1279). In "Landor's Cottage," a "lakelet" that is nearly an exact double of the basin in "Arnheim" likewise exhibits photographic properties. It too has white pebbles, which "could be distinctly seen" on its bottom (3: 1333), and is *"so* clear" that "so perfectly, at times, did it reflect all objects above it" (3: 1333). Like a daguerreotype, this lakelet reflects "with a fidelity unsurpassed by the most exquisitely polished mirror" (3: 1333).

But it is the basin's quality of exercising the eye, more than in the sharpness or fidelity of its reflected images, where Brewster's influence is felt. In *Techniques of the Observer,* Crary liberates photography from a narrative that accounts for it in terms of classical models of vision—which assume a stationary, monocular viewer, and which privilege the type of truthful representation such as that realized in the qualities of sharpness and fidelity—and he places it in the context of scientific work on subjective vision. Brewster's understanding of the utility of looking at an object indirectly falls squarely within the category of subjective vision, for it is based on the isolation and study of the eye's behavior and the correlation of the eye's physical properties with the optical effects it is capable of perceiving.

In this sense, Brewster's analysis of oblique vision is part of the same enterprise that led him to invent the stereoscope. In fact, Brewster's stereoscope builds directly on his observations regarding indirect vision. We are not normally aware of the indistinctness of indirect vision, Brewster reasons, because the eyes are constantly moving and compensating for that indistinctness. The eyes' movement then becomes central to Brewster's conception of binocular vision.[29] The stereoscope creates the illusion of three-dimensionality by recognizing that binocular vision—the use of both eyes—is required for depth perception. By placing two slightly different images before the eyes at slightly different angles, the stereoscope capitalizes on the fact that the eyes will move back and forth in rapid succession in order to unify the images and endow the result with the appearance of relief. When "Arnheim" orchestrates the movement of the eye of the beholder back and forth from the alabaster pebbles at the bottom of the basin to the images of inverted hills and duplicate trees on the basin's surface—a movement that is similar to the one that produces the illusion of depth in binocular vision—the tale likewise displays an interest in exploiting the idiosyncrasies of human vision to create fantastical effects.

These effects are most pronounced in the tale's representations of three-dimensional space, which simulate several of the effects of looking through a stereoscope. The text bids readers to enter the landscape as it might bid us enter the picture plane of a painting by suggesting an analogy between the art of landscape gardening and "such paradises" that are not "to be found in reality" but that "[glow] on the canvass of Claude" (3: 1272). Once the reader enters the space of the landscape, however, its similarity to painting ends. Where paintings use linear perspective (the convergence of parallel lines at a single point in the distance) to indicate recessional space, stereoscopic images organize space in successive planes. Objects appear to be lined up one behind the other, and the eyes move back through the image by jumping from one plane or object to the next.[30]

Like a stereoscopic image, the domain of Arnheim is revealed in successive planes. Recall that "the stream took a thousand turns, so that at no moment could its gleaming surface be seen for a greater distance than a furlong" (3: 1279). The eye cannot travel smoothly from foreground to background but must move piecemeal through the landscape. The domain feels claustrophobic, not only because the walls of the ravine on the side of the river are steep, blocking peripheral views, but also because the vanishing points keep disappearing. A "limitless vista seen through [a] chasm-like rift in the hills" is revealed but only in the moments before the voyager "quits the vessel." This vista is transfigured into a "rocky gate" that must be physically approached before its "depths can be more distinctly seen." Then again, what the narrator calls "the gate of the vista" loses its "chasm-like appearance" as a bay "is discovered on the left," but "down this opening the eye cannot penetrate very far" (3: 1280–82). As in a stereoscopic image, the eyes are forced by the contours of the landscape to maneuver their way from one plane to the next by locking onto objects in the foreground, never quite able to take in the whole. Recessional space is repeatedly blocked. In one case, "the vision is impeded by an impenetrable screen of foliage" (3: 1282); in another, the voyager "finds his progress apparently barred by a gigantic gate or rather door" (3: 1282). Depth is then reconstituted in reverse—in the foreground—as tree limbs reach forward "and dip their pendent extremities into the water" (3: 1282).

The effect in "Arnheim," in which the eyes must proceed cautiously from plane to plane, is analogous to what Crary calls "the desired effect of the stereoscope": "not simply likeness, but immediate, apparent *tangibility* . . . a tangibility that has been transformed into a purely visual experience" (122-24). Oliver Wendell Holmes, the inventor of the Holmes stereoscope, describes the experience of looking at a stereoscopic image in precisely these terms: "The mind, as it were, *feels round* [an object] and gets an idea of its solidity. We clasp an object with our eyes, as with our arms, or with our hands, or with our thumb and finger, and then we know it to be something more than a surface."[31] For Holmes, as for visitors to Arnheim, this experience of "clasping an object with our eyes" is not altogether comfortable. As the eyes reach into the image, so do the objects portrayed there threaten to reach back: "The first effect of looking at a good photograph through the stereoscope is a surprise such as no paintings ever produced. The mind feels its way into the very depths of the picture. The scraggy branches of a tree in the foreground run out at us as if they would scratch our eyes out. The elbow of a figure stands forth so as to make us almost uncomfortable" (77–78). Holmes's "scraggy branches" reach dangerously forward, just as the "frequent limbs" (1282) of the black walnut trees in Arnheim encroach on the reader.

Although Poe probably never saw a stereoscope, it is quite possible that he read about them. Brewster's lenticular stereoscope became commercially available in 1850, just after Poe's death, but Brewster submitted papers on the subject to the Royal Society of Edinburgh in 1843 and 1844, and exhibited the instrument in 1849. Binocular vision had been acknowledged since Euclid, and scientists and inventors constructed and wrote about stereoscopes even before photography was invented in 1839.[32] In 1838, Charles Wheatstone exhibited a reflecting stereoscope and published the account, complete with diagrams, in the *Philosophical Transactions of the Royal Society of London* under the title "Contributions to the Physiology of Vision: Part the First: On Some Remarkable, and Hitherto Unobserved, Phenomena of Binocular Vision." Poe almost certainly encountered this piece when he conducted an intensive study of the *Philosophical Transactions* between the years 1835 and 1840, as he prepared to revise "Hans Phaall."[33] Wheatstone explains why a two-dimensional painting, even if it applies the laws of linear perspective and uses lights and shadows to create modeling, can never "show a relievo equal to that of natural objects, unless these be viewed at a distance and with a single eye."[34] To show depth in the foreground—a project obsessively repeated by "Arnheim"—requires acknowledgement of the properties of binocular vision. Wheatstone later refutes Brewster's explanation—which appears in letter V of *Natural Magic*, and which Poe knew well—of why the eyes can be easily fooled into mistaking elevations or cameos for depressions or intaglios and vice versa (384).

Whether Poe knew of or read about stereoscopes per se is ultimately less important than what his longstanding interest in the science of human vision enabled him to imagine in "Arnheim." Through his reading of *Natural Magic*, Poe was familiar with the idea that illusions "have their origin in the eye" (*NM* 21), and he was exposed to many of the ways such illusions might be produced.[35] In projecting illusions into three dimensions for a beholder who moves through the landscape, Poe consolidates his knowledge of optics within the familiar narrative form of the journey. He had attempted something similar as early as 1835 with "Hans Phaall," where Hans's vision in space is distorted by changes in atmospheric pressure and extreme distances. "Arnheim" takes the next step by telescoping distance and forcing an optical encounter between the voyager and an obstacle-strewn landscape. The text's optical construction of space can be further understood as Poe's fictional contribution to a more widespread cultural fascination with technologies designed to elicit "realistic" optical experiences by setting the observer in motion. The diorama, which Poe knew well, places spectators on a moving platform, which rotated them through the scenery. As Tom Gunning argues, railway journeys provided an early template for the visual experiences created later in the century by cinema. A camera placed on the front of a train would appear to penetrate the space behind the screen; even more interestingly, a train rushing toward the audience would rupture the cinematic frame.[36] Gunning places "Arnheim" within this larger cultural preoccupation with the penetration of space. In creating a text in which the eye feels its way through space by moving from plane to plane, Poe responds to this cultural preoccupation in a way that parallels almost exactly the effects of the stereoscope.

"Arnheim" contains one exception to the withholding of perspectives and blocking of recessional space that typifies stereoscopic vision. This circumstance comes at the apotheosis of the reader's journey, when "the whole Paradise of Arnheim bursts upon the view." A castle appears, "a mass of semi-Gothic, semi-Saracenic architecture, sustaining itself as if by miracle in mid air" (3: 1283). Just as the source of the glimpse can be found in Brewster's discussion of indirect vision in *Natural Magic,* so too does his discussion of apparitional castles supply Poe with a way of thinking about vision. Though there is no single castle that floats in mid-air in *Natural Magic,* the castle of Ellison's domain can be seen as the composite of several "aerial spectres" catalogued by Brewster in Letter VI (*NM* 125). M. Haue and a companion saw the specters of three human figures of monstrous size hovering above the horizon in 1797; the eminent Baron von Humboldt *"saw cows suspended in the air"* at the Mesa de Pavona; and the list goes on (*NM* 137). Most relevant here is a sighting by "Professor Vance of Cambridge and another gentleman on the 6th August 1806 at Ramsgate" of the whole of Dover Castle on a hill, when from their position, only its four turrets should have been visible. Brewster reports that the upward projection of the castle "was so very singular and unexpected that at first sight Dr. Vance thought it an illusion; but upon continuing his observations, he became satisfied that it was a real image of the castle" (*NM* 130). Likewise, while attempting to view the coast of Greenland through a telescope in 1820, a Mr. Scoresby saw a shimmering image that was "alternately a castle, a cathedral, or an obelisk" suspended above the shoreline. In Scoresby's own words, "some of the hills seemed to be surmounted by turrets, battlements, spires, and pinnacles; while others, subjected to one or two reflections, exhibited large masses of rock, apparently suspended in the air, at a considerable elevation. . . . The whole exhibition was a grand phantasmagoria. Scarcely was any particular portion sketched before it changed its appearance, and assumed the form of an object totally different" (*NM* 136). Brewster attributes Professor Vance's sighting of Dover castle and Mr. Scoresby's vision of the castle/cathedral/obelisk, along with the other reports of aerial specters, to a related series of facts having to do with the ability of water in the air, when heated or cooled, to act as a convex or convex lens and project an inverted or erect image, respectively, above the horizon (*NM* 141–42).[37]

Not only does Brewster's text supply Poe with an iconographic model of the castle's style—semi-gothic, semi-saracenic—it provides a history of and a template for the eye's receptivity to illusion. Jeffrey A. Hess makes a strong case that Poe based the appearance of Ellison's castle on one that appears in Thomas Cole's "Youth," the second in the series of four canvases that comprise *The Voyage of Life*.[38] In linking Ellison's castle to Brewster's aerial specters, I am positing an additional source for the image that accounts for it in terms of its phenomenal status as an illusion rather than its architectural features. For Brewster, to call something an illusion in no way detracts from its reality. Just as Dr. Vance was satisfied that what he saw was "a real image" of Dover Castle, so Mr. Scoresby relates that his vision, despite being "a grand phantasmagoria," "had all the distinctness of reality" (*NM* 136). Brewster endorses these views by understanding illusions as "real phenomena of nature" that call for "a distinct and satisfactory knowledge of the causes which gave them birth" (*NM* 140). Because Brewster takes these visions seriously, he emphasizes the credibility of his sources, detailing the times, places, and circumstances of his witnesses' experiences, and often, as in the cases of Dr. Vance and Mr. Scoresby, quoting their testimony.

Brewster's discussion of optical illusions rests on the conviction that they are real, or rather, along the lines suggested by Johannes Müller's experiments, that the opposition between illusion and reality does not hold. To the perceiver in Müller's experiments, the sensation of light, whether caused by the actual presence of light or some other stimulus (electrical or chemical), is the same. As Crary argues, the discovery that many stimuli could produce the same sensation suggested that the relation between sensation and stimulus was arbitrary. "Vision," then, is not the perception of the material world but an effect created by the physiology of the eyes and their interaction with the mind. As Crary puts it, "the very absence of referentiality is the ground on which new instrumental techniques will construct for an observer a new 'real' world" (91).

Indeed, both the Brewster and Wheatstone stereoscopes make this absence of referentiality graphically clear. The eyes combine two dissimilar images—which in the Wheatstone model do not even appear directly in the viewer's line of sight, but off to the sides, so that there is literally nothing in front of the beholder—into a single three-dimensional image that has no physical existence, no referent in the material world. Though Brewster had not yet invented his stereoscope when he wrote *Natural Magic*, it contains the basic premise that vision does not rely on the external world:

> Dr. Hibbert has shown that spectral apparitions are nothing more than ideas or recollected images of the mind, which in certain states of bodily indisposition have been rendered more vivid than actual impressions; or to use other words, that the pictures in the "mind's eye" are more vivid than the pictures in the body's eye. This principle has been placed by Dr. Hibbert beyond the reach of doubt; but I propose to go much further, and to show that the "mind's eye" is actually the body's eye, and that the retina is the common tablet on which both classes of impressions are painted. . . . Nor is this true merely in the case of spectral illusions: it holds good of all ideas recalled by the memory or created by the imagination. (53–54)[39]

Brewster is saying here that "pictures in the mind" and objects in the external world are registered on the retina in analogous ways. Even remembered or imagined images have a somatic manifestation, for the retina is "the common tablet" shared by mind and body. In proposing that "the 'mind's eye' is actually the body's eye," Brewster widens the net, as it were, so that the arbitrary relation between sensation and stimuli includes not only physical excitations but mental ones as well. Spectral apparitions—images of the mind—are therefore as real to the retina as any other type of vision.

In Brewster's insistence that "the 'mind's eye' is actually the body's eye," we can begin to see the logic by which Ellison's concern with the mortal "eyes which behold" becomes consistent with Poe's notion that the poetic sentiment is best apprehended in the body's transcendence. In isolating and addressing the organ of the eye, the landscape—and the text that contains it—simulates an experience so purely optical that other physical senses such as touch are folded into the visual. The landscape (the domain of Arnheim) and the text ("The Domain of Arnheim") treat the human eye in the same way that scientists of Poe's day did—as simultaneously material and disembodied—inducing a state of transcendence in the visitor/reader that coincides with the ideal state of receptivity to the poetic sentiment. The science of vision is thus completely compatible with Poe's notions of poetic transcendence and, in fact, provides the mechanisms by which that transcendence might be induced. And if, as Brewster asserts, "the 'mind's eye' is actually the body's eye," there is no reason to maintain the distinction between viewer and reader or between landscape and text, which the text works so manifestly to collapse. In Brewster's view, objects in the physical landscape and their representations in the reader's mind share equal status on the "common tablet" of the retina. To read, to create a "picture in the mind," is in effect to see.

Finally, then, Brewster's assurance that "pictures in the mind" are as real to the eye as worldly objects provides a scientific rationale for Poe's well-known formulation about reading: that "during the hour of perusal, the soul of the reader is at the writer's control" (*ER* 586). Brewster explains that "with persons of studious habits, who are much occupied with the operations of their own minds, the mental pictures are much more distinct than in ordinary persons; and in the midst of abstract thought, external objects even cease to make any impression on the retina" (*NM* 55). In Poe's view, the author is responsible for creating the conditions under which external objects and events cease to make impressions on the retina and therefore cease to interfere with the mental pictures suggested by the text. He prescribes the circumscription of space and the creation of a single effect as the techniques most likely to create these conditions. "By such means," writes Poe, "with such care and skill, a picture is at length painted which leaves in the mind of him who contemplates it with a kindred art, a sense of the fullest satisfaction" (*ER* 586). Though Poe notoriously disliked the use of allegory, I am tempted to conclude that "The Domain of Arnheim" gives us a narrator who, in guiding the visitor to Arnheim through the engulfing three-dimensional space of the text's simulated landscape, allegorizes the act of reading as the reception of optical illusions. As the "literary histrio" who orchestrates this experience of textual optical effects, Poe demonstrates the way a text might enact its own kind of natural magic.

NOTES

1. Edgar Allan Poe, "The Domain of Arnheim," in *Edgar Allan Poe: Tales and Sketches*, ed. Thomas Ollive Mabbott et al., 3 vols. (Cambridge: Belknap, 1969–1978), 3: 1273. Unless noted, all of Poe's tales are from Mabbott, and will be cited by page number parenthetically in the text.
2. Edgar Allan Poe, "The Poetic Principle," in *Edgar Allan Poe: Essays and Reviews*, ed. G. R. Thompson (New York: Library of America, 1984), 77. *Essays and Reviews* will be cited parenthetically as *ER*.
3. Zen chants and the recitation of the rosary are other examples of the contemplative mode. Thanks to Steven R. Nuss for helping me think about this point.
4. Other examples are "The Facts in the Case of M. Valdemar" and Poe's three dialogues, "The Conversation of Eiros and Charmion," "The Colloquy of Monos and Una," and "The Power of Words," in which knowledge of or unity with the eternal is hastened through the abandonment of the body in death.
5. Jeffrey A. Hess, "Sources and Aesthetics of Poe's Landscape Fiction," *American Quarterly* 22, no. 2 (Summer 1970): 177–89. Mabbott notes that Poe quoted directly from "American Landscape Gardening," an article that appeared in *Arcturus* in June 1841 (Mabbott 1: 702).
6. Catherine Rainwater, "Poe's Landscape Tales and the 'Picturesque' Tradition," *The Southern Literary Journal* 16, no. 2 (Spring 1984): 30–43.
7. Though Ellison's theories allude to the language of the picturesque, it is not clear that he desires to create a picturesque garden. When he chooses a site for his domain, he explicitly rejects one that affords a "panoramic prospect" even though it contains "all of the true elements of the picturesque" (1278). To complicate matters, Ellison then suggests that this "prospect" is marked by "grandeur" and an "excess of . . . glory," features that characterize the sublime rather than the picturesque. Whether Poe is mocking Ellison or theorists of the picturesque is difficult to determine.

8. Poe writes: "Taste informs us of the Beautiful while the Moral Sense is regardful of Duty. Of this latter, while Conscience teaches the obligation, and Reason the expediency, Taste contents herself with displaying her charms:—waging war on vice solely on the ground of her deformity—her disproportion—her animosity to the fitting, to the appropriate, to the harmonious—in a word, to Beauty" (*ER* 76). Thus, taste has only an indirect relation to morality. In viewing Ellison's garden as morally neutral, I implicitly agree with Hess, who argues that Poe's landscape stories are "by no means evidence that Poe had faith in the possibility of artistic perfectability" (Hess, "Sources and Aesthetics," 178). For a full discussion of Poe's opposition to the doctrine of human perfectibility, see Richard Fusco, "Poe and the Perfectibility of Man," *Poe Studies* 19, no. 1 (June 1986): 1–6.

9. Rainwater quotes Joseph Addison's interest in "the eye of the beholder" ("Poe's Landscape Tales," 38). For an extended discussion of Addison's focus on the eye in his discussions of the imagination in *The Spectator* (June 21 through July 3, 1712, nos. 411–21), see Walter John Hipple, Jr., *The Beautiful, the Sublime, and the Picturesque in Eighteenth-Century British Aesthetic Theory* (Carbondale: Southern Illinois University Press, 1957), 13–24. Addison's thought helps lay the groundwork for writing about the picturesque.

10. Christopher Hussey, *The Picturesque: Studies in a Point of View* (London: Frank Cass and Company Limited, 1983 [1927]), 4.

11. Martin Price, "The Picturesque Moment," in *From Sensibility to Romanticism: Essays Presented to Frederick A. Pottle*, ed. Frederick W. Hilles and Harold Bloom (New York: Oxford University Press, 1965), 260. For a discussion of the literary importance of the picturesque that concurs with Price and Hussey, see Nancy Armstrong, *Fiction in the Age of Photograph: The Legacy of British Realism* (Cambridge, MA: Harvard University Press, 1999), 32–74.

12. E. W. Pitcher argues persuasively that in order to envision the garden, Poe first needed to understand how a work of art might partake simultaneously of the divine and the human, a question Poe pursues in his colloquies. See "The Arnheim Trilogy: Cosmic Landscapes in the Shadow of Poe's *Eureka*," *The Canadian Review of American Studies* 6, no. 1 (Spring 1975): 27–35.

13. From Poe, "Elizabeth Barrett Browning" (1845). Poe is citing Bacon, and as Mabbott notes, he substitutes "exquisite" for "excellent" in Bacon's original, which reads, "There is no excellent beauty that hath not some strangeness in the proportion" (quoted in Mabbott, 2: 331). Poe repeats the formulation often. See "Ligeia" (1838) (Mabbott, 2: 311–12); "William Ellery Channing" (1843) (*ER* 460); *Marginalia* (1846 and 1849) (*ER* 1381, 1445); "Anastatic Printing" (1845), *The Complete Works of Edgar Allan Poe*, vol. 14, ed. James A. Harrison (New York: AMS Press, 1965), 153.

14. Joan Dayan, *Fables of the Mind: An Inquiry into Poe's Fiction* (New York: Oxford University Press, 1987), 89.

15. Kent Ljungquist correlates the "picturesque intricacy of the landscape" with "the problematic nature of the narrator's vision." See *The Ground and the Fair: Poe's Landscape Aesthetics and Pictorial Techniques* (Potomac, MD: Scripta Humanistica, 1984), 132.

16. Jonathan Crary, *Techniques of the Observer: On Vision and Modernity in the Twentieth Century* (Cambridge, MA: MIT Press, 1990), 9.

17. Crary, *Techniques of the Observer*, 89–91. Müller discusses these phenomena in *Elements of Physiology* (1833).

18. I am indebted to Anna Henchman for the following list of ways the human visual system perceives distance: stereopsis (each eye provides a different "view" to the brain, which combines them into a three-dimensional image), the relative size of objects, perspective (the convergence of parallel lines in the distance), clues from lights and shadows, and parallax (the relative motion of near and far objects). Henchman relies on the writings of Brewster and Hermann von Helmholtz for this list; see also David Hubel, *Eye, Brain, and Vision* (New York: Scientific American Library: W. H.

Freeman, 1988); Richard L. Gregory, *Eye and Brain: The Psychology of Seeing* (Princeton: Princeton University Press, 1990); and Richard L. Gregory, *The Intelligent Eye* (New York: McGraw Hill, 1970).

19. See for instance Mary-Jo Haronian, "Margaret Fuller's Visions," *ESQ* 44, nos. 1–2 (1998): 35–59; Larry J. Reynolds, "Subjective Vision, Romantic History, and the Return of the 'Real': The Case of Margaret Fuller and the Roman Republic," *South Central Review* 21, no. 1 (Spring 2004): 1–17; Laura Dassow Walls, *Emerson's Life in Science: The Culture of Truth* (Ithaca: Cornell University Press, 2003); and Eric Wilson, *Emerson's Sublime Science* (New York: St. Martin's Press, 1999). Thanks to Noelle Baker for reminding me that the Transcendentalists were as strongly influenced by the new visual paradigms as Poe was, using them to draw slightly different conclusions about transcendent vision.

20. Ellison's garden remains remarkably true to his intention of addressing "the eye which beholds it," almost to the complete exclusion of the other senses. The domain is silent until the later stages of the journey, when the landscape emits "melancholy music" from an "unseen origin" (3: 1281). The journey then culminates in "a gush of entrancing melody" and "an oppressive sense of strange sweet odor" (3: 1283). At only one other point on the journey is the reader made aware of senses other than vision. Early on, flowers in the landscape present a "sea of odorous and fluctuating color" (3: 1280). Even here, the flowers' smell is reconstituted in visual terms as "odorous . . . color." Immediately following this passage, all of the senses seem to collapse in on one another in an inchoate impression of "richness, warmth, color, quietude, uniformity, softness, delicacy, daintiness, voluptuousness, and a miraculous extremeness of culture" (1280).

21. The first American edition of *Natural Magic* was published in New York by Harper's in 1832. All citations here are from Sir David Brewster, *Letters on Natural Magic, Addressed to Sir Walter Scott, Bart* (New York: Harper and Brothers, 1843), which will be cited parenthetically as *NM* hereafter.

22. Poe's debt to Brewster extends from 1833, with "MS Found in a Bottle," until the end of his career, with the publication of *Eureka* in 1848. For the most complete list of Poe's borrowings from Brewster, see Roberta Sharp, "Poe's Chapters on 'Natural Magic,'" in *Poe and His Times: The Artist and His Milieu*, ed. Benjamin Franklin Fisher, IV (Baltimore: The Edgar Allan Poe Society, 1990), 154–66. See also Burton Pollin, "'MS. Found in a Bottle' and Sir David Brewster's *Letters*: A Source," *Poe Studies* 15 (1982): 40–41; William K. Wimsatt, Jr., "Poe and the Chess Automaton," *American Literature* 11, no. 2 (May 1939): 138–51; Walter Shear, "Poe's Use of an Idea about Perception," *American Notes and Queries* 21 (May/June 1983): 134–36; and William J. Scheick, "An Intrinsic Luminosity: Poe's Use of Platonic and Newtonian Optics," in *American Literature and Science*, ed. Robert J. Scholnick (Lexington: University Press of Kentucky, 1992), 77–93.

23. Quoted in Mabbott, 2: 573; Mabbott finds this passage in an early edition of Brewster's *Optics* (Edinburgh, 1828), 43. David Brewster, *Optics* (London: 1851), 297. See also Mabbott, 2: 573, who finds this passage in the first American edition of *Optics* (Philadelphia, 1833), 249, and locates Herschel's original discussion of oblique vision in *The Philosophical Transactions of the Royal Society* part III, 1825, 15–16. Mabbott also traces most of the appearances of indirect vision in Poe's fiction, including in "Al Aaraaf" (1829), "Hans Phaall"(1835), reviews of Coleridge (1831) and Alexander Slidell (1836), *The Narrative of Arthur Gordon Pym* (1838), "The Murders in the Rue Morgue" (1841), and "The Island of the Fay" (1841). In addition to these instances, Poe uses the trope of indirect vision in "Arnheim," a review of Macauley (1841), *Eureka* (1848), and the *Marginalia* (entry for June 1849).

24. David Ketterer, *The Rationale of Deception in Poe* (Baton Rouge: Louisiana State University Press, 1979), 1–45.

25. Poe similarly retains the connection to optics and astronomy when he uses the trope in "Hans Phaall." Hans muses that "in the contemplation of heavenly bodies it struck me very forcibly that I could not distinguish a star with nearly as much preci-

sion, when I gazed upon it with earnest, direct and undeviating attention, as when I suffered my eye only to glance in its vicinity alone. I was not, of course, at that time aware that this apparent paradox was occasioned by the centre of the visual area being less susceptible of feeble impressions of light than the exterior portions of the retina." See "Hans Phaall: A Tale," *Southern Literary Messenger* 10, no. 1 (June 1835), 567.

26. Alan Trachtenberg, "Mirror in the Marketplace: American Responses to the Daguerreotype, 1839-1851," in *The Daguerreotype in America: A Sesquicentennial Celebration*, ed. John Wood (Iowa City: University of Iowa Press, 1989), 65.

27. Quoted in Samuel Irenaeus Prime, *The Life of Samuel F. B. Morse, LL.D., Inventor of the Electro-Magnetic Telegraph* (New York: D. Appleton and Company, 1875), 401.

28. Edgar Allan Poe, "The Daguerreotype" (1840), reprinted in *Classic Essays on Photography*, ed. Alan Trachtenberg (New Haven: Leete's Island Books, 1980), 38.

29. This fact is also a major point of dispute between Charles Wheatstone, who invented the reflecting stereoscope, and Brewster. See Wheatstone's "Contributions to the Physiology of Vision: Part the First: On Some Remarkable, and Hitherto Unobserved, Phenomena of Binocular Vision," *Philosophical Transactions of the Royal Society of London* part 2 (1838): 371–94, where he argues against the eyes' movement as a playing a role in binocular vision, and Brewster's response in *The Stereoscope: Its History, Theory, and Construction, with Its Application to the Fine and Useful Arts and to Education* (London: John Murray, 1856), 20–28.

30. See Crary's discussion of the difference between viewing a painting and a stereoscopic image on 124–25.

31. Oliver Wendell Holmes, "The Stereoscope and the Stereograph" (1859), reprinted in Trachtenberg, *Classic Essays*, 75.

32. For a chronology of the stereoscope, see Brewster, *The Stereoscope*, 5–37. At least two people, Wheatstone and a Mr. Elliot of Edinburgh, exhibited stereoscopic images before photography was invented. Photographic processes, because they produce near-exact duplicates of images, advanced stereoscopic technology tremendously. Early stereoscopic images were made in both daguerreotype and paper formats.

33. See Margaret Alterton, *Origins of Poe's Critical Theory* (New York: Russell and Russell, Inc., 1965), 134. Poe used some of the notes made during those years when he wrote *Eureka* as well.

34. Wheatstone, "Contributions," 372. Wheatstone is quoting Leonardo da Vinci's *Trattato della Pittura*. See also Brewster's discussion of how easily cameos and intaglios can be converted one into the other in *Natural Magic*, 96–103.

35. For example, in "The Sphinx" (1846), a monster "of hideous conformation" (1247) is revealed to be a tiny insect when the viewer is made aware that the size of the animal is due wholly to his nearness to it. The lesson is almost the same as in "Rue Morgue," that "the principle source of error in all human investigations, lay in the liability of the understanding to under-rate or to over-rate the importance of an object, through mere misadmeasurement of its propinquity" (3: 1249–50). The illusion is purely optical.

36. Tom Gunning, "Landscape and the Fantasy of Moving Pictures: Early Cinema's Phantom Rides," in *Cinema and Landscape*, ed. Graeme Harper and Jonathan Rayner (Wayne State University Press, 2007). On railway journeys more generally, see Wolfgang Schivelbusch, *The Railway Journey: The Industrialization of Time and Space in the Nineteenth Century* (Berkeley: University of California Press, 1986). On the connection between "Arnheim" and both industrialization and westward expansion, see Jules Zanger, "Poe's American Garden: 'The Domain of Arnheim,'" *American Transcendental Quarterly* 50 (Spring 1981): 93–103. For an analysis that contrasts Poe and Emerson's views on the relations between man/culture and nature, see Jochen Achilles, "Edgar Allan Poe's Dreamscapes and the Transcendentalist View of Nature," *Amerikastudien/ American Studies: A Quarterly* 40, no. 4 (1995); 553–73.

37. Coleridge makes use of a similar optical illusion in a poem Poe knew well, "Constancy to an Ideal Object." There, Coleridge refers to the famous natural phenomenon called the Brocken Spectre: "the viewless snow-mist weaves a glistening haze,"

which produces "an image with a glory round its head." See Samuel Taylor Coleridge, *Samuel Taylor Coleridge: The Major Works*, ed. H. J. Jackson (Oxford: Oxford University Press, 2000), 123. Thanks to Peter Norberg for pointing out this connection.

38. Hess, "Sources and Aesthetics," 184.

39. See Scheick, "An Intrinsic Luminosity," for a discussion of the way Brewster's notion that "the 'mind's eye' is actually the body's eye" affects Poe's representation of narrators and characters such as Egaeus in "Berenice," who cannot distinguish between dreams and reality.

TEN

"A Species of Literature Almost Beneath Contempt": Edgar Allan Poe and the World of Literary Competitions

Leon Jackson

In 1829, two down at heel poets met in a bookstore in Baltimore and traded insults. Their dispute might have ended in blows or a duel, but before it could do so, a different sort of challenge was issued. "I'll bet you five dollars," said one, "I can write more stanzas in one hour than you can in a day." The other picked up the gauntlet with a sneer. Pencils and paper were produced and so began one of the period's stranger "tourna-ment[s] of rhymes." The challenger was the wretchedly obscure John Lofland, also known as the Milford Bard; his competitor was Edgar Allan Poe.[1] Familiar though we are with Poe's contentious personality, and even with his habit of competing with his peers, we have failed until now to appreciate the extent to which Poe was also engaged in the world of formal literary competitions. Over the course of his career, Poe acted as a competition entrant, organizer, and judge; he reviewed prize-winning plays and poetry; he became involved in competition scandals, lawsuits, even fistfights; and, crucially, he wove the central themes of competition into his poetry and fiction, as well as into his nonfictional prose. Few figures, in fact, were involved so intimately in so many aspects of the competitive world as Poe, and, importantly, perhaps none more fully dramatized the tensions inherent in literary competitions.

Poe's engagement with the world of competitions is more than a foot-note to literary history, moreover, because to an extent that we have failed to appreciate, writing competitions were themselves a vitally important part of the antebellum literary terrain. The impact of competitions was immense. Those who entered and won included writers as prominent as Susan Warner, Lydia Sigourney, Sarah Hale, Nathaniel P. Willis, Henry Wadsworth Longfellow, William Cullen Bryant, John Greenleaf Whittier, Sarah Helen Whitman, and Harriet Beecher Stowe. Indeed, when we include the writing competitions organized by schools, academies, and colleges, then it would be fair to say that almost every American author with a diploma or degree participated in this mode of economic and cultural exchange. Nor was the competitive impulse limited to literary productions alone. There were competitions organized to encourage animal breeding, agricultural innovation, scientific development, and domestic manufactures. There were prize jellies and jams, prizefights, prize races, and prizes for binding books and setting types. Early national, and, especially, antebellum America were dominated by a culture of competitions.[2]

Considering competitions helps us see a new—an other—Poe, but, still more, considering Poe helps us understand something new about competitions. A curiously torn figure, Poe could neither embrace literary competitions nor leave them wholly alone. When he won, he endorsed their operating assumptions enthusiastically; when he lost, he submitted them to blistering and uniquely insightful critiques. Finally, Poe not only participated in the world of literary competitions, but he also hastened their transformation, treating them less as chances for personal improvement and more as opportunities for financial gain. Poe, in other words, offers us a unique vantage point from which to consider this forgotten but immensely important activity.

A VERY BRIEF HISTORY OF COMPETITION THEORY AND PRACTICE

When competitions first began to appear in America in the 1780s, their appeal and success were explained by reference to two psychological drives with which Poe would have been intimately familiar: these were emulation and approbation. Although emulation today suggests the desire to imitate, in the eighteenth century it was defined, according to John Adams, as "imitation and something more—a desire not only to equal or resemble, but to excel." Emulation, in other words, was not the desire to do one's best but to surpass the best of another, even while working within a shared, or imitative, frame of reference. It was regarded as a powerful, and indeed almost uncontrollable, impulse. The urge to emulate, however, was driven by what pundits believed to be the still more fundamental and compulsive need for approbation, which Adams described as "the desire to be observed, considered, esteemed, praised, beloved, and admired." Individuals sought to emulate one another in order to garner the approbation that success brought them.[3] Emulation was widely praised stimulating every achievement in the arts and sciences and also for its capacity to ennoble those who were moved by it, yet it was feared, too, for its tendency to promote ruthlessness, hostility, and envy, and—in those who did not succeed—a hopeless loss of motivation. Approbation, likewise, was seen as a powerful spur to effort and, at the same time, as a selfish and superficial impulse. Emulation has been well described as a "slippery virtue that always hovered on the brink of a vice," and the same might be said of approbativeness too. Rather than rejecting either of them, however eighteenth-century thinkers sought to harness them and play off one against the other through what Adams called "the checks of emulation and the balances of rivalry." Literary competitions were just such a system of checks and balances, in which one passion (the urge for approbation) was used to propel another (the urge to excel).[4]

The competitive ideal informed a number of informal literary jousts that flourished through the eighteenth century, such as Crambo, or verse capping, in which a group of friends took turns adding improvised lines to a group poem, the players being eliminated as they faltered or failed to come up with a suitable rhyme.[5] Formal literary competitions differed from such games, however, in two important ways. In the first place, they entailed prizes, sometimes of money. Although the sums could be fairly substantial, such premiums were meant only to be symbolic—to give some tangible manifestation to the approbation the winner would receive. Money was never the point of a competition; the goal, rather, was emulation, and, indeed, to the extent that everyone did their best, the assumptions was that everyone "won." Secondly, formal competitions required judges who were not, as in Crambo, also players. Competition judging was predicated on Enlightenment notions of scrupulous, disinterested objectivity, impeccable taste, and absolute fairness, all of which were guaranteed by the gentility of the judges and anonymity (or pseudonymity) of the entrants. Of course, not everyone necessarily agreed with the judges of a competition, and one of the genres that grew out of the competitive world was the volume of "rejected addresses," the first example being Horace and James Smith's spoof volume of that title, published in England in 1812.[6] By that time, competitions were just beginning to take off in America. By the 1820s, they had become common—fuelled by a vibrant nationalist impulse—and poet Charles Sprague, who won every contest he entered, became a household name. They became still more prominent in the 1830s, after actor Edwin Forrest launched and bankrolled lavishly a series of contests for plays in which he would act. Between 1828 and 1852, there were no less than twenty playwriting contests organized in New York City alone. While competitions eventually generated hostility and boredom, in the antebellum period, few aspiring authors were either able, or willing, to ignore them. Poe, certainly, could not.

"I WOULD BEG YOU TO JUDGE ME IMPARTIALLY"

Poe's engagement with competitiveness began early. His classmates at Joseph Clarke's academy in Richmond remembered the thirteen-year-old Poe as being "eager for distinction" and "inclined to be imperious," while Clarke himself invoked the textbook definition of emulation in describing his young charge as being "ambitious to excel." In 1821 or 1822, Poe won his first competition: a public elocution contest, or exhibition, held in Richmond. By the time he entered William Burke's academy in 1823, he had become an expert at "capping verses," and it was at this time, too, that he swam an alleged six miles up the James River against the tide, in deliberate emulation of Lord Byron's famous swim of the Hellespont. (Byron was, of course, and would remain for some time, *the* figure whom Americans emulated.) Even at the University of Virginia, Poe showed no let up in his competitive drive. He "grew noted as a debater," as one student recalled, and also participated in boxing and jumping competitions.[7]

Poe's relentless drive to compete and succeed, according to Kenneth Silverman, can be traced back directly to his status as an orphan and to his need to be recognized and approved of by figures of authority. It was a lifelong and, apparently, insatiable hunger. Years later, a friend recalled of Poe that "no man living loved the praises of others better than he did . . . whenever I happened to communicate to him anything touching his abilities as a writer, his bosom would heave like a troubled sea."[8] What the world of competitions gave him was a stage on which to act out these deep-seated needs; what the concepts of emulation and approbation gave others was a convenient language with which to explain his actions. So far from seeming aberrant, then, Poe's emulative drive was seen as, in fact, quite admirable, at least initially.

Unfortunately for Poe, his chief judge—at least in his own mind—would always be his guardian, John Allan, a bitter man who was determined not to see him win. Poe's early letters to Allan are filled with anguished pleas, in which he asks to be judged, but flinches from the judgment: "you can judge for yourself," "I will give you the reason . . . then judge," "suspend your judgement until you hear *of* me again," "I begged that you would suspend any judgement," "If you conclude upon giving me a *trial* please enclose me the letter," "I would beg you to judge me impartially," and, revealingly, "I have offended only in asking your approbation."[9] But Allan was unwilling to give his approbation. An orphan himself, he bore an unresolved grudge at his own foster father's failure to support his intellectual development, and he seemed determined to inflict on Poe the neglect he had himself received. No matter what Poe achieved, it was rarely ever enough to merit his flinty foster father's approval, and as Poe entered his mid teens, their relationship grew increasingly tense. A man who could in private admit to his own "pride and ambition," Allan came to revile those same traits in his young charge, and he left Poe with a painfully skewed view of the world: one in which he felt it necessary to win the approval of those who judged him, but which at the same left him convinced that he would never be judged fairly. Life, for Poe, was a rigged competition in which he nonetheless had no choice but to participate. [10]

Fittingly enough, Poe's first published poem, "Tamerlane," which appeared mere months after he had fled Allan's household, both denounced "the folly of even *risking* the best feelings of the heart at the shrine of Ambition" and at the same time vaunted that very impulse as a means of achieving greatness. It was, in fact, a text utterly characteristic of Poe's ambivalent feelings concerning competitiveness, and it would directly inform his engagement with the world of formal literary competitions. [11]

Poe makes a fascinating case study, then, both because he felt such a powerful need to compete with others, and because he betrayed an equally powerful contempt for such competitions and, indeed, for competitiveness as a whole. His conflicted feelings, moreover, were only exacerbated by the fact that he tended to enter writing contests at moments of acute financial and emotional vulnerability, when the promise of winning prizes seemed to hold out redemption on several distinct levels: monetary, vocational, and emotional. The prize money, for Poe, was *never* merely symbolic. The great irony for Poe is that his feelings about competitions were so wholly conflicted that even when he was a winner he lost, never able to accept fully either the premises or the practitioners. Yet Poe's loss is our gain, so to speak, for his curious blend of blindness and insight concerning the world of competitions makes him an almost unique informant: engaged and detached, starry-eyed and cynical, both in and out of the game.

1831: A DECIDED LOSS

Poe's entry into the world of adult competitions came in May 1831, when he learned of a contest in the Philadelphia *Saturday Courier* offering a premium of one hundred dollars for the best American tale submitted. [12] Poe submitted five. That he was driven by something like emulation and approbation is apparent, but he was driven just as much if not more by poverty, for he was in desperate straits, living in a tiny Baltimore apartment with his impoverished aunt, Maria Clemm, and several others. At a period in time when it was common for periodical authors to receive little more than two dollars a page, the opportunity to win one hundred dollars must have been hard to resist.[13]

Poe's decision to enter the competition, however, should not be taken as an indication that he approved of such events. Many dozens of contests were advertised over the twenty or so years Poe was writing to sustain himself, but he entered only three of which we are aware, and in every case he entered at a time of absolute financial desperation, treating the contests as a high stakes gamble. Indeed, there is reason to believe that he experienced a deep humiliation at having to hawk his wares in such a way. That Poe's feelings about competitive success were conflicted was apparent from the tales themselves, one of which, "A Decided Loss," featured a few well-placed swipes at Edwin Forrest, John Augustus Stone, and their prize-winning script, *Metamora* (1829). Whatever he thought of Indian dramas—and the evidence is that he thought very little of them indeed—it is clear that he resented the pair's prize-driven celebrity. The approbation and money that came with being a star were precisely what Poe wanted, and lacked, and therefore despised. The fact that one of the *Courier*'s judges—Richard Penn Smith—was a friend of Forrest's who had himself just won (and very likely fraudulently) a Forrest prize of one thousand dollars for his play *Caius Marius* would have galled Poe deeply, and simply reinforced his conviction that all competitions were rigged, had he been aware of it.[14] Poe, as it turns out, was neither as lucky, nor as well connected, as Penn Smith. He lost the competition and, with it, control over his five stories; while all of them were published in the *Courier* in 1832, he received no money from them and, besides, very little cachet, for his name appeared over only the first, and none indicated that they had been competition entries. If, as I am arguing, Poe entered the world of competitions with a well-entrenched prejudice against them on the score of fairness, then his first experience simply reinforced such beliefs.

1833: A QUALIFIED LOSS

By 1833, Poe was in yet more desperate straits, writing to Allan in April of that year that he was "perishing—absolutely perishing for want of aid." Allan never replied. Starved for both attention and money, Poe could hardly have ignored the news that the *Baltimore Saturday Visiter* was also running a competition, this time with a fifty dollar premium for the best short story and twenty-five for the best poem submitted. He knew that the competition again represented a serious gamble. If he won in both the prose and poetry divisions, he stood to make seventy-five urgently needed dollars—or, if he chose, two "Silver medals"—but if he lost, his submissions automatically became the "property of the Publishers." Risking much, Poe again employed a saturation technique, sending in six short stories and a poem entitled "The Coliseum."[15]

Ironically, the six tales Poe submitted to the *Visiter* formed the nucleus of his new and still unpublished story collection, *Tales of the Folio Club*, which evinced a deeply critical suspicion of the entire axiological process on which literary contests were predicated. The narrative that frames the collection describes the inner workings of the intensely competitive Folio Club. Each month, the narrator of the frame explains, the members of the Club convene over food and wine, read aloud their stories, critique one another, and then vote on the works read. "Much rivalry will ensue," he adds, for the members of the Club compete not merely to win, but also to avoid losing, since while the winner is made club President, the loser is compelled to pay for the food and wine at the club's next meeting. The organization of the Club's meetings seems a striking and pointed commentary on Poe's view of competitions. In the first place, it suggests that he saw the competitive world as an incestuous clique where authors wrote for, and judged, one another. More important still, it indicates that Poe saw contests less as noble and emulatory events in which, to the extent that one tried one's best, "everyone won" and more as zero sum games with losers as well as winners. Losing, indeed, seemed to be both costly and humiliating. When the narrator of the frame loses the contest, however, he does not submit to the decision of the members; rather, he grabs all of the manuscripts, "and, rushing from the house, determines to appeal, by printing the whole, from the decision of the Club, to that of the public." It is these stories, then, together with the Club's comments, that comprise Poe's volume, and from which he selected six for the *Visiter*.[16]

While scholars have seen the roots of Poe's projected volume in works as diverse as Plato's *Symposium*, Thomas Moore's *Lalla Rookh* (1817), and Washington Irving's *Tales of a Traveler* (1824), the parallels with the rejected address tradition are hard to miss. Like the aggrieved participants in that genre, the narrator of the Folio Club collection seeks to shift the center of axiological gravity from a small group, or club, of judges to the opinion of "the public." Poe's decision to frame his narrative in this way was anything but arbitrary; he was familiar with the works of Horace and James Smith and more generally with the history of British theater, so his reliance on this axiological maneuver, and especially in the context of his own entry into a literary contest, is telling indeed. If nothing else, it suggests his deep ambivalence about competitions and makes clear the irony of his engagement in a zero-sum authorial economy in whose fairness he reposed so little trust.[17]

In the instance, Poe ended up being both winner *and* loser. The committee of judges—whose meeting sounded remarkably like that of the Folio Club, complete with cigars, wine, and balloting—unanimously voted Poe's story collection the best, selecting one tale, "MS. Found in a

Bottle," for the prize. The judges also admired Poe's poem and they came close to voting for it too, but in the end they settled on another, entitled "The Song of the Wind," written by one Henry Wilton. [18]

Poe, recalled *Visiter* editor John Hill Hewitt many years later, was "greedy for fame, as well as in need of money," and in winning this competition, he managed to gain a combination of both. [19] Desperately as he needed the money, however, he seemed to need fame, and the approval it suggested, still more. In 1835 he sent Thomas Willis White, the proprietor of the *Southern Literary Messenger*, a copy of the *Visiter* containing the judges' warm praise of his work and begged him to have it "copied into any of the Richmond papers." White immediately printed it in his own magazine. Indeed, Poe continued to harp on his competition successes long after others might have left them behind, and he milked them for all they were worth. An 1843 biographical sketch ghost-written by Poe claimed that the author had received "first honours" at the University of Virginia, "headed every class" at West Point, jumped "the distance of twenty-one feet, six inches, on a dead level, with a run of twenty yards," swam the James in an effort that made "Byron's paddle across the Hellespont" look like "mere child's play in comparison," and, significantly, won "*both* premiums" in the *Visiter* contest. Almost every statement was a falsehood. [20]

In fact Poe might well have felt that he *had* won the poetry as well as the prose division, for shortly after the awards were announced, he discovered that the poetry winner, "Henry Wilton," was none other than John Hill Hewitt himself, the editor of the very paper in which the competition had been run. He discovered, too, that the judges had initially favored his poem over Hewitt's but had felt uncomfortable awarding all the prizes to one entrant and so had given Hewitt's poem first place instead. [21] The fact that Hewitt had entered pseudonymously and that his pseudonym was not even known to the judges until after they had selected his poem seemed irrelevant to Poe. Attuned, as he was, to even the slightest taint of bias in the act of judgment and, moreover, predisposed to see competitions as zero sum games, Poe felt that, in some ill-defined way, Hewitt had defrauded him of a prize that was rightly his.

Days later, Poe confronted the editor on the street and an ugly scene ensued. "You have used underhanded means, sir, to obtain that prize over me," said Poe. Hewitt vehemently denied the accusation. "Then why did you keep back your real name?" Poe persisted. Hewitt explained that he had had his "reasons," but Poe pushed on. "But you tampered with the committee, sir," he said. "The committee are gentlemen," retorted Hewitt, "and above being tampered with; and if you say that you insult them." This was too much for Poe. "I agree that the committee are gentlemen," he said, "but I cannot place *you* in that category." On hearing this, Hewitt turned and punched Poe in the face, and a fight was only averted by the interference of friends. It was hardly the most decorous conclusion to what was, in many respects, the most important moment in Poe's literary coming of age, but in some sense it is typical. The committee, for Poe, was both above reproach and yet also capable of being tampered with. Winning a prize was both priceless (to the extent that it validated Poe) and worthless (to the extent that it could also, for whatever reason, validate a scoundrel like Hewitt). When Poe's poem was reprinted in the *Southern Literary Messenger* two years later, Poe very pointedly retitled it, "The Coliseum, a Prize Poem."[22]

As the aftermath of the *Visiter* affair suggests, Poe evinced a curious double consciousness regarding competitions. When he won, he not only endorsed the justice of the judges, but he bragged endlessly of his attainments, magnified them, and at times simply fabricated 'facts' that were not true. When, by contrast, he lost, or when he was commenting on competitions in which he was not an entrant, he cast scorn on the proceedings in their entirety, vilifying the judges, belittling the entrants, and ridiculing the winner. At times, he offered up witheringly cynical and, the truth be told, devastatingly accurate critiques of the hypocrisy and deceit on which many such competitions were based. The fact that he so often saw deceit where none was to be detected does not mean that his analyses of those situations that *were* fraudulent lacked bite. They did not.

In the case of the *Visiter* competition, for example, Poe was perhaps right to suspecting dishonesty but wrong laying the charge at Hewitt's door. In submitting his poem pseudonymously, Hewitt had, in fact, been operating strictly within the conventions of the traditional competition; in choosing to spread the wealth among the entrants, however, the judges had not.[23] (That Poe did not criticize the judges was directly a result of their having awarded him first place in the story contest and, equally, of his continuing reliance on their largesse).

Of course, it is quite possible that both Hewitt *and* the judges colluded in rigging the competition, as Poe might have suspected deep down. If this was the case, it would have been neither the first nor the last time that such a fait accompli had taken place. Just six months after the announcement of the *Visiter* results, the *New Yorker* ran a similar contest, with a one hundred dollar premium for best short story and fifty dollars for the best poem and the best essay. Contest judge Lewis Gaylord Clark arranged for his friend, a Bowdoin College professor named Henry Wadsworth Longfellow to win the contest, but in the end, the panel (Clark, H. W. Herbert, and Samuel Woodworth) decided to give him only half the prize, the other being given out of pity to none other than Poe's recent publisher Eliza Leslie: a combination of deceit, then, and meddling.[24] Although it is highly unlikely that Poe ever learned of the machinations that took place in this event, he already had his eye on Clark and would very soon accuse him, and a small cadre of fellow writers, of orchestrating a generally corrupt clique that rigged everything from contests and contracts to puffs and plagiarism. One of the authors whom he accused of benefiting from this incestuous world of critics and editors was none other than Henry Wadsworth Longfellow.[25]

But the problem went further, in fact, than even this isolated incident. While there were honest competition judges, there were just as many — and probably more — who bent, if they did not outright break, the rules, typically though nepotism. Although there were few cut-and-dried cases of cheating, many savored of dishonesty and collusion. Consider: Nathaniel P. Willis won several poetry competitions in a newspaper edited by his father; Harriet Beecher won a prize in the school essay contest run by her sister Catharine; Judge James Hall later begged Harriet to enter a story in his *Western Literary Magazine* contest after deciding that the submissions entered on time were inadequate and then promptly awarded her first prize; Ann Stephens won first prize in a contest run by *Snowden's Ladies' Companion*, a journal she co-edited; and Edwin Forrest routinely awarded prizes to plays that had not yet been written, that had been written years earlier, or that had not been submitted formally to his contests.[26]

Such juxtapositions are highly suggestive of deceit or collusion but no more than that. Yet definitive evidence of competition rigging does exist. In 1847, Maine author Elizabeth Oakes Smith received a remarkable and remarkably frank letter from magazine editor Alice B. Neal. With little apology, Neal explained that her periodical, *The Gazette*, had organized a competition with a hefty $150 premium for the best tale on the American Revolution, and with only three weeks left before the deadline no submissions had been made that were worthy of the award. Completely unwilling to either cancel the contest or extend the deadline, Neal decided to commission a story from Smith. "Will you not be so good," asked Neal, "if previous engagements do not interfere — as to write one, for which we guarantee you shall receive the prize." Completely undaunted, Smith cranked out a story — "The Bald Eagle" — for which she was duly awarded first place. Poe's sense that committees were, from time to time, tampered with, turns out, then, not have been so far-fetched.[27]

When Poe began to write for the *Southern Literary Messenger* in late 1834, he was propelled in part by a campaign designed to expose this kind of literary fraud in all its manifestations, and while he did not challenge the results of competitions specifically during his tenure in Richmond, he would perhaps never have begun his campaign had it not been for his own competition disappointments. Poe raged against puffing, plagiarism, and the power of ruthless literary cliques. Even his benign essays, such as "Maelzel's Chess Player," were designed to unveil hidden machinations, or, to quote Willis himself, to reveal "who pulls the wire to all the literary puppets."[28] Upon firing Poe in 1836, *Messenger* owner Thomas W. White heaved a sigh of relief that he was now free of this self-appointed "Judge or Judge Advocate." Poe had, indeed, made it his mission to judge judges. All that remained now was for him to become, himself, a judge.[29]

1840: JUDGE OR JUDGE ADVOCATE

Poe's conflicted feelings concerning competitions and their judging were merely reinforced by his experiences as an editorial assistant for *Burton's Gentleman's Magazine* between 1839 and 1840. In November 1839, the magazine announced its own competition with one thousand dollars in prizes, editor William Burton's novel twist on the literary competition being to dispense altogether with the typical committee of judges, who, he opined, "generally select, unread, the effusion of the most popular candidate as the easiest method of discharging their onerous duties." The submissions in this case, he said, would be read "by the Editors alone." Poe was horrified, not because this scheme dispensed with even the semblance of objectivity held out by most competition organizers, but also because he had nothing but contempt for Burton's critical prowess. If Burton was to be judge, then everyone was in trouble. Poe suspected, too, that Burton intended not to make any awards, a suspicion that was simply reinforced when Burton decided to cancel the competition and sell his magazine. Several of the submissions were not returned and appeared later in *Graham's Magazine*, unpaid for. Poe's view from within the world of competitions was as disappointing as the view from without.[30]

Yet as we have seen, Poe was unable to walk away from the need to compete. Even as he was deploring the fraudulence of Burton's premium scheme in letters to friends, he was establishing his own informal and eccentric competition, which, much like Burton's, dispensed with a committee of judges in favor of a more singular form of adjudication. The venue for this contest was *Alexander's Weekly Messenger*, a newspaper at which Poe moonlighted between December 1839 and May 1840. (It was, fittingly enough, published by the same firm that issued *Burton's*.) In the issue for December 18, 1839, Poe claimed rather boldly that there was no cryptogram that he could not solve. "Let this be put to the test," he announced. "Let any one address us a letter in this way, and we pledge ourself to read it forthwith—however unusual or arbitrary may be the characters employed."[31] Poe's readers immediately leapt to the challenge, and his throwaway comment became a strange two-way competition: the readers challenging Poe to decode their ciphers, and Poe challenging his readers to figure out how he did it. Prizes, too, entered the equation, as Poe offered to reveal his secret in exchange for forty subscribers, and one reader promised him "ten subscribers and the cash" if he could solve his puzzle.[32]

Poe's "competition" differed from the usual events in many ways. In the first place, rather than pitting a group of entrants against one another, Poe sought to compete against the entrants, taking on all comers; as such, Poe's contest had absolutely nothing to do with emulation, which was meant to be a collectively ennobling venture. In the second place, where a typical contest involved acts of creation, Poe's claim was that he could take apart any cryptogram presented him; it was not an act of encoding but an instance of decoding, less creative, on other words, than destructive. Thirdly, and most significantly, Poe's contest was predicated on a deep-seated need to reveal precisely the kind pretense he saw going on in other competitions. For every cryptogram he solved, he showed several more to be based upon deceit or dishonesty: using inconsistent codes, foreign words, and so on. It was Poe's ideal competition: one in which he not only won (being the only competitor) but which, in so doing, he managed to defeat everyone else and show how mendacious and deceitful most of the entrants were. He was also the judge, passing summary judgment on the coding abilities of the entrants.[33]

Poe's dual strategy of critique and engagement continued into the 1840s when he became an editorial assistant at *Graham's Magazine*. It was at this time that he issued perhaps his sternest criticism of the competitions by attacking the nation's best known prize poet, Charles Sprague. In an 1841 review of Sprague's writings, Poe derided "Prize Odes for Festivals and Opening Nights of new theatres" as "a species of literature almost beneath contempt," noting only that inasmuch as "all prize articles are bad *ex officio*," the most that could be said of Sprague's "Shakespeare Ode" was that it was "the best of them." Angrily criticized by pundits in Boston, Poe repeated the claims again in 1842, describing the "Shakespeare Ode" as "mawkish, *passé*, and absurd," and noting that it was "just such a one as would have obtained its author an Etonian prize some forty or fifty years ago," an ironic comment for a man who had still not finished trumpeting his teenaged achievements as a jumper and swimmer. In a review of Robert Walsh's *Sketches of Conspicuous Living Characters of France*, published in April 1841, Poe continued his attack on competitions, noting several anecdotes in that text recounting instances in which French competition judges had defrauded authors of their rightfully won prizes.[34]

Again, however, and even as he denounced competitions as corrupt and competition genres as beneath contempt, Poe was reviving his own cryptography competitions, issuing new challenges and even offering a year's free subscription to the reader who could decode a cryptogram that Poe himself had just succeeded in decoding. In December 1841, Poe printed a letter from a reader named W. B. Tyler, whom many critics believe to be Poe himself, dubbing the author "the king of 'secret-readers.'" If Tyler really was Poe's stand-in, then this was a remarkable act of self-consecration; if not, it was an even more compelling act of vindication.[35]

1843: A QUALIFIED SUCCESS

Poe's final competitive entry was, again, spurred by crushing poverty and a sense of desperation. In January 1842, his wife, Virginia, had begun to show the first signs of tuberculosis. Rather than battening the hatches, however, Poe threw all caution to the wind, drinking heavily and resigning his position at *Graham's Magazine*. By June, he was jobless and penniless, writing to a correspondent that his "pecuniary embarrassments" were driving him "to distraction." It would be another two years before he found steady, salaried employment.[36]

In March 1843, the *Dollar Newspaper* announced a short story competition with two hundred dollars in prizes: one hundred for the best story, sixty for the second best, and forty for the third. Everything about Poe's engagement with this competition seems familiar. He was, again, desperately poor; the panel of judges again included a recent Forrest prize winner; and again he made a rash gamble, buying back a story he had already sold to his former employer, George Graham. For Poe, the one hundred dollars he believed that he *might* win were more appealing than the fifty-two that Graham had already paid him and which he was compelled to pay back with other materials. Poe's gamble, however, paid off; in June, the *Dollar Newspaper* announced that Poe's short story, "The Gold-Bug," had won first prize. There followed a giddying period of celebrity, in which Poe saw the paper containing his story sell out within one day, go into a second and then a third authorized printing, appear elsewhere in pirated form, and occasion enthusiastic reports and extensive summaries in publications around the nation. Poe had the immense satisfaction, too, of seeing the story reprinted in the Philadelphia *Saturday Courier*, scene of his impoverishing competition loss in 1831, while the *Baltimore Saturday Visiter* obligingly reprinted an abridgement of his ghost-written and exaggeration-filled biography, leaving uncorrected his assertion that he had won both poetry and prose divisions in their 1833 contest. The prize-winning tale was even adapted for the stage and performed twice in August 1843. In a letter to a friend written much later, Poe claimed that he had written his story "for the sole purpose of running," an allusion to his own childhood racing experiences perhaps; for a while, at least, "The Gold-Bug" ran far and fast. Yet even this was not enough for Poe. In a revealing indication of his insatiable hunger for praise, he claimed in private that he had only submitted the tale to the

Dollar Newspaper after it had been rejected by Graham, seeking thereby to amplify both his consecration and vindication still more by making it seem as if his achievement was a success d'estime.[37]

Yet Poe's satisfaction was hardly unalloyed. Less than a fortnight after the results of the contest had been announced, the *Daily Forum* published a letter from Francis Duffee claiming that the competition had been rigged and that the judges had arranged to offer Poe first prize if he was willing to accept fifteen dollars. It was a stunning and extraordinarily clever accusation, since it implied both the corruption of the judges and the stinginess of Poe, who was willing to sell himself for so trifling a sum. Poe filed suit and Duffee retracted his claim but not before another pundit suggested that Poe had plagiarized his story from a thirteen-year-old girl, Ann Humphreys Sherburne, who had written a story entitled "Imogene; or the Pirate's Treasure" in 1839. The accusations were, again, retracted, but they cast a pall over Poe's achievement, depreciating the prestige he might otherwise have accumulated. Although Poe claimed a year after the contest that more than 30,000 copies of his story had been disseminated, the story was never completely free of the taint of scandal.[38]

In a sense, Poe brought this misery upon himself. His relentless criticism of the achievements of others and his carping accusations that the entrants and organizers of contests were in cahoots was being turned back upon him. While Poe was correct in assuming that many contests of the 1830s and 1840s were rigged, he could hardly make such accusations and not expect recriminations. His criticisms notwithstanding, it was becoming increasingly clear to his enemies how desperately Poe relied on competitions when at his most economically and emotionally vulnerable moments, and so it was with some satisfaction that they set about discrediting his own competitive achievements. Duffee's assault on the integrity of the *Dollar Newspaper* competition was only the first instance. Penning his infamous "Ludwig Article" immediately after Poe's death, Rufus Griswold not only savaged Poe's character and morality but also claimed that his success in the *Saturday Visiter* competition was based solely on his handwriting, the judges having "unanimously decided that the prizes should be paid to the first of the geniuses who had written legibly," adding as a coup a grace: "Not another MS. was unfolded." When John Hill Hewitt, the winner of the *Visiter's* poetry section, recalled in his 1877 memoirs Poe's tipsy rhyming tournament with John Lofland, then, he was simply joining the company of those who were motivated to discredit every element of Poe's competitive endeavor.[39]

Perhaps the most striking example of how the antebellum critical establishment was of Poe's position on competitions is the fact that it took so long for him to be invited to judge one. While most prize winners were invited to serve as judges soon after having won their own competitions, it was a dozen years before Poe was extended that privilege. In 1845, finally, he received the call, but even here he was dogged by embarrassment. The competition in question was at the Rutgers Institute, a private girl's school in New York: hardly the prestigious venue for which he might have hoped. More frustrating still, the other judge, Rufus Griswold, who would later tarnish his reputation, backed out at the last moment, leaving one of Poe's many other enemies, Henry Tuckerman, to take his place. The two "sat alone" together for most of the afternoon, reading the students' manuscripts. For Charles Fenno Hoffman, writing to Griswold, it was "a good joke," but for Poe, it must have been excruciatingly embarrassing. It was a fitting finale to his engagement with the competitive world. Poe would never again become involved with a competition.[40]

Poe's engagement with literary competitions in the 1830s and 1840s reflect an attitude completely at variance with the ideal expounded in the 1820s and exemplified by an author like Charles Sprague. Where Sprague competed for honor, Poe dueled for money. The premium from the "MS. Found in a Bottle" represented something like three months' room and board in Baltimore at the time he lived there. At the same time, Poe understood that no matter what the dollar amount of the premium, the prestige it accrued offered both status, social connection, and further potential earnings. For these rewards, too, Poe fought vigorously, fuelled by his insatiable need for approbation, yet he fell afoul of the social networks that reproduced and protected social and cultural distinction. Poe was simply too belligerent and too poorly connected to capitalize effectively on the dynamic potentialities of the competitions. His good will, that is, ran out almost as fast as the cash he received. It is little wonder that Poe was as much repelled by as drawn to contests. No honors could appease this brilliantly talented author, because he was dueling as much with the dead as with the living, and the dead, as his stories showed time after time, could never be beaten.

NOTES

1. William F. Gill, *The Life of Edgar Allan Poe* (New York: D. Appleton, 1877), 49. There is another version of this story in which the setting is a tavern, Poe rather than Lofland throws down the challenge, and the wager—significantly, in light of the Folio Club narrative—is for the loser to pay for everyone's drinks. See William W. Smithers, *The Life of John Lofland, "The Milford Bard"* (Philadelphia: Wallace M. Leonard, 1894), 108. In both versions, Poe loses.

2. For an extended discussion of literary competitions in this period, see chapter 5 of my book, *The Business of Letters: Authorial Economies in Antebellum America* (Stanford: Stanford University Press, 2008).

3. John Adams, *Discourses on Davila*, in *The Political Writings of John Adams*, ed. George W. Carey (Washington, DC: Regnery, 2000), 347, 311. For a broad survey of ideas on emulation and approbation, see Arthur O. Lovejoy, *Reflections on Human Nature* (Baltimore: Johns Hopkins University Press, 1961); G. W. Pigman III, "Versions

of Imitation in the Renaissance," *Renaissance Quarterly* 33 (1980): 1–32; and Howard D. Weinbrot, "'An Ambition to Excell': The Aesthetics of Emulation in the Seventeenth and Eighteenth Centuries," *Huntington Library Quarterly* 48 (1985): 121–39.

4. Laura Auricchio, "The Laws of *Bienséance* and the Gendering of Emulation in Eighteenth-Century French Art Education," *Eighteenth-Century Studies* 36 (2003): 231; Adams, *Discourses on Davila*, 356.

5. On Crambo and verse capping, see David S. Shields, *Civil Tongues and Polite Letters in British America* (Chapel Hill: Institute of Early American History and Culture, 1997), 165–69; and Joseph Strutt, *The Sports and Pastimes of the People of England* (London: Thomas Tegg, 1831), 398–99.

6. On the rejected address tradition, see Dennis Hall Sigmon, Jr., "Rejected Addresses and the Art of Poetic Parody" (Ph.D. diss., Purdue University, 1976).

7. Eugene Didier, *The Life and Poems of Edgar Allan Poe* (New York: A. C. Armstrong, 1882), 32; J. T. L. Preston, "Some Reminiscences of Edgar A. Poe as a Schoolboy," in Sara Sigourney Rice, *Edgar Allan Poe: A Memorial Volume* (Baltimore: Turnbull Brothers, 1877), 40; Didier, *Life and Poems*, 30. See also Kenneth Silverman, *Edgar A. Poe: Mournful and Never-ending Remembrance* (New York: HarperCollins, 1991), 23–24, 29–30, 41; and Arthur Hobson Quinn, *Edgar Allan Poe: A Critical Biography* (Baltimore: Johns Hopkins University Press, 1998), 84–85. On capping verses: Preston, "Some Reminiscences," 39–40. For Poe's very deliberate *emulation* of Byron's feat, see "Swimming," *Southern Literary Messenger* 1 (May 1835): 468.

8. See Silverman, *Edgar A. Poe*, 25, 458 (on competition); 155 (quotation).

9. See Poe to Allan, September 21 1826; March 19, 1827; December 1, 1828; December 28, 1828; May 29, 1829; June 25, 1829; July 26, 1829, *The Letters of Edgar Allan Poe*, ed. John Ward Ostrom (New York: Gordian Press, 1966), 1:6, 7, 10, 12, 20, 22, 26. All italics are in the originals.

10. Silverman, *Edgar A.* Poe, 11–14 (Allan's adoption); 22 (quotation). A slightly more nuanced argument along the same lines has been made by J. Gerald Kennedy, "The Violence of Melancholy: Poe against Himself," *American Literary History* 8 (1996): 533–51.

11. Edgar Allan Poe, "Tamerlane," *Complete Poems*, ed. Thomas Ollive Mabbott (Urbana: University of Illinois Press, 2000), 22.

12. The announcement, rules, and results are reproduced in John Grier Varner, *Edgar Allan Poe and the Philadelphia Saturday Courier* (Charlottesville: University of Virginia, 1933).

13. See Poe to Allan, October 16, 1831; Poe to Allan, November 18, 1831; Poe to Allan, December 15, 1831; Poe to Allan, December 29, 1831, *Letters of Edgar Allan Poe*, 1:46–49. On typical per page rates, see John Ward Ostrom, "Edgar Allan Poe: His Income as Literary Entrepreneur," *Poe Studies* 15 (1982): 1–7.

14. Smith had written his play in the 1820s; when he sent it to Forrest for feedback, the actor promptly awarded it first prize in his contest. See Marshall, "Playwriting Contests," 105; Moody, *Edwin Forrest*, 100. On Poe's generally contemptuous attitude toward Native American-themed literature and Forrest's brand of racial cross-dressing in particular, see Leon Jackson, "'Behold Our Literary Mohawk, Poe': Literary Nationalism and the 'Indianation' of Antebellum American Culture, " *ESQ: A Journal of the American Renaissance* 48 (2002): 97–133.

15. Poe to Allan, April 12, 1833, *Letters of Edgar Allan Poe*, 1:49–50; "Premiums," *Baltimore Saturday Visiter*, June 15, 1833. For a brief discussion of the competition, see John C. French, "Poe and the *Baltimore Saturday Visiter*," *Modern Language Notes* 33 (1918): 257–67.

16. For the frame of the collection, which was never published, see Edgar Allan Poe, "The Folio Club," *Tales and Sketches*, ed. Thomas Ollive Mabbott (Urbana: University of Illinois Press, 2000), 1:200–207 (quotation 204). Poe developed the frame narrative further in Poe to Joseph T. and Edwin Buckingham, May 4, 1833; and Poe to

Harrison Hall, September 2, 1836, *Letters of Edgar Allan Poe*, 1:54, 103–4 (quotation 104), and I have used these descriptions too. It is clear, however, that the basic idea was established by the time Poe entered the *Visiter* contest.

17. On the origin, organization, and final disposition of the collection, see Alexander Hammond, "A Reconstruction of Poe's 1833 *Tales of the Folio Club*: Preliminary Notes" *Poe Studies* 5 (1972): 25–32; Hammond, "Further Notes on Poe's Folio Club Tales," *Poe Studies* 8 (1975): 38–42; Hammond, "Edgar Allan Poe's *Tales of the Folio Club*: The Evolution of a Lost Book," in *Poe at Work: Seven Textual Studies*, ed. Benjamin Franklin Fisher IV (Baltimore: Edgar Allan Poe Society, 1978), 13–43; and Kenneth Alan Hovey, "'These Many Pieces Are Yet One Book': The Book-Unity of Poe's Tale Collections," *Poe Studies* 31 (1998): 3–5. Poe's familiarity with Horace and James Smith is established by Burton R. Pollin, "Figs, Bells, Poe, and Horace Smith," *Poe Newsletter* 3 (1970): 8–10.

18. "The Premiums," *Baltimore Saturday Visiter*, October 12, 1833. The details of the judging emerge from two accounts of judge John H. B. Latrobe. See his "Reminiscences of Poe" [1875], in *Edgar Allan Poe: A Memorial Volume*, 57–62; and Latrobe to Burr, December 7, 1852, reprinted in Jay B. Hubbell, "Charles Chauncey Burr: Friend of Poe," *Publications of the Modern Language Association* 69 (1954): 837–39 (quotation 838).

19. Hewitt, quoted in Vincent Starrett, "One Who Knew Poe," *Bookman* 66 (1927): 200.

20. Poe to White, 20 July 1835, *Letters of Edgar Allan Poe*, 1:65; "The Poets and Poetry of Philadelphia. Number II. Edgar Allan Poe," *Philadelphia Saturday Museum*, 4 March 1843.

21. The decision to award the prize to Hewitt was explained by Latrobe in "Reminiscences of Poe," 59–60.

22. John Hill Hewitt, *Recollections of Poe*, ed. Richard Barksdale Harwell (Atlanta: The Library, Emory University, 1949), 19. For a briefer account of the affair, see Hewitt, *Shadows on the Wall, Or, Glimpses of the Past* (Baltimore: Turnbull Brothers, 1877), 40–43, 154–59. There exists a rumor that Poe initially confronted Hewitt and told him that he could keep the prize money if he was willing to concede the contest, since he "only wanted the honors." Gill, *Life of Edgar Allan Poe*, 69–70 (quotation 69). For the reprinting of "The Coliseum," see *Southern Literary Messenger* 1 (August 1835): 706. Within the world of competitions, to call a piece a "prize poem" was to imply, quite unambiguously, that it had *won* a prize.

23. The judges might perhaps have responded that in spreading the prizes, they were more generally rewarding (and hence promoting) emulation. Kevin Hayes's argument that Poe's dispute with Hewitt was really a matter of editorial professionalism seems to me to miss the point, inasmuch as entering a contest anonymously obviates, at least in theory, any taint of professional indecorum. See Hayes, *Poe and the Printed Word* (Cambridge: Cambridge University Press, 2000), 41–42.

24. See "Literary Notice," *New Yorker*, March 22, 1834; Lewis Gaylord Clark to Henry Wadsworth Longfellow, November 2, 1834, quoted in Lawrence Thompson, *Young Longfellow (1807–1843)* (New York: Macmillan, 1938), 201; and James Taft Hatfield, "An Unknown Prose Tale by Longfellow," *American Literature* 3 (1931): 136–48.

25. For Poe's feud with Clark, and his circle, see Sidney P. Moss, *Poe's Literary Battles: The Critic in the Context of his Literary Milieu* (Carbondale: Southern Illinois University Press, 1963).

26. On Willis: Thomas N. Baker, *Sentiment and Celebrity: Nathaniel Parker Willis and the Trials of Literary Fame* (Oxford: Oxford University Press, 1999), 21–22. On Catharine Beecher: Catharine E. Beecher, *Truth Stranger than Fiction* (Boston: Phillips, Sampson, 1850), 18–20; Vivian C. Hopkins, *Prodigal Puritan: A Life of Delia Bacon* (Cambridge, MA: Belknap Press of Harvard University Press, 1959), 24. On Harriet Beecher: "The Proprietors of the Western Monthly Magazine Offer a Premium of Fifty Dollars," *Western Monthly Magazine* 1 (September 1833): 429; "To Readers and Correspondents," *Western Monthly Magazine* 1 (December 1833): 592; Forrest Wilson, *Crusader in Crino-*

line: *The Life of Harriet Beecher Stowe* (Philadelphia: J. B. Lippincott, 1941), 125–26. On Stephens: Madeleine B. Stern, "Ann S. Stephens: Author of the First Beadle Dime novel, 1860," *Bulletin of the New York Public Library* 64 (1960): 306–7. On Forrest: Marshall, "Playwriting Contests," 105; Moody, *Edwin Forrest*, 100.

27.   Alice C. Neal to Elizabeth Oakes Smith, December 16, 1847, John Neal Correspondence, Maine Historical Society.

28.   Nathaniel P. Willis, "Editor's Table," *American Monthly Magazine* 1 (November 1829), quoted in Baker, *Sentiment and Celebrity*, 44.

29.   Thomas Willis White to Nathaniel Beverley Tucker, January 24, 1837, quoted in *Poe Log*, 214.

30.   See Dwight Thomas, "William E. Burton and his Premium Scheme: New Light on Poe Biography," *University of Mississippi Studies in English* 3 (1982): 68–80 (quotation 73); Thomas S. Marvin, "'These Days of Double Dealing': Edgar Allan Poe and the Business of Magazine Publishing," *American Periodicals* 11 (2001): 81–94.

31.   "Enigmatical and Conundrum-ical," *Alexander's Weekly Messenger*, December 18, 1839, reprinted in Clarence S. Brigham, "Edgar Allan Poe's Contributions to *Alexander's Weekly Messenger*," *Proceedings of the American Antiquarian Society* 52 (1942): 58.

32.   "Another Poser," *Alexander's Weekly Messenger*, January 22, 1840; "Our Puzzles Once More," *Alexander's Weekly Messenger*, February 26, 1840, both reprinted in Brigham, "Edgar Allan Poe's Contributions," 66, 92 (quotation).

33.   William K. Wimsatt, Jr. has pointed out that Poe only grudgingly acknowledged when other readers were able to decode the ciphers he presented, a practice consistent with his habit of embellishing his own competitive successes even as he deplored the practice in others. See "What Poe Knew About Cryptography," *Publications of the Modern Language Association* 58 (1943): 757–59.

34.   "Writings of Charles Sprague," *Graham's Magazine* (May 1841), *Complete Works of Edgar Allan Poe*, ed. James A. Harrison (New York: AMS Press, 1965), 10: 140; "An Appendix on Autographs," *Graham's Magazine* (January 1842), *Complete Works*, 15: 248–49; "Sketches of Conspicuous Living Characters of France," *Graham's Magazine* (April 1841), *Complete Works*, 10:133–39. For retorts to Poe's Sprague bashing, see [Rufus W. Griswold], *Boston Notion*, May 22, 1841, quoted in B. Bernard Cohen and Lucian A. Cohen, "Poe and Griswold Once More," *American Literature* 34 (1962): 98–99; and Cornelia Wells Walter, *Boston Evening Transcript*, March 5, 1845, quoted in Moss, *Poe's Literary Battles*, 176n80.

35.   "Secret Writing," *Graham's Magazine* (August 1841), *Complete Works*, 14:134; "Secret Writing," *Graham's Magazine* (December 1841), *Complete Works*, 14:141. For the suggestion that Tyler was Poe, see Louis A. Renza, "Poe's Secret Autobiography," in *The American Renaissance Reconsidered: Selected Papers from the English Institute, 1982–83*, ed. Walter Benn Michaels and Donald E. Pease (Baltimore: Johns Hopkins University Press, 1985), 86–87n14; and Shawn Rosenheim, "The King of 'Secret Readers': Edgar Poe, Cryptography, and the Origins of the Detective Story," *English Literary History* 56 (1989): 393–95. I am less certain than other critics that Tyler was Poe, a scepticism I share with John A. Hodgson and that is additionally supported by Stephen Rachman's recent discovery of several possible Tyler pieces in both *Graham's Magazine* and *Alexander's Weekly Messenger*. See Hodgson, "Decoding Poe? Poe, W. B. Tyler, and Cryptography," *Journal of English and Germanic Philology* 92 (1993): 523–34; and Rachman, "Poe, Secret Writing, and Magazine Culture: In Search of W. B. Tyler" (unpublished essay, 2003). I am grateful to Rachman for sharing a copy of his essay with me.

36.   Poe to James Herron, June 1842, *Letters of Edgar Allan Poe*, 1:198.

37.   Poe to Frederick W. Thomas, May 4, 1845, *Letters of Edgar Allan Poe*, 1:287. For a concise account of the publication and controversies surrounding "The Gold-Bug," see *Tales and Sketches*, 1:799–806.

38.   Poe to James Russell Lowell, May 28, 1844, *Letters of Edgar Allan Poe*, 1:253; W. T. Bandy, "Poe, Duane, and Duffee," *University of Mississippi Studies in English* 3 (1982): 87–89.

39.   "Death of Edgar A. Poe," *New York Daily Tribune*, October 9, 1849.

40. Hoffman to Griswold, July 11, 1845, quoted in *Poe Log*, 549.

ELEVEN

Poe's Early Criticism of American Fiction: *The Southern Literary Messenger* and the Fiction of Robert Montgomery Bird

Justin R. Wert

I

The fiction of Robert Montgomery Bird was reviewed in the *Southern Literary Messenger* on four occasions between February 1835 and September 1836. We know for certain that Poe was author of the first two of these reviews (of *Calavar* and *The Infidel*), although the other two (of *The Hawks of Hawk Hollow* and *Sheppard Lee*) may have been written or cowritten with Poe by others on the *Messenger* staff.[1] Bird was a major figure in early American fiction, a man who in Poe's words had "risen . . . to a very enviable reputation."[2] Bird's popularity was nearly on par with that of Simms, Kennedy, Paulding, and other contemporaries who are better known today. In fact, Robert Jacobs reinforces Poe's opinion of Bird by listing Bird with Cooper and Simms as "the best of the [American] novelists of Poe's time."[3] Moreover, Bird was not only a novelist but also a prize-winning playwright. In fact, four of Bird's dramas were awarded substantial prizes (of as much as $1,000) by the preeminent producer/actor of the era, Edwin Forrest. Today, however, Bird is little known. With the exception of *Nick of the Woods*, his writings are out of print, and none appear in modern literature anthologies. His literary reputation, ironically in contrast to Poe's, has fallen considerably from its "enviable" height.

However obscure Bird's literary achievements may appear today, the *Messenger* reviews of Bird's fiction help to illuminate Poe's emergence as a leading American literary critic. First, the reviews of *Calavar* and *The Infidel* shed light on the critical criteria employed by American reviewers like Poe during the 1830s: criteria relating to the novel and related genres such as the romance and historical romance. Although Jacobs claims that Poe "was not prepared, in [his] review [of Bird's *The Hawks of Hawk-Hollow*] or in later ones, to make any significant contribution to the theory of the novel [and that] to him it was not a true art form,"[4] Poe certainly made significant contributions to the art of literary criticism and more specifically to the art of reviewing novels and romances. In reviewing Bird's work, Poe previews his later theory of the short story, in which the "single effect" is all-encompassing.

Poe's reviews of Bird's works establish some critical reviewing practices concerning the novel and romance, based to some degree on his own theories of how to write and narrate "a tale"—concepts that are particularly vivid in the *Sheppard Lee* review. While Poe may have refused to accept the novel as a unified art form, he reviewed numerous novels during his tenure at the *Messenger* with a sharp critical wit. Even though Poe may not have been "prepared" to make a "significant contribution to the theory of the novel," his reviews of *Hawks* and *Sheppard Lee* demonstrate the complex relationship between Poe's development as a literary critic and fiction writer during the changing American literary-publishing environment of the 1830s.

The *Southern Literary Messenger* reviews of Bird's works also help us better understand the nineteenth-century uses of the terms "romance" and "novel." While the reviewers at the *Messenger*—Poe, Thomas Willis White, Edward Sparhawk, and Edward Heath—did not formally agree on their exact uses, the genres were frequently reviewed by the *Messenger* staff. Moreover, these literary terms were well-established; they had long been used to categorize long works of fiction on both sides of the Atlantic. In brief, I will explore some definitions and examples of both genres as represented in American literature, then demonstrate the *Messenger's* expressions of criticism relating to *the novel* and *the romance*, assessing Poe's limited use of the terms "historical romance" and "romance" in his terminology and other similar terms and related criteria. I will also explore possible reasons why Poe did not establish a finely tuned criticism of long fictional works, although he lavished exquisite detail upon all aspects of his criticism and delineated terminology for his own theories of short fiction and poetry while he worked at the *Southern Literary Messenger* between 1835 and the beginning of 1837.

II

The first two *Messenger* reviews of works by Bird help to define what a "novel," "romance," or—in the case of *Calavar* and *The Infidel*—a "historical romance" is. The word "novel," however, was beginning to be the preferable term for reviews of all long narratives, as Jacobs explains, because by the 1830s the novel was taking precedence over the romance as a literary form. The *Messenger* review of Bird's *Calavar* is a good gauge by which to determine where American literary criticism stood regarding the genre. As Jacobs notes, the review is useful "as an illustration of the standards applied to the novel [in the 1830s]. The reviewer examined the works in terms of verisimilitude, characterization, and style, and concluded that, although '[*Calavar*] is certainly the very best American novel, excepting one or two of Mr. Cooper's . . . ,' it fails in one respect because it is 'too unnatural even for romance.'" [5]

The *Messenger* reviewer's criticism of *Calavar* as being "too unnatural even for romance" is of particular interest. As Northrop Frye states, the chief difference between the novel and the romance "lies in the conception of characterization. The romancer does not attempt to create 'real' people so much as stylized figures which expand into psychological archetypes." [6] In other words, the romance writer's characters should be "natural" or have compelling psychological aspects but not realistic appearances or "verisimilitude," unless one is concerned with "historical romance" and actual historical figures—such as with the historically based characters in many of Simms's works. Jacobs further explains that Poe, like his fellow *Messenger* reviewer Beverly Tucker, also "employed the standard of *nature* in regard to the novel." Although there were "no rules of the novel" per se, the standard for American reviewers of the time was to examine whether a romance or novel achieved a uniform "nature" (romances) or "verisimilitude" (novels and historical romances) as Michael D. Bell also notes. [7] In the *Messenger* reviewer's comparison of Bird's and Cooper's uneven attempts to achieve "nature" or "verisimilitude" in their "novels," one should read the term "novels" as *romances* or more specifically *historical romances*. In other words, neither Bird nor Cooper is very capable of depicting "stylized" female characters. As a result their characters were objectionable to the reviewer, much as they are to modern readers, because Bird's and Cooper's female characters seem to be mere constructs, not "stylized" characters or "psychological archetypes" like Hawthorne's Hester Prynne, or Phoebe in *The House of the Seven Gables*: two more "natural" characters in two more celebrated, contemporaneous romances.

By contrast, Cooper's and Bird's female characters wander "through the forests, unmussed in clothing and deportment, swooning at frequent intervals." Moreover, Jacobs says, "the reviewer of the 1830s was also annoyed by the somnambulism of Cooper's females,"[8] a sentiment that this particular reviewer, be it Poe or Tucker, also finds objectionable in Bird's *Calavar*: "The author [Bird], who is vastly superior to Cooper in dialogue, is we fear, equally unqualified with that writer [Cooper], to depict the female character in all its exquisite traits and attractive graces."[9] For a particular example of Bird's uneven representation of female characters, the reviewer faults Bird for not giving "more than a mere glimpse at the daughter of Montezuma . . . whose image we behold as in a 'glass darkly,' and whose wretched fate we regard with less anguish, knowing so little as we do of the fair and unfortunate victim."[10] Herein one can detect the reviewer's standard of both "verisimilitude" and "stylized" characterization, two definitive requirements of the historical romance. Poe uses these critical criteria in his reviews of Simms' *The Partisan* and Bulwer-Lytton's *Rienzi*: historical romances that present actual historical figures within a fictional context, demanding realistic characters in a kind of bas-relief or "verisimilitude" against a "stylized," mysterious and/or melodramatic backdrop.[11]

Concerning "verisimilitude" and other literary terms in use during the 1830s, Jacobs suggests that Poe, like other American reviewers of the time, had to "borrow" critical standards/terms from "other genres"[12] since "there were no rules for the novel." If a true "novel" "departed too obviously from verisimilitude,"[13] or made use of Gothicism or excessive imaginative, as opposed to "natural" (realistic) elements, then the novel "could be considered a romance and the demand for verisimilitude was mitigated."[14] Both *Calavar* and *The Infidel* were "romances," as Bird's subtitles for both works reveal. Moreover, Bird's subject matter in both books is Cortez's conquest of Mexico—lending a factual context that suggests the kind of historical realism made popular by Scott, Cooper, and Simms. Hence, *Calavar* and *The Infidel* could loosely be termed "historical romances," much as Simms, Parks, and Bell suggest.[15]

Furthermore, the reviewer recognizes *Calavar* as a "historical romance" but makes measured critical points about the work's value as such. On the one hand, the reviewer takes issue with the probability of some of Bird's rendering of historical events: "There is too much improbable and miraculous agency in the various life-preserving expedients, and extraordinary rescues which are constantly occurring,—and which . . . impart to a tale founded on historical truth, an air of oriental fiction which is not agreeable." For the most part, however, the reviewer praises Bird's historical accuracy and twice delineates the genre of *Calavar*, not only as "romance" but as "historical romance." He also contends that, should Bird follow up this "success in the region of historical romance," he would "assuredly outstrip all his competitors on this side of the Atlantic": a lofty evaluation of Bird's literary potential. More to the point, Bird's novel is termed a good "historical romance" because it represents "a faithful delineation of Cortez," so much so that the reviewer proclaims that, in this regard, Bird "has been wonderfully successful."[16] In other words, Bird's rendering of history brought accolades from the reviewer because Bird's "verisimilitude" has faithfully recreated history and historical figures in this "historical romance."

The *Infidel* review offers up more praise of Bird's "powers as a writer of fictitious narrative."[17] In fact this review also praises an aspect of Bird's narrative abilities that the reviewer found defective in the preceding romance: "The principal female character is drawn with far greater vigor, than marked the heroine of *Calavar*," he writes.[18] This is measured praise, however, since the reviewer does comment, that much as in *Calavar*, "we think it problematical whether the author is capable of success in a purely feminine picture of female character."[19] Once again the reviewer returns to the criticism of characterization, especially the lack of effective female characterization in both Bird and Cooper's works.

The reviewer concludes that *The Infidel* will enjoy the popularity of *Calavar*, confirming "public opinion as to the abilities of the author, who has suddenly taken proud station in the van of American writers of romance."[20] While this comment further supports the *Calavar* reviewer's assessment of Bird as a major literary talent on the rise, it also firmly labels Bird as a genre writer. The reviewer also defines the creative elements of the romance as opposed to the novel, and compares Bird with Simms and Cooper:

> [Bird] possesses a fertility of imagination rarely possessed by his compeers. In many of their works, there is a paucity of events; and incidents of small intrinsic importance, are wrought up by the skill of the writer so as to give the factitious interest to a very threadbare collection of facts. Great ability may be displayed in this manner; but our author seems to find no exertion necessary. The fertility of his imagination displays itself in the constant recurrence of dramatic situations, striking incidents and stirring adventures; so much so, that the interest of the reader, in following the characters through the mazes of perils and enterprises, vicissitudes and escapes, which they encounter, is often painfully excited. If this be a fault, it is one which is creditable to the powers of the author, and indicates an exuberance of invention, which will bear him through a long course of literary exertions, and insure to him great favor with the votaries of romance.[21]

The reviewer distinguishes Bird from "his compeers" according to Bird's heightened "fertility of imagination"—as opposed to other writers' lesser engagement of the factual, in which they merely "give the factitious interest to a very threadbare collection of facts." This analysis is fascinating not only for what it reveals about Bird's writing and emerging status as an author, but also for what it reveals about the reviewer. Bird is admirable as a "romance" writer because he favors treading in the realm of the "imagination" as opposed to trudging through the merely factual, which

Simms and Hawthorne thought to be the modus operandi of the "romance" writer. According to the reviewer's assessment, Bird is a writer of superior "imagination" and thus a superior writer of "romance."[22]

In this assessment of Bird's *Infidel*, the reviewer seems Poesque (perhaps it is indeed Poe) in his descriptions of the imagination as *the* writer's tool to induce a concentrated effect upon the reader: "the fertility of his imagination displays itself . . . so, that the interest of the reader in following his characters . . . is often painfully excited."[23] In other words, through his use of concentrated and well-orchestrated imagination, Bird achieves what Poe would later term a "unified effect" upon the reader. Poe never claimed, however, that a novel, "romance" or otherwise, could attain a "unified effect"; only short lyric/narrative poems and tales could achieve this desired effect. The initial source for this critical terminology is Poe's December 1835 *Messenger* review of *Tales of the Peerage and the Peasantry*.

Between the *Messenger* reviews of Bird's *Calavar* and *The Infidel*—which helped to establish the budding magazine's critical stance concerning the novel and romance—and the reviews of *The Hawks of Hawks Hollow* and *Sheppard Lee*, Poe's February 1836 review of Bulwer's *Rienzi* provides a key example of Poe's use of the terms "novel" and "romance." Once again, Poe avoids delineating many particularities about what a "novel" and a "romance" entail, but Poe does describe the difference between the two genres to some extent. As Jacobs notes, "Poe discriminated carefully between the author's 'scrupulous fidelity to all the main events in the *public* life of his hero' and 'the relief afforded through the personages of pure romance which form the filling in of the picture.'"[24] In addition, Poe understands that *Rienzi* is an epic, historically based account, and thus encompasses what his contemporaries would ordinarily call an "historical romance."

Edd Winfield Parks claims that *Rienzi* is "considerably more than a novel. In sweep and character of composition it is essentially epic rather than dramatic; it is also, in the truest sense, a History. Poe digresses to note that 'we shall often discover in Fiction the essential spirit and vitality of Historic Truth—while Truth itself, in many a dull and lumbering archive, shall be found guilty of all the inefficiency of Fiction.'"[25] Poe's use of the terms "Fiction" and "Historic Truth" is similar to the use of "imagination" (i.e., "Fiction and Historic Truth") and "factitious" (i.e., "Truth itself") in the reviews of *Calavar* and *The Infidel*. As such Bird's *Calavar* and *The Infidel* are "historical romances," as is Bulwer's *Rienzi*. Also interesting is the similarity in effect of downplaying the importance of the "factitious": that is, the novel with its emphasis on the "factual" as juxtaposed with the romance/historical romance or "fiction," which might contain "the vitality of Historic Truth."

Especially important to Poe's developing views of American literary criticism was the seemingly contradictory role of two elements: one, his drive to establish American magazines in an effort to publish short fiction, poetry, and critical reviews; and two, the overwhelming necessity of publishing book-length works to establish his own literary reputation. His tendencies as a fictionist fit the magazine's venue of short fiction and poetry; Poe's strengths as a writer are undoubtedly in his fiction, poetry, and literary criticism. Yet Poe knew the road to literary visibility and financial viability was through publishing a book, perhaps even a long narrative. While Poe worked at the *Messenger* his difficulties in publishing a book-length volume must have weighed heavily upon his mind.

For instance, Poe attempted to publish *Tales of the Folio Club* by enlisting the help of James K. Paulding. Paulding was a literary insider, having published many successful and critically acclaimed works. Moreover, he admired Poe and the *Messenger* for their high literary standards and agreed to solicit his publishers, Harpers. Poe hoped that Paulding's influence—Harpers had just entered into a contract with Paulding to release a twelve- to fifteen-volume set of Paulding's works—would boost his chances of publishing the *Folio Club*. But he apparently overestimated Paulding's sphere of influence. In June 1836, Poe's manuscript was rejected, partly because it was too satiric about the literary establishment. However, there were also market forces at work, as Harpers noted in its rejection letter: "Readers in this country have a decided and strong preference for works (especially fiction) in which a single and connected story occupies the whole volume, or number of volumes."[26] In Harpers' estimation, the novel/romance was superior to collections of short stories in terms of marketability, and thus Poe's *Tales of the Folio Club* would not sell. As a result of this rejection, it became all the more clear to Poe that he had to write a novel in order to succeed as a writer: as Kevin J. Hayes points out, "he was still struggling for literary fame, and he knew well that contemporary novelists [like Paulding, Bird, Simms, Kennedy] were garnering more attention than other imaginative writers."[27] This recipe for success ran counter, however, to Poe's developing literary principle that the tale was superior to the novel/romance since only the tale could deliver "a unified effect" to the reader.

A few months before Harpers turned down *Tales of the Folio Club*, Poe reviewed Bird's "novel" *The Hawks of Hawk Hollow*. In the December 1835 review, Poe referred to *Hawks* as a "novel" and *Calavar* as a "romance" but he did not explain what he meant by these terms. One can propose, however, three possible causes for Poe's using the term "novel" almost exclusively. First, he did not admire long works of fiction as much as he did "the tale." Second, Poe saw no need to distinguish between these two terms for his own fiction-writing purposes—unlike Simms and Hawthorne, who were deeply invested in defining the "romance" since it was their preferred prose genre. To Poe, the distinctions between the terms added little if any necessary clarification about a particular work's literary merit—his key concern as a critic.

The term "historical romance" was also waning in popularity among American reviewers during this period. Beyond Cooper's era, a shift in reviewing vocabulary occurred in part as a reaction by American reviewers bent on distinguishing American long works of fiction (novels) from their British counterparts (romances).[28] Certainly Poe, like any other American critic of the time, clamored to distinguish American belle lettres from its European counterparts. Poe, however, refused to engage in "puffing" or inflating the value of an American literary work, just because it was American. Rather, he attempted to develop a systematic approach to assessing literary works—as his later essays, "The Philosophy of Composition" and "The Rationale of Verse" clearly indicate. While Poe did not establish a set of critical terms to distinguish novels from romances, he did indicate some critical criteria for what makes for a good romance or novel, which in turn reveals much about Poe's developing theories of the short story.

III

Poe's standard reviewing style is evident in his comments on *Hawks* and *Sheppard Lee*. He applauds merit but condemns structural, mechanical, or stylistic errors and inconsistencies. These commentaries, while less scandalous and contentious than some of Poe's more infamous "tomahawk" reviews, were more typical of his reviewing style at the *Messenger*.

In his review of *Hawks*, Poe begins by commending Bird for *Calavar* and *The Infidel* and assesses his literary reputation by noting that it is "very enviable." This method of reminding the reader of an author's previous literary works and their critical approbation was standard procedure for reviewers of the time. Poe also says that others in literary circles had "asserted that [Bird's] last novel, *The Hawks of Hawk-Hollow*, will not fail to place his name in the very first rank of American writers of fiction." Neither Poe's preliminary commendation of Bird nor others' early estimates of *Hawks*, however, softened Poe's sharp sword of criticism from cutting through the artificial surface of literary commendations to expose weak aspects of Bird's novel. In fact, this balanced praise and criticism—despite what Poe's acerbic review of Theodore S. Fay's *Norman Leslie* and his condemning reviews of William Leete Stone's *Ups and Downs* or Laughton Osborne's *Confessions of a Poet* might have seemed to indicate—was Poe's modus operandi when a deficient novel crossed his desk. Balanced critiques far outnumbered harsh or laudatory reviews, indicating that Poe was far more considerate and civilized in his reviews than his "tomahawk" reputation would indicate.[29]

Poe's review of *Hawks*, while certainly not as vitriolic as his review of *Norman Leslie* in the same issue (Dec. 1835) of the *Messenger*, contains some sharp criticism. Poe's review of *Norman Leslie* was intentionally scandalous to attract notice, his sarcasm filling his cup to overflowing: "Well—Here we have it! This is the book—the book par excellence—the book bepuffed, beplastered and be-Mirrored!"[30] By contrast, Poe's review of *Hawks* uses a milder-mannered, lighter sarcastic style. At first, Poe pretends that *Hawks* was written by Sir Walter Scott in order to criticize Bird for his heavy-handed imitation of that popular author: "It is unnecessary to tell us that this novel is written by Sir Walter Scott; and we are really glad to find that at length he ventured to turn his attention to American incidents, scenery, and manners. We repeat that it was a mere act of supererogation to place the words 'By the author of *Waverly*' in the title page. The book speaks for itself."[31] Poe's sarcastic mode is in line with his affinity for parody since at the time he was writing the *Folio Club*. Moreover, the sarcastic critique illuminates his condemnation of American literary works that were more imitative than original.

Poe's comments also reveal his objective critical criteria. He comments on Bird's "style" of writing by first defining what he means by style: "The style vulgarly so called—the manner properly so called—the handling of the subject to speak pictorially, or graphically, or as a German would say plastically—in a word the general air, the *tout ensemble*, the prevailing character of the story, all proclaim, in words which one who runs may read, that these volumes were indited 'By the author of *Waverly*.'"[32] In other words, what Poe calls the "manner" of a work is its style, its "prevailing character." In *The Hawks of Hawk Hollow*, Bird's manner is imitative of Scott and "by no means in the best manner of its illustrious author . . . it is a positive failure."[33] By comparing Bird's "novel" to Scott (implying by inference Scott's preference for the romance), Poe indicates that a novel cannot compare to a romance, especially one written by Scott, the master of the genre. In addition one wonders if Poe might not be lampooning the forced similarity of style between Bird's *Hawks* and Scott's books, such as *Waverly*, in an attempt to ride on the coattails of Scott's popularity. In this case perhaps, Bird's book fails in that it is an inferior imitation of Scott and that it is more "novel" than "romance."

Poe's critique of Bird's "manner" and mechanics reveals something significant about Poe's standards for good fiction. Bird's characters are unevenly drawn according to Poe: some are admirable, some execrable. While one female character is "one of the sweetest creations emanating from the fancy [imagination] of poet or of painter," yet another is "forced, unnatural, and overstrained." The characterization of the first female figure in the book emanates "from the fancy of poet or of painter"; the latter character violates one of Poe's tenets for "a tale," a principle that he shares with the romancers: a character should seem "natural," not "forced" or "overstrained."[34]

According to Poe, Bird's style is uneven. Poe attributes Bird's stylistic vacillations in this novel to "moments of the most utter mental exhaustion."[35] This is an astute observation, as Bird *was* laboring at his writing table under extreme exhaustion. Between 1834 and 1837, Bird wrote five novels, including *Hawks*, while editing *The American Monthly* magazine and writing for the theatre. As a result Bird's health was "adversely affected by the late, strenuous hours he was keeping."[36] In fact Bird had to recuperate from this period of "exhaustion" for the next two years, and eventually he moved away from Philadelphia and his strenuous schedule. Perhaps Poe was beginning to know the rigors and exhaustion of writing and reviewing himself.

Poe concludes by comparing *Hawks*, a "true" novel in many respects, to Bird's two previous efforts, both of which were "romances." Poe states, "Like *Calavar* and *The Infidel*, [*Hawks*] excels in the drama of action and passion, and fails in the drama of colloquy. It is inferior, as a whole, to *The Infidel*, and vastly inferior to *Calavar*."[37] So Bird's "novel" falls short of his "romances." This inferiority is based mainly on Bird's unevenness of "manner": it is not a complete failure but an effort that lacks the virtuosity of the previous two works, both "romances." Poe's evaluation of *Hawks* might very well indicate his preference for the "romance" over the "novel," certainly in terms of what Poe refers to as "colloquy." This evenhanded evaluation of *Hawks* demonstrates Poe's developing critical abilities and his willingness to evaluate a novel on its merits and deficiencies in an objective manner—a hallmark in most of Poe's reviews.

IV

Poe's review of *Sheppard Lee* shows us his appreciation of humor and social satire. In it we also see a range of perceptions about science, slave insurrections, abolition, and superstition in serious fiction. In addition, as Mabbott has noted, Poe's "The Gold-Bug" and *Sheppard Lee* share some similarities.

Poe's review of *Sheppard Lee* is more laudatory than his review of *Hawks*: "this novel is an original in *American Belle Lettres*," he announces at the start of the review.[38] Concerning Sheppard Lee's soul migrations, Poe had already used metempsychosis in his own tale, "Morella," and would use it again later in many other stories, including "Ligeia," "The Facts in the Case of M. Valdemar," "Mesmeric Revelation," and "A Tale of the Ragged Mountains." So it is of considerable interest that Poe reviewed Bird's novel; he had discovered a novel with some similar subject matter, singular subject matter for an original American fictionist to explore and, for Poe, a "true" novel— a "work of profundity" rather than mere "play of the mind."[39]

Poe is disappointed with Bird's ending, however, where the narrator reveals that Sheppard Lee's soul transmigrations were all just a dream, a delirium caused at the beginning of the novel by Lee accidentally striking his foot with a mattock. Poe believes that this plot maneuver does not create the most effective *bizarrerie*. Bird, Poe argues,

> conceives his hero endowed with some idiosyncrasy beyond the common lot of nature, and thus introduces him to a series of adventures which, under ordinary circumstances, could occur only to a plurality of persons. The chief source of interest in such narrative is, or should be, the contrasting of these varied events, in their influence upon a character *unchanging*—except as changed by the events themselves. This fruitful field of interest, however, is neglected in the novel before us, where the hero, very awkwardly, partially loses, and partially does not lose, his identity, at each migration. The sole object here in the various metempsychoses seem to be, merely the depicting of seven different conditions of existence, and the enforcement of the very doubtful moral that every person should remain contented with his own. But it is clear that both these points could have been more forcibly shown, without any reference to a confused and jarring system of transmigration, by the mere narrations of seven different individuals.[40]

Poe is pointing out Bird's means of narration and its weakness: that Sheppard Lee remains unchanged after his many unusual "transmigrations." Moreover, Poe sees Bird's plot resolution—it was all just a hallucination, a dream—as a deus ex machina, an artificial resolution of loose plot ends and difficulties, violating "the tone of the novel with incongruities," as Jacobs explains.[41] Poe saw that this flawed narrative device deprives "the reader of the emotional effect he had secured through identification with the character."[42] This concept is similar to what one sees in the previous *Messenger* reviews of Bird's works concerning effective characterization.

Bird's narration, in Poe's opinion, was effective on some counts, but it might have been better handled as a novel with multiple narrators: "it is clear that both these points could have been more forcibly shown, without any reference to a confused and jarring system of transmigration, by the mere narrations of seven different individuals."[43] Poe does not seriously entertain this idea, however—a modernist narrative mode like that of Faulkner, for instance. Poe preferred the first person and third-omniscient narrative techniques. More important, Poe refers to the critical standard of "nature" in a *romance* as establishing believability, a standard that relates to his own theories of fiction writing: "all deviations, especially wide ones, from nature, should be justified to the author by some specific object—the object, in the present case, might have been found, as above-mentioned, in the opportunity afforded of depicting widely-different conditions of existence actuating *one* individual."[44] Poe's remarks here anticipate his theory of the short story as based around a single effect. According to Poe, Bird is not only undermining the creation of "totality of effect" on the reader by saying it was all a dream, but also by claiming that writing *bizarreries* requires that "all deviations . . . from *nature should be justified to the author by some specific object*" (emphasis mine). In Bird's case this "specific object" is the effect of these various soul transmigrations on *one* particular soul, on "one individual"—that of Sheppard Lee. What Poe desires as a reader/critic is to feel the singular effect of Lee's soul migrations rather than diffuse and multifarious effects, as multifaceted and interesting as they are. Furthermore, although Bird's narrative method "is managed with unusual ingenuity,"[45] Poe says that "having been worried to death with incongruities (allowing such to exist) until the concluding page, it is certainly little indemnification for our sufferings to learn that, in truth, the whole matter was a dream, and that we were very wrong in being worried about it at all."[46]

As another means of narration, Poe suggests a "second general method": to avoid "that directness of expression which we have noticed in *Sheppard Lee*, and thus leaving much to the imagination."[47] Here Poe shows how his fiction-writing and literary criticism were interdependent. Poe was just developing as a fiction writer; one could argue that much of his best work lay ahead of him. The analysis of Bird's narrative technique points to Poe's preferences for a narrative style that "leav[es] much to the imagination" and creates the singular narrative. To Poe, it is "as if the author were firmly impressed with the truth, yet astonished at the immensity, of the wonders he relates, and for which professedly, he neither claims nor anticipates credence—in minuteness of detail, being at variance with indirectness of expression—in short by making use of the infinity of arts which give verisimilitude to a narration—and by leaving the result as a wonder not to be accounted for."[48]

One need not look any further than Poe's most familiar tales—say, "The Tell-Tale Heart" or "The Black Cat"— to find pertinent examples of what he describes here. The purpose of this narrative is "to place before the world, plainly, succinctly, and without comment, a series of mere household events"—that is, "without explaining away the singularity, the 'romance' of the situations." This does not mean that an author should never explain bizarre incidents in a *bizarrerie* (especially when using a first person narrator-criminal perpetrator as in the tales mentioned above), but rather that their ultimate "nature"—that is, their occurrences and causes—should remain mysterious to the reader: "*bizzareries* thus conducted, are usually far more effective than those otherwise managed. The attention of the author, who does not depend upon explaining away his incredibilities, is directed to giving them the character and the luminousness of truth. The reader, too, readily perceives and falls in with the writer's humor and suffers himself to be borne on thereby."[49] The "unified effect" then, while not possible in the novel form according to Poe, certainly is possible in the tale as long as the fictional lens of the author focuses on presenting everything with "the luminousness of truth" or verisimilitude and does not explain away the singular situations and characters the narrator relates to the reader.

Poe ends his critique of *Sheppard Lee* by claiming that stories that do not follow the aforementioned narrative method will not create a "single effect" upon the reader: "what difficulty, or inconvenience, or danger can there be in leaving us [readers] uninformed of the important facts that a certain hero *did not* actually discover the elixir vitae, *could not* really make himself invisible, and *was not* either a ghost in earnest or a bona fide Wandering Jew?"[50] While Poe may at times overstate his own brand of narration as the best method of writing *bizarreries*, his own tales clearly exemplify them.

V

Although far more subtle than his "tomahawk" onslaughts, Poe's critiques of Bird's romances and novels in the *Southern Literary Messenger* demonstrate his more standard, evenhanded reviewing practices. They also show his unwillingness to "puff" a work merely because it is American: to Poe a flawed work is flawed, an inferior work inferior. To Poe, a literary critic was not supposed to be a circus sideshow advertiser for good and bad fiction alike, puffing the latest works of established authors, renowned individuals waxing literary or powerful publishing houses. If a work is overly imitative, poorly plotted or narrated, riddled with grammar, diction or punctuation errors, Poe says so. In this manner, Poe helped to establish literary criticism as more objective than subjective—a timely transformation, helping to further American literature's "renaissance." Moreover, the *Messenger*'s four reviews of Bird's works demonstrate the established critical criteria concerning novels and romances, illuminating some of Poe's own literary techniques and standards for the short story or "tale," leading up to his theory of the "single effect."

NOTES

1. Two earlier *Messenger* reviews—that of *Calavar* (Feb. 1835) and *The Infidel* (June 1835)—have not been conclusively attributed to Poe, but are variously included or excluded from the canon.
2. Edgar Allan Poe, *Collected Writings of Edgar Allan Poe*, vol. 5, ed. Burton R. Pollin and Joseph V. Ridgely (New York: The Gordian Press, 1997), 50.
3. Robert D. Jacobs, *Poe: Journalist and Critic* (Baton Rouge: Louisiana State University Press, 1969), 189.
4. Jacobs, 100.
5. Jacobs, 100.

6. Northrop Frye, "Anatomy of Criticism: Four Essays" in *Collected Works of North-rop Frye*, vol. 22, ed. Robert D. Denham (Toronto: University of Toronto Press, 2006), 285. For definitions and discussions of the "Romance" see also Richard Chase, *The American Novel and Its Tradition* (Baltimore: The Johns Hopkins University Press, 1957); Michael Davitt Bell, *The Development of American Romance* (Chicago: University of Chicago Press, 1980); and Joel Porte, *The Romance in America* (Middletown, CT: Wesleyan University Press, 1969).

7. Jacobs, 73; see also Bell, 3–39.

8. Jacobs, 74.

9. Edgar Allan Poe, "Poe's Criticisms" in *Works of Edgar Allan Poe*, Edgar Allan Poe Society of Baltimore, www.eapoe.org/works/criticism.htm, 315.

10. Poe, "Criticisms," 315.

11. Jacobs, 73.

12. Jacobs, 73.

13. Jacobs, 73.

14. Jacobs, 73.

15. See William Gilmore Simms, *The Yemassee* (Fayetteville: University of Arkansas Press, 1993); Edd Winfield Parks, *Edgar Allan Poe as Literary Critic* (Athens: University of Georgia Press, 1964), and *William Gilmore Simms as Literary Critic* (Athens: University of Georgia Press, 1961); Bell, *Development of American Romance*.

16. Poe, "Criticisms," 315.

17. Poe, "Criticisms," 315.

18. Poe, "Criticisms," 582.

19. Poe, "Criticisms," 582.

20. Poe, "Criticisms," 582.

21. Poe, "Criticisms," 585.

22. Poe, "Criticisms," 585.

23. Poe, "Criticisms," 585.

24. Jacobs, 100.

25. Parks, *Poe as Literary Critic*, 41.

26. David K. Jackson, *Poe and the Southern Literary Messenger* (New York: Haskell House, 1970), 212.

27. Kevin J. Hayes, *Poe and the Printed Word* (Cambridge: Cambridge University Press, 2000), 61.

28. See Chase, 16; and Bell, 3–39.

29. See Jacobs.

30. Poe, *Collected Writings*, 60.

31. Poe, *Collected Writings*, 50.

32. Poe, *Collected Writings*, 50.

33. Poe, *Collected Writings*, 50.

34. Poe, *Collected Writings*, 52.

35. Poe, *Collected Writings*, 53.

36. Justin R. Wert, "Robert Montgomery Bird," *Dictionary of Literary Biography* 202 (1999): 36–41.

37. Wert, 53.

38. Poe, *Collected Writings*, 282.

39. Poe, *Collected Writings*, 285.

40. Poe, *Collected Writings*, 286.

41. Jacobs, 173.

42. Jacobs, 173–74.

43. Poe, *Collected Writings*, 286.

44. Poe, *Collected Writings*, 286.

45. Poe, *Collected Writings*, 286.

46. Poe, *Collected Writings*, 286.

47. Poe, *Collected Writings*, 286.

48. Poe, *Collected Writings*, 286.

49. Poe, "The Black Cat" in *Works*, 37.
50. Poe, *Collected Writings*, 286.

TWELVE

Mad Ravings or Sound Thinking?: "The Philosophy of Composition" and Poe's Parodic Raven

Dennis W. Eddings

Back in 1990 I suggested that "The Raven" was a parody of the poetic school known as the Spasmodics, an argument based on the poem itself and on Poe's January 1845 review of Elizabeth Barrett's *The Drama of Exile, and Other Poems* in the January 4 and 11, 1845, issues of the *Broadway Journal*. I would now like to suggest that further support for my argument can be found in "The Philosophy of Composition," wherein Poe carefully, perhaps too carefully, describes the deliberate, step-by-step process involved in writing "The Raven." Juxtaposing these three works will help us see that they combine to create a powerful critical statement about poetry and its uses and abuses.

I

A brief summary of that 1990 article, "Theme and Parody in 'The Raven,'" will provide a necessary starting point. I commenced by pointing to several critical remarks regarding infelicities in the poem and asked how Poe, given his oft-stated critical standards regarding poetry, could have allowed such. My answer is that the flaws are deliberate, a means of creating parody.

Central to my argument is the notion that, as a dramatic monologue, "The Raven" can be seen, at least from one angle, as a product of the narrator. True, Poe hides behind the narrative flow and manipulates the strings of his puppet for all he's worth, as "Philosophy" makes clear, but in the imaginative, narrative world of the poem the student is both speaker and poet. As I stated, "'The Raven,' like many other satires, masquerades as a product of its narrator and its absurdities are the means of revealing the error of the narrator's ways," a point supported by Leland S. Person, Jr. when he refers to the narrator as the "speaker-writer of the poem."[1]

I next examined the three six-stanza sections of the poem, delineating the narrator's insistence upon exacerbating his angst and pointing to his deliberate turning from rationality to the mad speculations of his uncontrolled Romantic imagination. His first reaction to the Raven's "Nevermore," that it's the bird's "only stock and store," is absolutely dead on. But that rational explanation doesn't meet the narrator's desire to rub the salt of denial into the wounds of his grief. So he imaginatively conjures up a scenario of an unhappy master filled with Usherian gloom and disaster. Doing so "pulls together bird, former master and himself in a melancholy lament that simply flies in the face of reason."[2] Rejecting the sane notion that "Nevermore" is a conditioned reflex, the narrator plunges into speculating what the bird *meant* in "croaking" that word. (Notice how the harsh "croaking" comically undercuts the idea of "meant.")

In the final six-stanza section, the narrator follows to its inevitable dead-end his plunge into the deep caverns of his uncontrolled Romantic imagination, asking questions that will inevitably be answered in the negative, thus lacerating even more the pageant of his bleeding heart. We last see the Raven perched on the bust of Pallas, throwing its shadow over the soul of the narrator. The Raven dominates reason, Pallas, but it is the narrator who has elevated it to that position through his own abdication of reason for the masochistic pleasure of wallowing in his grief.

The narrator, I then argue, follows a progression seen in many of Poe's tales where the abdication of reason in favor of the dark side of the imagination is ultimately destructive. What does that have to do with parody, however? My reply is, simply, everything. When "The Raven" is seen as a product of the narrator, the many infelicities mentioned in the onset of the essay take on far greater meaning than mere poetic lapses on Poe's part. If those infelicities are deliberate, and I'm convinced they are, then Poe is doing far more in "The Raven" than just returning to one of his favorite themes. He is, I suggest, giving us a poem that parodies the wretched verse produced by an imagination that has overwhelmed reason.

Which is where Poe's review of Barrett comes into play. Keeping in mind that that review appeared the same month as "The Raven," we can readily identify the poets being parodied:

From the ruins of Shelley there sprang into existence, affronting the Heavens, a tottering and fantastic pagoda, in which the salient angles, tipped with mad jangling bells, were the idiosyncratic faults of the great original. . . . Young men innumerable, dazzled with the glare and bewildered with the *bizarrerie* of the divine lightning that flickered through the clouds of the Prometheus, had no trouble whatever in heaping up imitative vapors, but for the lightning, were content, per-force, with its *spectrum*, in which the *bizarrerie* appeared without the fire.[3]

The review reveals that while Poe professes great respect for Barrett, he also clearly sees the faults in her work that suggest her flirtation, at the very least, with the Spasmodics.[4] More intriguing, though, is that Poe's detailed dissection of Barrett's poetry, including "Lady Geraldine's Courtship," the work from which he borrowed the form and meter of "The Raven,"[5] is readily applicable to his own poem.

Barrett's "multiplicity of inadmissible rhymes" is replicated in "The Raven," as is her being "not infrequently guilty of repeating herself." Even Barrett's "deficiencies of *rhythm*"[6] are mimicked in Poe's poem. A look into "Lady Geraldine's Courtship" reveals even more resonance—we find a purple chamber, perfumed air, window casement, "silken stir-ring," "open windows flung," "With a murmurous air uncertain, in the air the purple curtain," and "Ever, evermore"[7] —demonstrating that no matter what else Poe may have had in mind in writing "The Raven," he deliberately used Barrett's poem as a vehicle for parody.

The review of Barrett, then, provides a roadmap for reading the infe-licities in "The Raven" and demonstrates that Poe was well aware of them. To drive the point home, he dedicated the 1845 volume, *The Raven and Other Poems,* to Barrett, calling her "the fairest of her sex" but also deliberately pointing to her authorship of *The Drama of Exile and Other Poems* as a means of drawing attention back to his review. The process is, I suggest, precisely the same Poe employed in using his second review of Hawthorne's *Twice-Told Tales* in the May, 1842, issue of *Graham's* to point to his plundering of Hawthorne material in "The Masque of the Red Death," as is so meticulously delineated by Robert Regan.[8]

The evidence, I believe, is overwhelming that Poe had a clear grasp on what he was up to in "The Raven," that he deliberately wove into his poem jarring, incongruous notes as a means of indicting the narrator and his fellow ilk of perpetrating really, really bad poetry on an audience that deserved better. (Well, at least the more discerning deserved better.)

I do not mean to imply that other readings that take "The Raven" seriously and at face value are misguided. Poe was an incredibly complex writer capable of taking on many issues within the confines of a single tale or poem. Making him even more complex is how those many issues

resonate, creating layers of meaning that are often so intricately intercon-
nected that the reader at times becomes frustrated by the task of sorting
them out. Poe, I believe, would have it no other way.

Let us keep in mind his seemingly detached, almost dismissive references to "The Raven." There is his apparently offhand statement to F. W.
Thomas: "'The Raven' has had a great 'run,' Thomas—but I wrote it for
the express purpose of running—just as I did the 'Gold-Bug,' you know.
The bird beat the bug, though, all hollow."[9] (The gist and wonderful
expression of this comment would have brought a smile of appreciation
to the face of even a veteran Poe detractor such as Mark Twain.) Nor
should we forget Poe's "Preface" to *The Raven and Other Poems* where he
refers to the contents as "trifles," adding, "I think nothing in this volume
of much value to the public, or very creditable to myself."[10] On the other
hand, he also told more than one person of his belief in the greatness of
"The Raven,"[11] and there is no question that Poe relished reciting the
poem and playing the role of "the author of 'The Raven'" to the hilt. Such
contradictions are the stuff of Poe's life and oeuvre and we frequently
make a great mistake in forgetting that.

II

So how, then, does "The Philosophy of Composition" fit into all this? By
falling at the other end of the spectrum from his review of Barrett. While
the review points forward to the poem, "Philosophy" looks backward
upon it. The review deals with concrete instances of poetic lapses replicated in "The Raven." "Philosophy" ignores those lapses, concentrating,
at least on the surface, on the sequential steps involved in writing the
poem. I doubt if many really believe Poe wrote "The Raven" in such a
mechanical fashion and there are hints that he didn't in "Philosophy."
But the essay, I wish to argue, does address issues raised in the Barrett
review and "The Raven" itself.

I would like to commence with what appears to be a rather strange
statement coming from one usually labeled a Romantic poet: "Let us
dismiss, as irrelevant to the poem *per se*, the circumstance—or say the
necessity—which, in the first place, gave rise to the intention of composing a poem that should suit at once the popular and the critical taste."[12]
Dismiss as irrelevant that inner fire that compels the writing of a poem,
that "sweet hell within" as Whitman has it? By all means, for Poe's osten-
sible purpose in writing "The Philosophy of Composition" is critical, not
poetic. As Kenneth Burke observes, "regardless of how any work
arose . . . the critic should aim to formulate the principles of composition
implicit in it."[13] Poe recognizes and addresses this issue in "Philosophy,"

stating "the interest of an analysis . . . is quite independent of any real or fancied interest in the thing analyzed."[14] Poe's dismissal of the necessity for writing "The Raven," then, is critically sound.

But the idea of "the necessity" of writing a poem brings up another interesting possibility. I suspect that Poe wrote "The Raven" precisely for the reason he told Thomas—to run. That is, to make some money. And how did Poe usually go about that? By writing tales geared to a popular taste he basically scorned. In "The Raven," as in so many of his tales, Poe deliberately subverted the form he was ostensibly mining by hiding within it literary jokes and hoaxes that criticized and/or ridiculed the very taste to which he was pandering. I have no doubt that the huge success of "The Raven" was a source of great satisfaction to Poe, not just for the notoriety it brought him but also for the sense of superiority he would gain in having pulled one over on his audience.

There is another way of looking at this seemingly strange statement, however. Since Poe's focus in the essay is on compositional process (among other things), then the impetus for writing a poem *is*, as he says, irrelevant. Indeed, making such a dismissive statement draws attention to the process rather than the poem, as the first part of "Philosophy" makes clear. By the end of the essay, however, the "thing" being analyzed has become paramount, even furnishing the end of the essay. And that end contradicts the beginning, for it occurs two stanzas after the denouement Poe identifies at the beginning of "Philosophy" as the necessary starting point before composition can even begin. Such contradiction again subverts what Poe sets forth, just as the hidden parody in "The Raven" subverts that poem.

Furthermore, as we shall see, the compositional process Poe describes in "Philosophy," as well as some very direct and specific statements, reveal precisely where the narrator/writer of "The Raven" goes astray. That revelation pulls the relationship between poem and essay even closer.

Finally we need to consider more fully Poe's comment about intending to write for both the popular and the critical taste. Poe's basic contempt for popular taste is widely enough known not to need documentation.[15] But if he is writing a potboiler, as his letter to Thomas suggests, why bother with the critics at all? I suspect because those with critical taste would be the most likely to read his review of Barrett and to see the analogies to "The Raven," to catch, in other words, Poe's literary joke. They are also those most likely to read "Philosophy" and apply it to the poem. In other words, Poe is basically cross-referencing his own works.

III

"Philosophy" is meticulous in describing the steps Poe says he followed in writing "The Raven." All proceeds mathematically, inevitably, almost as though the writer is not a thinking organism but some type of automaton, an authorial mechanism somewhat akin to Maelzel's Chess Player. Such is not the case, of course. Poe did not write "The Raven" as "Philosophy" depicts. As Burke puts it, we can "flatly assume that his account of how he wrote the poem is completely false."[16] But while the process described in "Philosophy" is factually nonsensical, it is also metaphorically true, and that metaphor takes us right back to "The Raven."

The narrator/writer of that poem, as Poe states in "Philosophy," is "impelled . . . by the human thirst for self-torture, and in part by superstition, to propound such queries to the bird as will bring him, the lover, the most of the luxury of sorrow."[17] To reap that luxury the narrator plunges into the dark abyss of his imagination, an abyss which Poe warns of in *Marginalia*: "the Imagination of Man is no Carathis, to explore with impunity its every cavern. Alas! The grim legion of sepulchral terrors can*not* be regarded as altogether fanciful; but like the Demons in whose company Afrasiab made his voyage down the Oxus, they must sleep, or they will devour us—they must be suffered to slumber, or we perish."[18] The narrator of "The Raven" ignores the warning, which leads us back to "Philosophy."

In that essay, Poe insists that a poem is as much a product of reason as of insight: "Most writers—poets in especial—prefer having it understood that they compose by a species of fine frenzy—an ecstatic intuition."[19] Poe believes otherwise, as his remarks on the Spasmodics make clear.[20] His delineation of the mathematical process of composing "The Raven" is his way of demonstrating where the poem's narrator/writer errs, for while he most surely experiences a fine frenzy, the resultant poem is full of poetic lapses in language and meter that reveal his failure to apply reason to his flayed feelings. "Philosophy," then, can be seen in terms of Dupin. It metaphorically insists that great poetry results from imagination (an element in the "necessity" that gives rise to a poem) and reason. Bad poetry results when either is omitted. Thus the delicious paradox of "The Raven." As a product of the narrator/writer, its lapses represent bad poetry. As a product of Poe, those lapses represent good poetry, or at least good craftsmanship.

Poe makes the point specifically several times in "Philosophy," drawing a careful distinction between himself and the narrator of "The Raven," who, as noted above, composes his poem in a "fine frenzy—an ecstatic intuition." Poe insists that he well knows practically no author is in any "condition to retrace the steps by which his conclusions have been attained. In general, suggestions having arisen pell-mell, are pursued and forgotten in a similar manner," while he, on the other hand, has never had "the least difficulty in recalling to mind the progressive steps of any of my compositions."[21] I doubt the veracity of this statement, but if Poe in both poem and essay is attacking the Romantic dogma of the supernal nature of poetic inspiration, and I believe he is, then positioning himself as a type of alternative makes perfect sense. As Dennis Pahl puts it, "Philosophy" becomes "Poe's attempt to manufacture an image of himself that would serve to counter, if not completely contradict, whatever romantic image is suggested by 'The Raven.'"[22]

We are not finished with how "Philosophy" looks back on "The Raven" and helps to reveal the parody lurking below the poem's surface. For instance, in "Philosophy" Poe cites lines from the poem that are themselves examples of the poetic lapses he catalogs in the Barrett review, a type of triple cross-referencing. Perhaps most telling is his citation of the lines—"Much I marveled *this ungainly fowl* to hear discourse so plainly," and "But the Raven, sitting lonely on that placid bust, spoke only, etc."[23] These lines represent precisely the type of bad poetics Poe refers to in the Barrett review: "the natural rhythmical division, occurring at the close of the fourth trochee, should never be forced to occur, as Miss Barrett constantly forces it, in the middle of a word, or of an indivisible phrase."[24] My scansion (by no means a precise art) tells me "ungainly" and "lonely" respectively mark the close of the fourth trochee and that "Much I marveled *this ungainly fowl* to hear discourse so plainly" and "sitting lonely on that placid bust" are indivisible phrases. Other examples of this specific lapse in "The Raven," though not mentioned in the review, occur in lines 13, 15, and 33.

Poe claims in "Philosophy" that he points to these lines to mark where he shifts the tone of the poem from "the fantastic" to "the most profound seriousness,"[25] and it's true that no such lapses occur after line 55. But why does he italicize the phrase *"this ungainly fowl"*? To demonstrate its fantastic tone? Given the italics he also provides in quoting lines 52 and 53, the answer is surely yes. But Poe's ability to double-deal is well known and he could just as surely be demonstrating how the line violates his dictum in the Barrett review regarding where the caesura properly belongs.

The Barrett review figures into "Philosophy" in another way. Poe claims great originality in the combination of lines making up the stanzaic form of "The Raven": "what originality the 'Raven' has, is in their *combination into stanza*; nothing even remotely approaching this combination has ever been attempted."[26] Remotely? What of Barrett's "Lady Geraldine's Courtship" which consists of four line stanzas alternating between eight and seven-and-a-half feet? True, Poe adds two more lines to his stanzaic pattern and incorporates internal rhyme, but that is not the point. His remarks on the metrics of "The Raven" in "Philosophy" echo familiarly to those who have read his close analysis of the metrics of

"Lady Geraldine's Courtship" in the Barrett review, belying his claim that "nothing even remotely approaching this combination has ever been attempted."

Also in the Barrett review, Poe goes to great lengths to defend her from charges that many of her lines lack sense, although the fact that he has to paraphrase the lines suggests the charges may have some merit. Yet lines from "The Raven" cited in "Philosophy" demonstrate Poe's ability to create lines that simply fly in the face of rationality. When the raven enters, we are told, as cited in the essay, "Not the *least obeisance made he*—not a moment stopped or stayed he, / But with *mien of lord or lady*, perched above my chamber door."[27] Daniel Hoffman suggests in reading "The Raven" that we need to "let [our] mind fight back, just a little, against the maniacal regularity, the hypnotic fanfare in which the same combinations of rhyme recur with the inexorability of a Chinese water torture—just *resist* the spell a little bit, and the whole contraption suddenly comes apart at the seams. . . . A body'd have to be stark raven mad to go along with Poe's ludicrous poem!"[28] The lines Poe cites above are a prime example of what Hoffman refers to.

Why on earth would the raven bow when it enters the room? How can what is later described as an "ungainly fowl" have the "mien of lord or lady"? Poe's italics in the essay help highlight the ludicrous nature of the words. And how did the raven get to the perch above the chamber door? Flew, I suspect, and that would be quite a sight in a small room, for ravens are by no stretch of the imagination small. The lines may sound fine in recitation, but they don't stand up well under close examination. By taking them out of the context of their "maniacal regularity" the absurdity of the lines is emphasized.

Other lines Poe cites in "Philosophy," and emphasizes through italics, are just as loopy. How can the countenance of a raven be described as "grave and stern"? Why on earth would the raven's crest be "shorn and shaven" and how can that possibly lead to the conclusion that the bird is "sure no craven"? Were one to turn from "Philosophy" to "The Raven" itself, such examples would multiply. I don't mean to deny Poe's point in "Philosophy" about using the fantastic to heighten the contrast to the poem's somber ending. The lines he emphasizes do help accomplish that. When it comes to his works, however, Poe was no monotheist. He could weave a great many threads in the warp and woof of his tales and poems. The lines he places before our eyes in "Philosophy" are as susceptible to being read as clues to his hoax as they are to the purported purpose for their placement there.

"The Philosophy of Composition," then, does look back on "The Raven" in terms of the Barrett review, helping pull all three together in an attack on a Romantic sensibility that exalts intuition and feeling above poetic control. That attack is specified in the review, exists as an undercurrent of meaning in the poem through its being a parody of the bad poetics that sensibility creates, and is then again made specific in the essay.

IV

"The Philosophy of Composition" mirrors "The Raven" in other ways. One such mirror has been neatly pointed out by Leland S. Person, Jr.: "It may be simply a coincidence that the raven first appears in stanza seven of the poem and that Poe first mentions 'The Raven' in the seventh paragraph of the essay."[29] I am not sure that this is "simply a coincidence." Such pairing represents the type of cipher Poe relished. Perhaps a more significant mirroring, however, is that, like the poem it purports to analyze, "Philosophy" is both hoax and not hoax, precisely the type of paradox Poe delighted in perpetrating.

The hoaxical nature of "Philosophy" has been noted by many. Part of that literary practical joke is that Poe most obviously did not concoct "The Raven" in the detailed fashion he describes in the essay. Anyone who has tried his or her hand at writing creatively (or critically, for that matter) is well aware of the fits and starts, the inspired forward motion and difficult retrograde that make up the compositional process. Poe admits as much in the above-cited reference to suggestions arising to authors "pell-mell" and being "pursued and forgotten in a similar manner." Yet, again setting himself off from the common herd, Poe insists such is not the case in his particular instance, an insistence that is most difficult to swallow.

"Philosophy" hoaxes in other ways than merely setting forth a compositional method that belies reality. Poe insists that everything in "The Raven" proceeded logically, proceeded "step by step, to its completion with the precision and rigid consequence of a mathematical problem," but as Person points out, such is not the case. As presented by Poe, we see not "the precision and rigid consequence of a mathematical problem," but a process that appears to be akin to the "accident or intuition" "Philosophy" purports to debunk.[30] The language is a dead giveaway. Poe is led "at once" to a one-word refrain; led "inevitably" to "the long *o*"; the single word "Nevermore" is "the very first" he thinks of; the notion of a "*non*-reasoning creature" arises "immediately."[31] This sense of inevitability undercuts the professed rationality of Poe's method.

"Philosophy" belies itself in other ways as well. Putting itself forth as a critical essay describing a rational process, its language frequently descends into the disjointed, almost frenzied rhetoric Poe appears to attack. As Dennis Pahl remarks, "Rather than the semblance of sober reflection, we find . . . a kind of ecstatic writing that tends often to erupt amidst the more 'obvious' arguments concerning the poet as the embodiment of rational self-control." Pahl goes on to note that "we perhaps witness no better example of frenzied writing than at that precise moment when Poe, ironically, is refuting the idea that it is within a state of frenzy that most writers compose their works."[32] The passage Pahl refers to follows:

> Most writers—poets in especial—prefer having it understood that they compose by a species of fine frenzy—an ecstatic intuition—and would positively shudder at letting the public take a peep behind the scenes, at the elaborate and vacillating crudities of thought—at the true purposes seized only at the last moment—at the innumerable glimpses of idea that arrived not at the maturity of full view—at the fully matured fancies discarded in despair as unmanageable—at the cautious selections and rejections—at the painful erasures and interpolations—in a word, at the wheels and pinions—the tackle for scene-shifting—the step-ladders and demon-traps—the cock's feathers, the red paint and the black patches, which in ninety-nine cases out of the hundred, constitute the properties of the literary *histrio*.[33]

Pahl's point is that the essay is "contaminated by the very poetry from which it pretends to be coolly detached,"[34] an idea with which I fully concur, for such "contamination" is the vehicle for hoax.

This passage resonates in another way, however, specifically in the stage metaphor that dominates it. Poe, the literary *histrio* par excellence, was well aware of the double world of the stage. While it may present a glittering front to the audience, behind the stage are all the flats and props constituting a make-believe world. Inhabiting that stage, much as Poe inhabited his world, actors exist simultaneously in two interdependent worlds—the show and the props that make the show work. If one prop is missing, if one stage trick misfires, the whole pretend world collapses. The stage metaphor, I suggest, is yet another clue to "Philosophy" being a hoax, for it insists there are at least two worlds in a literary work—the surface façade we all recognize (the popular taste) and another side hidden, for the most part, from the popular taste and that is to be ferreted out by the critical taste.

In other words, doubleness pervades "Philosophy." We have popular and critical taste, a work that exhibits the very rhetoric it denies, a work, as Person demonstrates, that "parodies the critical or analytical process. It is not poems that are 'composed' through the process Poe describes, after all, but critiques of poems."[35] Finally, "Philosophy" asserts its doubleness by insisting that a poem must have "some amount of suggestiveness—some under current [*sic*], however indefinite of meaning."[36] The plethora of Poe hoaxes that the "critical taste" has exposed makes abundantly clear that one of his common undercurrents of meaning are literary jokes. Those jokes have a serious import, however, that further ties "The Raven" and "The Philosophy of Composition" together.

Poe's hoaxes are frequently critical in nature; that is, they function as a type of literary criticism. Such is the case with "Ligeia" in Clark Griffith's seminal reading.[37] And, as Robert Regan so ably demonstrated, "The Maskque of the Red Death" could well be subtitled "How to Write a Hawthorne Story."[38] So it is, as I have suggested, with "The Raven," where the narrator/writer constructs a poem full of jarring dissonance, cockamamie rhymes, and sonorously stupid phrases, all as a means of Poe's denouncing the type of poetics created by the type of Romantic sensibility attacked in "Philosophy." As Person remarks, "It is only the worst of works of art, it turns out, that can be reconstructed; the meaning of the best works remains indeterminate."[39]

The hoaxing in "Philosophy," as in "The Raven," carries critical import. The parody in the poem attacks products of a type of frenzied, self-indulgent Romanticism represented by the narrator. The slyly brilliant construction of the poem by Poe, on the other hand, demonstrates the craftsmanship with which he built that duplicitous work. The appeal of the poem to popular taste, measurable in its incredible lasting popularity, suggests that, critically, popular taste is pretty lousy when it comes to assessing accurately the value of a poem. This suggestion would not represent a radical departure from Poe's many statements to this effect.

The same idea is mirrored in "Philosophy," where Poe specifically delineates the critical statement implicit in the poem's hoax by debunking the idea that poetry is the result of raging emotions rather than reason; where Poe, in other words, specifically shows where the poem's narrator errs. The metaphoric truth lurking behind the eyebrow-raising process Poe so carefully describes in the essay demonstrates that poetry *is* a craft and like all crafts it is the end result of insight and labor. The insight can come at any time, but the labor occurs when putting that insight into form and language. For Poe, a gushing forth of spontaneous emotion simply doesn't cut it, as "The Raven" exemplifies. The true poet is a craftsman as well as a seer. Poe's poem, not the narrator's, demonstrates that, as does the careful construction of "Philosophy."

V

All of which, I suspect, leads to an inevitable question: Why bother? Why take the time and effort to write such elaborate works that function in such a multilayered fashion?

First, I would suggest, for the fun of it. Poe enjoyed writing and solving puzzles, so it should be no surprise that he was capable of creating puzzles within the context of his creative work. I am sure that he took great delight in fooling his readers by slipping literary jokes and hoaxes into even his most ostensibly Gothic works.

Furthermore, those jokes and hoaxes become a way of asserting superiority, of distancing self from those who are taken in by them. Such distancing, as noted, is part of the construction of "Philosophy." Poe is unlike other poets because he can reconstruct his creative process. He is unlike other poets because he creates rationally rather than in a moment of frenzy. He is unlike other poets because he can satisfy both popular and critical taste. In this sense "Philosophy" is a most immoderate document, for Poe holds himself up as a poetic standard.

There is another reason for concealing his jokes and hoaxes that goes far beyond such ego-satisfying explanations. I quote from Michael J. S. Williams: "As Poe was aware, once published, the writer's work acquires an independent existence with only a tenuous relationship to its author."[40] Poe's hoaxes, I suspect, were an attempt to establish control in a world where, once published, a work became the domain not of its author, but of its readership. To make matters worse, those who exhibit what Poe in "Philosophy" refers to as "the popular taste" were capable of gross misinterpretation, of completely misunderstanding what a writer was really up to. To compound the problem, some who staked a claim to having "the critical taste" were also capable of such gross misreading. Poe's frequent jibes at fellow critics exemplify his awareness of this fact.[41] Even worse, such misunderstanding could extend beyond the work, attaching itself to the author as well. Poe's somewhat unsavory reputation during and after his lifetime testify to this reality.

In this context, the hoax, by definition a literary joke, became perhaps an inevitable means by which Poe could maintain a degree of control over his work after it left his hands. He could not prevent misreadings and misinterpretations, but he could serve up a duplicitous work that lay beyond the ken of the popular and much of the critical taste. As stated by Williams: "[Poe's] well-known predilection for hoaxing his readership is clearly a gesture compounded both of resentment at their presumed usurpation of his control over his 'literary property' and of an attempt to retain ultimate control—even if it can be recognized only by an ever-narrowing circle of 'insiders,' which, at its minimal point, is reduced to a readership of one—himself."[42]

Which brings up yet another intriguing element in "Philosophy." By ostensibly explaining precisely how he wrote "The Raven," Poe attempts to exercise control over *his* poem after its publication at the same time he constructs a hoax that enables him to exercise control over *his* essay. For those readers who misunderstood the poem, falling for the angst he rejects as proper for poetry in "Philosophy," Poe supplies (perhaps) the correct reading: "The reader begins now to regard the Raven as emblematical—but it is not until the very last line of the very last stanza, that the intention of making him emblematical of *Mournful and Never-ending*

Remembrance is permitted distinctly to be seen."[43] Such a statement imposes *Poe's* interpretation of the poem back on the reader of "The Raven," taking it back from the reader.

The reader of "The Philosophy of Composition" who takes the essay at face value is also fooled, also misses its point. Only a careful, close reading—as demonstrated by Person and Pahl—can bring out the carefully inserted contradictions, the rhetorical betrayals, that help to make the essay a hoax while simultaneously emphasizing its metaphoric point: authorial control is vital in composition. Poe, beyond question, exercised such control in both "The Raven" and "The Philosophy of Composition," just as he did in writing the Barrett review. Consequently, he could bring all three together in a type of unified statement rebuffing a stereotypical Romantic temperament in a delicious complexity that positively boggles the mind. I have no doubt that he found the effort greatly rewarding, highly gratifying, and, ultimately, vastly amusing.

NOTES

I would like to thank Professor Benjamin Franklin Fisher for his willingness to read a draft of this paper and for his suggestions regarding both substance and style.

1. Dennis W. Eddings, "Theme and Parody in 'The Raven,'" in *Poe and His Times*, ed. Benjamin Franklin Fisher IV (Baltimore: The Edgar Allan Poe Society, 1990): 209. Leland S. Person, Jr., "Poe's Composition of Philosophy: Reading and Writing 'The Raven,'" *Arizona Quarterly* 46 (Fall 1990): 9. Those errors are manifest both in action and in language.

2. Person, "Poe's Composition of Philosophy," 7.

3. Person, "Poe's Composition of Philosophy," 6.

4. Poe, "The Philosophy of Composition," in Thompson, *Essays and Reviews*, 25.

5. Thomas Ollive Mabbott, ed., *Collected Works of Edgar Allan Poe*, 3 vols. (Cambridge, MA: The Belknap Press of Harvard University Press, 1969–1978): I:356–57.

6. All three quotations are from Poe, "Elizabeth Barrett Browning," 134–35.

7. Elizabeth Barrett Browning, "Lady Geraldine's Courtship: A Romance of the Age," www.caxton.stockton.edu/browning/ (Part 1, 5 Nov. 2004; Part 2, 6 Nov. 2004), I: 1, 2, 3, II:5.

8. Robert Regan, "Hawthorne's 'Plagiary'; Poe's Duplicity," *Nineteenth Century Fiction* 25, no. 3 (1970): 281–98.

9. Edgar Allan Poe, *The Letters of Edgar Allan Poe*, ed. John Ward Ostrom, 2 vols. (Cambridge, MA: Harvard University Press, 1948), I: 287.

10. Mabbott, *Collected Works*, I: 579.

11. Mabbott, *Collected Works*, I: 351.

12. Edgar Allan Poe, "The Philosophy of Composition," in Thompson, *Essays and Reviews*, 15.

13. Kenneth Burke, "The Principle of Composition," *Poetry* 99 (Oct. 1961): 51.

14. Edgar Allan Poe, "The Philosophy of Composition," in Thompson, *Essays and Reviews*, 14.

15. To cite one instance, see Michael J. S. Williams, *A World of Words: Language and Displacement in the Fiction of Edgar Allan Poe* (Durham, NC: Duke University Press, 1988): 62–79.

16. Burke, "Principle," 47.

17. Poe, "The Philosophy of Composition," in Thompson, *Essays and Reviews*, 24.

18. Edgar Allan Poe, "Marginalia," *The Complete Works of Edgar Allan Poe*, ed. James A. Harrison, 17 Vols. (1902; rpt. New York: AMS Press, 1965), 16:167.

19. Poe, "The Philosophy of Composition," in Thompson, *Essays and Reviews*, 14.

20. See Jacobs, *Journalist & Critic*, 339, 361–64.

21. Poe, "The Philosophy of Composition," in Thompson, *Essays and Reviews*, 14.

22. Person, "Poe's Composition of Philosophy," 7.

23. Person, "Poe's Composition of Philosophy," 7.

24. Person, "Poe's Composition of Philosophy," 7.

25. Person, "Poe's Composition of Philosophy," 7.

26. Person, "Poe's Composition of Philosophy," 7.

27. Person, "Poe's Composition of Philosophy," 7.

28. Person, "Poe's Composition of Philosophy," 7.

29. Person, "Poe's Composition of Philosophy," 7.

30. Person, "Poe's Composition of Philosophy," 6.

31. Person, "Poe's Composition of Philosophy," 6.

32. Person, "Poe's Composition of Philosophy," 6.

33. Person, "Poe's Composition of Philosophy," 6.

34. Person, "Poe's Composition of Philosophy," 6.

35. Person, "Poe's Composition of Philosophy," 6.

36. Person, "Poe's Composition of Philosophy," 6.

37. Person, "Poe's Composition of Philosophy," 6.

38. Person, "Poe's Composition of Philosophy," 6.

39. Person, "Poe's Composition of Philosophy," 6.

40. Poe, "The Philosophy of Composition," in Thompson, *Essays and Reviews*, 25.

41. Poe, "The Philosophy of Composition," in Thompson, *Essays and Reviews*, 25.

42. Poe, "The Philosophy of Composition," in Thompson, *Essays and Reviews*, 25.

43. Poe, "The Philosophy of Composition," in Thompson, *Essays and Reviews*, 25.

Index

About the Contributors

Amy C. Branam is an assistant professor of English at Frostburg State University. Her research areas include transatlantic nineteenth-century literature and women's studies. She has published in the *Edgar Allan Poe Review*, *ANQ*, *JFA*, and various edited collections.

Dennis W. Eddings, a longtime scholar of Poe and Mark Twain, as well as numerous other American authors, is retired from the faculty of Western Oregon University. He is the editor of *The Naiad Voice: Essays on Poe's Satiric Hoaxing* and past president of the Poe Studies Association.

Benjamin F. Fisher IV received his M.A. and Ph. D. degrees from the English Department at Duke University in 1963 and 1969, respectively. He has published numerous books on Poe including *The Very Spirit of Cordiality: The Literary Uses of Alcohol and Alcoholism in the Tales of Edgar Allan Poe*; *Poe and Our Times: Influences and Affinities*; *Poe and His Times: The Artist in His Milieu*; and *The Cambridge Introduction to Edgar Allan Poe*. In 1993, Fisher was awarded a Governor's Citation from the State of Maryland for his contributions to Poe studies. He has also published on such authors as Mary Wilkins Freeman, Frederick Irving Anderson, Edith Wharton, Stephen Crane, and Frank Norris and been active in the leadership of numerous literary societies and professional organizations, including the Poe Studies Association, which awarded him honorary membership for his service.

Peter Goodwin is a lecturer in English at the University of California, Berkeley, and San Francisco State University. He is currently working on a book about the gentleman, the dandy, and the cosmopolitan in nineteenth-century American literature.

Kevin J. Hayes, professor of English at the University of Central Oklahoma, is the author or editor of several books including *Poe and the Printed Word* (2000), *The Cambridge Companion to Poe* (2002), and *Edgar Allan Poe* (2009).

James M. Hutchisson, editor of this volume, is professor and director of graduate studies in English at The Citadel in Charleston, South Carolina. He has published widely on nineteenth- and twentieth-century American authors. His most recent book is *POE*, an acclaimed biography (2005), which earned starred reviews from major newspapers, magazines, and academic journals.

Leon Jackson is associate professor of English at the University of South Carolina. He is the author of *The Business of Letters: Authorial Economies in Antebellum America* (2008), as well as many essays on nineteenth-century American literature and the History of the Book. His current book project is a history of blackmail from the sixteenth century to the present.

John F. Jebb teaches writing and American literature at the University of Delaware. He co-authored, with J. K. Van Dover, *Isn't Justice Always Unfair? The Detective in Southern Literature* (1997). He also graduated from the New Castle County (Delaware) Citizens' Police Academy.

Daniel J. Philippon is associate professor of English at the University of Minnesota, Twin Cities, where he teaches courses in environmental literature, history, and ethics. He is the author of *Conserving Words: How American Nature Writers Shaped the Environmental Movement* (2004), the editor of *Our Neck of the Woods: Exploring Minnesota's Wild Places* (2009), and the co-editor of *Coming into Contact: Explorations in Ecocritical Theory and Practice* (2006), among other books. He is also past president of the Association for the Study of Literature and Environment (ASLE).

Laura Saltz is associate professor of art and American studies at Colby College, where she teaches courses on American visual culture. She has published on visual culture and the work of Henry James, Edith Wharton, Margaret Fuller, and Poe. She is working on a book about romantic and transcendental conceptions of photography and its relationship to the science of light in the early nineteenth century.

C. T. Walters has published in *The Edgar Allan Poe Review, The Automotive History Review, The Winterthur Portfolio, The Journal of American Culture,* and *The University of Michigan Museum Handbook*. He has contributed chapters to *Rituals and Ceremonies in Popular Culture* (1980) and *Pseudo-Science in Nineteenth-Century America* (1987).

Justin R. Wert is an assistant professor of English at Piedmont Virginia Community College in Charlottesville, Virginia. In 2009, he delivered the Edgar Allan Poe Annual Lecture in Baltimore, which will be published in 2010 as *A Tale of the Ragged Mountains: Of Mesmerism and Composition*, a monograph by the Edgar Allan Poe Society/University of Baltimore. He is the editor of a forthcoming Gothic edition of William Gilmore Simms's novel *Richard Hurdis* to be published by Udolpho Press in 2010. Wert is also the author of articles on Stephen Crane, Robert Montgomery Bird, and William Faulkner. At present, Professor Wert, who founded the Charlottesville-based Piedmont Writer's Group in 2008, is at work revising his own novels, *The Night Road* and *Both Sides Now*, for future publication.